Proverbs 3:3

ENDORSEMENTS

I love this devotional! It is the *My Utmost* for this generation. The Word is made clear and the Difference Maker challenge sticks with me throughout the day. I look forward to it every morning.

ROB McCLELAND, PhD
President, John Maxwell Leadership Foundation

Our deepest longing as human beings is for significance. *Make a Difference* isn't a luxury—it's at the core of our lives. Here, author and Bible scholar Ken Castor serves as an expert guide into a life of significance. Every day is a surprising exploration into a deep truth about Jesus, a reflection on his impact in the world, an intimate connection-point with him, and a simple challenge to live in his Spirit. Don't just read this book—do this book.

RICK LAWRENCE
Author of *The Jesus-Centered Life* and editor of the
Jesus-Centered Bible, simplyyouthministry.com

We're surrounded by a generation of emerging young leaders who are tired of watching, waiting for permission, and wondering when they will be called on to make a difference in this world for Jesus. Ken Castor understands their cry and provides a clear formula for daily empowerment and mobilization through this habit-forming devotional.

TIMOTHY ELDRED
President, Endeavor Ministries, endeavorministries.org

Ken continues to caringly but honestly encourage and drive people to grow deeper into what it means to follow Jesus. *Make a Difference* is another fantastic resource for anyone who desires a daily push to learn, grow, and live out their faith in a new way.

CHRIS THEULE-VANDAM
Regional Director, Young Life's Western Great Lakes Region,
westerngreatlakes.younglife.org

Too often our lives become so cluttered with selfish pursuits that we miss the opportunities right in front of our eyes to help people and change the world around us. In *Make a Difference*, Ken Castor reminds us every day what is good and what priority we ought to set first: to act justly, to love mercy, and to walk humbly with our God.

JOSHUA BECKER
Wall Street Journal best-selling author, Founder of Becoming Minimalist (becomingminimalist.com) and The Hope Effect (hopeeffect.com)

My favorite devotionals for forty-plus years have been crisply written hybrids, blending biblical encouragement and challenge. Their authors are word chefs, cooking up sweet swallows for the soul with lingering, satisfying aftertastes. Ken Castor uses this same tasty style with daily doable adventures for a year's worth of nourishment.

DAVE RAHN, PhD
Senior Vice President, Chief Ministry Officer, YOUTH FOR CHRIST®, yfc.org

I've learned from twenty-five-plus years of caring for orphans, the most valuable investment we can make is to give God the freshest (and the best) part of our day. It is harder for the enemy to sabotage our mind with irrelevant thoughts when we are committed to doing what God wants us to do. Ken's book is an extremely useful discipline in guiding us through a meaningful conversation with God, laying the foundation for a successful day.

THEA JARVIS
Founder and Director, The Love of Christ (TLC) Orphanage, South Africa, tlc.org.za

Do you want to be a positive force for good in this world? Form the simple practice of walking with Jesus—every. Single. Day. Grow in your faith and be challenged to take action. *Make a Difference* concisely yet brilliantly nourishes you with God's truth and then invites you to participate in what God is doing in the world.

KATHERINE WELCH, M.D.
Founder and Director, Relentless, gorelentless.org

MAKE

A

Difference

KEN CASTOR

BroadStreet
PUBLISHING

BroadStreet Publishing Group, LLC
Racine, Wisconsin, USA
BroadStreetPublishing.com

Make a Difference

ISBN-13: 978-1-4245-5231-3 (hardcover)
ISBN-13: 978-1-4245-5234-4 (e-book)

Cover by Chris Garborg at garborgdesign.com
Typesetting by Kjell Garborg at garborgdesign.com

Printed in China
16 17 18 19 20 5 4 3 2 1

INTRODUCTION

The life breath of our day should be spending time with Jesus so that we can make a difference in this world in which we live. Too many times, though, we push Jesus off like he's a vagrant: *Maybe I'll see you on Sunday and throw some money your way, Jesus.* Our attitude stems from an apathetic belief that displaced and broken people don't really matter, and a lethargic belief that Jesus is passive.

However, Jesus is not passive. He's passionate and he's proactive. And he doesn't want us to be lethargic about him or apathetic about people any longer. He wants to change us, and he wants to change the world through us.

Since I was a kid, Jesus has been active in my life. That doesn't mean I always noticed it. In fact, there were several moments where my focus was distracted and my steps were jumbled and my actions made the wrong kind of impact. But I've come to learn that Jesus has been intentionally seeking to change me every single day so that I can intentionally make a difference in this world through him.

I don't want to be a blob. Human blobs, who only think about doing something if they feel like it, are letting the world down. A disciple, however, is a learner. Our world needs fewer blobs and more learners of Jesus—people who are actively seeking him in a catalytic relationship, searching for his life around every corner and in every person.

My prayer is that this book will help kick you into that world-changing gear where God operates. This earth needs more people pursuing their radical God-created potential. People like you. It's a mess out there. And you have been called by God to take initiative, to do something about it.

Make a Difference helps you walk with Jesus and gives you encouragement to see the opportunities you have to deliver restoration where there is desperation. Through daily reflections (sometimes quirky, sometimes serious, hopefully always deep), verses, prayers, and "Difference Maker" challenges, I want you to discover ways to daily grow closer to Jesus and be spurred to make a difference in others as a result.

Oh, and note this: Many times when the Bible verses in this book say "you," it is plural. So even though this is a personal devotional book, remember that you are a part of a larger "you," a network of others who actively follow Jesus. In fact, you can go to my website (where, over the years, some of these daily entries originated) to find organizations and people who can help you follow through with many of the Difference Maker challenges in this book: kencastor.com.

It's your calling. It's your turn. It's your time. You can do it. Make a difference.

Ken Castor

January

Jesus,

Remind me that your eyes are on me.

And then help me to see what you see.

Amen.

START FRESH

Jesus wants you to have a fresh start in this world. In fact, he made this world with you in mind. He made it so that you could breathe in its air, marvel in its sunsets, surf in its waves, and wander in its paths with him. Be confident today in the one who made this world. While most people get caught up in their hectic schedules and busy lives, pause throughout this day to treasure what Jesus created for you and for me.

> The LORD merely spoke,
> and the heavens were created.
> He breathed the word,
> and all the stars were born.
> He gave the sea its boundaries
> and locked the oceans in vast reservoirs.
> Let everyone in the world fear the LORD,
> and let everyone stand in awe of him.
> For when he spoke, the world began!
> It appeared at his command.
>
> PSALM 33:6–9

Lord Jesus, let me see this world as you intended it to be. Thank you for making this world to be the place where I can be with you. Let me breathe in your creative power today. Amen.

DIFFERENCE MAKER

Notice something about this world that you may not have spotted before. Then tell somebody about it.

IN A MESS

There are some troubles that are massive in scale—like war, terror, disease, and death. And some of the troubles we see appear to be less intense, but they are the seeds that spawn disruption in our lives, such as hate, pride, jealousy, and selfishness. These things interfere with the amazing vision God has for his creation.

This is where you come in to play. First, God wants you to know something powerfully life changing: the problems of this world will one day fade away. Jesus is taking care of them. And second, God wants your words and actions to stand in contrast to the disruptive troubles of this world.

Live today in the freedom and power of Jesus. Don't allow the troubles around you to control your mind or your heart. Turn yourself toward your Creator today, knowing that he is taking care of all things.

> For sin is the sting that results in death, and the law gives sin
> its power. But thank God! He gives us victory over sin and
> death through our Lord Jesus Christ.
> So, my dear brothers and sisters, be strong and immovable.
> Always work enthusiastically for the Lord, for you know that
> nothing you do for the Lord is ever useless.
>
> 1 CORINTHIANS 15:56–58

Almighty Jesus, give me the strength today to stand against those destructive forces that seek to disrupt your plans in this world. And let me invite others into your victorious life. Amen.

DIFFERENCE MAKER

Here's a simple challenge that makes a big impact. If you see a mess today, clean it up. Just do it, whether someone notices or not.

GOD LOVES YOU SO MUCH

God has a track record of not giving up on his people. When they go lost, he pursued them. When they sinned, he made a plan to rescue them When they ran away, he actively looked for them. When they were in trouble he fought for them. When they continued to wander, he continued to see them. When they cried out, he gave them a Savior. And when they turned to him, he embraced them with his creative, unlimited life.

You are a person, are you not? The good news for you today is this: You are so loved by God, the very one who created this world so that he could be in relationship with you. He sent Jesus to find you, to pursue you, to search for you. He will never give up on you. In fact, he is thinking about you right now. He is calling out your name, and he wants you to call out his.

> "For this is how God loved the world: He gave his one and
> only Son, so that everyone who believes in him will not
> perish but have eternal life."
>
> JOHN 3:16

Lord Jesus, thank you for chasing after me. Let me be found by you. Here I am, Lord. I put my life in your hands. Use me to find others in your love. Amen.

DIFFERENCE MAKER

Look for someone who needs an extra chance today and find a way (through words or through actions) to share God's love with him or her.

DO SOMETHING

This world needs you to make a difference. This good world has veered a long way from what God created it to be. God did something about it, and he called you to do something about it with him.

Jesus, the Light of the world, calls you the light of the world too. You are a partner with Jesus in his mission on this earth. He wants everyone to see him, and he wants you to help shed some light for them. Jesus wants people to know the way to him. He wants you to offer to light the path. Jesus shines in brilliance. He wants you to shine his radiance upon your family, your friends, and all those you will encounter today.

Jesus spoke to the people once more and said, "I am the light of the world. If you follow me, you won't have to walk in darkness, because you will have the light that leads to life."

JOHN 8:12

Lord Jesus, Light of the world, let me reveal your life and light to others. Let me not be afraid. Let me stand tall in the confidence of your good news so that those around me would be blessed. Amen.

DIFFERENCE MAKER

Think of someone who is clouded by darkness today. Then take time right now to pray for them. And as you do, ask God to let you be a light in their life.

SPREADING IMPACT

You can't always see the impact you are having on those around you. The little things you do for Jesus that don't make you famous, and that seem to go unnoticed, may actually be a catalyst for something greater than you could ever imagine. Making a difference in this world sometimes means simply living every day in the creative light of Jesus. By doing this, people begin to be changed by the authentic truth and life that is evident in your integrity, in your joy, in your peace, in your words, and in your acts of kindness.

And here's a cool thing: While you are living out your faith in Jesus, there are millions of others who are also living out theirs. Millions of little actions become a gigantic world-changing movement. You are a part of something huge—the good news of Jesus transforming this world, one by one, little by little, person by person.

> This same Good News that came to you is going out all over the world. It is bearing fruit everywhere by changing lives, just as it changed your lives from the day you first heard and understood the truth about God's wonderful grace.
>
> COLOSSIANS 1:6

Jesus, let me be consistent in the little things of my life so that over time it will have a huge impact on others. Amen.

DIFFERENCE MAKER

Through either a message, a phone call, or a visit, share with someone a simple thing that God is doing in your life.

JESUS SHAPES YOU

Jesus shapes and tinkers and molds and forms. It's what he's good at. He walked the earth as a carpenter—trimming edges, nailing boards, and constructing treasured and useful items.

Jesus shapes people too. For instance, he radically changed a stuffy, murderous religious type named Saul. Jesus knocked his egotistical, self-righteous butt to the ground. He then healed the hatred and hurt that was in his heart. So deep was the transformation, in fact, that Jesus was able to use Saul (also called Paul) to shape others. He formed him into a life-giving example for people to follow.

You too can be changed by Jesus to become someone who changes others.

> Keep putting into practice all you learned and received from
> me—everything you heard from me and saw me doing.
> Then the God of peace will be with you.
>
> PHILIPPIANS 4:9

Lord Jesus, trim from me everything that gets in the way of your work in my life.
Let me be transformed as your agent in this world.

DIFFERENCE MAKER

Think of a habit in your life that is holding you back from fully serving God. Give it up to Jesus. Make a plan of action and let Jesus change you so that you can change others.

YOU ARE IN GOD'S PLANS

Even when things around you, or in you, are messed up, there is a remarkable truth that still reigns: Jesus created this world so that he could hang out with you. There is also a second truth that is just as remarkable: God doesn't give up on his plans. And no matter what you are experiencing today, no matter what you are facing in this moment, it just so happens that you are in the blueprint of God's plans for this planet. That is good news indeed. And good news is what Jesus is all about.

So turn to the Lord today. Call on his name. Ask him to re-create things around you and in you. This is what he wants for your life—it's why he created you in the first place. It is why he came for you, and it is why he called out on your behalf on the cross. It is why he conquered sin and death. Jesus made you, he loves you, and he plans to do great things through you. Call on Jesus today.

> For "Everyone who calls on the name of the Lord
> will be saved."
>
> ROMANS 10:13

Jesus, I call on your name today. Be with me in a renewed way. Make me right in your eyes. Make me mighty for your plans. And make me a light for this world that you love so much. Amen.

DIFFERENCE MAKER

Without placing any limits on yourself for a moment, imagine all that God wants for you. What desires has he placed on your heart that can make a positive impact on this world?

IMAGO DEI

An image is a reflection of the original. It has traits that resemble another, much like a mirror, a recording, or a picture. For instance, some people will look at a child and say, "You look and act just like your parents. It's like you're a spitting image of them."

So we can understand that it is an amazing announcement when the Bible declares that humans were created in God's image. *Imago Dei* is an old Latin term that describes how men and women were made in the image and likeness of God. Humans were made as reflections of the Creator. All of God's characteristics, desires, and abilities are on display in each and every one of us. His compassion, strength, wisdom, love, creativity, joy, and wonder are embedded in who we are. He endowed us with world-changing authority and entrusted us with life-giving responsibility. God made us to be his very representatives on the earth.

> Then God said, "Let us make human beings in our image, to be like us. They will reign over the fish in the sea, the birds in the sky, the livestock, all the wild animals on the earth, and the small animals that scurry along the ground."
>
> GENESIS 1:26

Dear Jesus, let everything I do today represent you. Let me not be a distraction, but let my words and actions reveal who you are. Amen.

DIFFERENCE MAKER

As you go throughout your day, make a note of how you, as a human being created in the *imago Dei*, look and act like a representative of God.

IMAGO EGO

Self-image problems began the moment humans rejected the *imago Dei* (image of God). Insecurity, embarrassment, frustration, confusion, self-hatred, shame, false thoughts, and self-harm—none of these things were characteristics humans were ever supposed to experience. In the beginning God created us with confidence, joy, clarity, innocence, and love. We were created with all of the great attributes of God embedded within us.

Instead of being people who represented God, we chose to be creatures who represented ourselves. And ever since we have suffered with our self-image. We stopped giving attention to God and we started focusing on ourselves instead. The result, of course, is a broken world—humans who are self-absorbed and self-destructive. Our world needs people who are brave enough to drop their ego and be re-created by Jesus again in the very image of God.

> Then he said to the crowd, "If any of you wants to be my follower, you must turn from your selfish ways, take up your cross daily, and follow me."
>
> LUKE 9:23

Lord Jesus, for the next twenty-four hours, help me take my attention off myself and place it on you. I give up my "self" so that you can use me to impact this world. Amen.

DIFFERENCE MAKER

Look in the mirror and ask yourself, "Whom will others see reflected in me? Whom will I represent today—myself or God?"

JESUS GAVE UP

To say that Jesus gave up is alarming. But it is also true. Jesus had everything. As the Creator, he owned everything—he was in charge of everything—but then he simply gave up. He gave himself up so that we can capture him. He surrendered his greatness so that we can embrace him. He let down his power so that we can enclose around him. Because we were unable to see him in all of his brilliant glory, he chose to lay aside his power so that we can know him personally once again.

Jesus doesn't ask us to do anything that he is unwilling to do himself. Rather, he asks us to follow his example, to do what he does, to be reflections of his attitude and actions on the earth today. He loves others so much that he willingly gave himself up so they—and we—could have life.

You must have the same attitude that Christ Jesus had.
Though he was God,
he did not think of equality with God
as something to cling to.
Instead, he gave up his divine privileges;
he took the humble position of a slave
and was born as a human being.
When he appeared in human form,
he humbled himself in obedience to God
and died a criminal's death on a cross.

PHILIPPIANS 2:5–8

Lord Jesus, thank you for giving yourself up on the cross. Thank you for thinking of us as you did that day. And thank you for inviting me to follow your heart.
Amen.

DIFFERENCE MAKER

What could you give up today that is more about you than God?

OTHERS FOCUSED

The first person on our mind in the morning is often ourselves, and the last person in our thoughts at the end of each night is often ourselves too. The primary person we're concerned about throughout the events of each day is often ourselves. Do you see a pattern here?

Do you want to change the world? Then try to think less of yourself and more about others. Consider what a friend is thinking about. Put yourself in your parents' shoes. Look at a situation through a hurting person's eyes. You see, Jesus calls us to be others focused. He doesn't want us to be so self-absorbed that we miss what is happening in the lives of our friends and family. He created us to be like him and to follow his example. Because he loves others and gave himself up for others, so should we.

> But we don't need to write to you about the importance of loving each other, for God himself has taught you to love one another.
>
> 1 THESSALONIANS 4:9

Lord Jesus, let me be more like you today by noticing the feelings and needs of others. Push me to do things for others that will give them encouragement and hope. Amen.

DIFFERENCE MAKER

Pick an important person in your life and, before you do anything else, call or text that person with a note of encouragement.

MIMIC

As a kid, did you ever play that fun but annoying game where you repeated everything someone said and did? If they moved an arm, then you would move your arm in the same way. If they spoke, you would repeat what they said verbatim. If they said, "Hey, stop it!" then you would say, "Hey, stop it!" too. It was funny (for a while, or unless you were the one being copied), and then it eventually got on everyone's nerves.

Imitating God is a lot different than that game. It's more like the moment when a little boy, after watching his dad shaving in the mirror, puts shaving cream on his face, picks up a razor (with the cap still on, of course!), and begins to practice the strokes up and down his face. Every father who has experienced this moment can't help but smile.

When we imitate God, we aren't playing a game where we merely repeat him like a robot responding to a command. When people copy God like that it can become really annoying really quickly. Instead, as we watch God, we learn to do what he does. When we follow his actions, his words, and his heart, we tend to put his movements into practice. In this way, when we mimic God, a smile spreads across his face, for we are becoming more and more like him.

> Imitate God, therefore, in everything you do,
> because you are his dear children.
>
> EPHESIANS 5:1

Lord Jesus, so much of my life doesn't imitate you. Align my thoughts,
my words, and my actions with yours. Amen.

DIFFERENCE MAKER

Think about your favorite characteristic of God. Then think of a way you can put that same characteristic into practical action today.

AMBASSADOR

An ambassador is a person who is sent by the leader of a kingdom to live in another kingdom as an official representative of the kingdom from which he or she was sent. In other words, what the ambassador speaks and does tells everyone, *This is what my leader is all about.* So it is important that the ambassador do and say only what their leader would want them to do and say.

Now imagine that Jesus has asked you to be his ambassador. He wants you to represent him where you live. As you interact with others, Jesus has given you his authority to share his words and customs with those with whom you live. It's as if you are a citizen of heaven and have been sent to your family, your friends, your career, and your community in order let others know what God is like. It's a lot of responsibility.

Unfortunately, throughout history, some people who have claimed to represent Jesus have done some terrible things, and, in the process, Jesus' message was misrepresented. Don't let the poor example of some people stop you from being a true ambassador for Jesus. Choose today to restore what it means to represent Jesus purely and share his message clearly.

So we are Christ's ambassadors; God is making his appeal
through us. We speak for Christ when we plead,
"Come back to God!"

2 CORINTHIANS 5:20

*Lord Jesus, let me represent you today in everything I say and everything I do.
Amen.*

DIFFERENCE MAKER

What can you speak on God's behalf today? What message has God given you the authority to share? And what would be the best way to share that message with someone else today?

MAKE ME LIKE YOU

Jesus celebrates when you follow him. In fact, it's his greatest joy. He came to this earth so that you could hear what he says and see what he does. He spoke with power so that you could see he is the source of all truth. He healed people so that you could know he is a God of restoration and love. He died on the cross so that you could have your sins forgiven and have a relationship with God. He gave you his Spirit so that you could be renewed every day and change this world with his authority. And he called you to follow in his steps, to walk in his ways, and to encourage others to become his followers too.

Heaven rejoices when you begin to look like Jesus in the way you live your life. This is God's original intent: making humans in his image, to be close to him in every moment. If you want to make a true difference in this world, one that matters forever, then today is a day to embrace God's re-creating work in your own life.

You made me; you created me.
Now give me the sense to follow your commands.

PSALM 119:73

Jesus, teach me to follow you in the little things of my life so that I can be entrusted to follow you in the big things too. Change me so that I can change the world for you. Amen.

DIFFERENCE MAKER

Pick something in your life that does not reflect God's image in you and give it over to Jesus today. Then use your new freedom to do something that gives life or joy to others.

GOD KNOWS YOU

Remember this truth: You are not forgotten. You are not alone. You are not unseen. You are not insignificant. You are not untested. You are not unknown. God has taken a remarkable interest in you. He examines you. Like a precision specialist finely tuned to your every joy or fear, God listens and searches and understands what is happening in you and to you. No matter what you are going through today, God knows and he is close.

David, the writer of Psalm 139, had incredible moments of victory, gut-wrenching moments of failure, endless hours of loneliness, and countless repetitions of everyday routines. Through his experiences, he grew to understand that everything he did throughout each day—every motion and emotion—was known by the Lord. Whatever your life is like today, know that God knows all about it. His attention is turned toward you in this very moment.

> O LORD, you have examined my heart
> and know everything about me.
> You know when I sit down or stand up.
> You know my thoughts even when I'm far away.

PSALM 139:1–2

Lord Jesus, let me know that you know me. Let me not forget that I am not forgotten. Let me stand up and sit down in that confidence today. Amen.

DIFFERENCE MAKER

Every time you sit down and stand up today, make a note in your mind that God's attention is on you in that very moment. And let that knowledge transform everything you think about and do.

GOD SEES YOU

Where are you going in the next twenty-four hours? Think about all of the places, near or far, that you will pass through. How will you get there? Will the travel be nerve racking? Whom will you meet? Will the locations be familiar or adventurous? Are you going to a classroom, coffee shop, or office? Gas station, highway, or sidewalk? Hallway, couch, or bathroom? Conversation, speech, or game?

Maybe you have trouble noticing God during a typical day. But God has no problem focusing on you, whether you are a moving blur or a still picture. God sees you when you are far away as clearly as he sees when you are at home. God also has no problem knowing what you're doing or what you're going to do when you are near or far. Jesus knew the thoughts of people (Matthew 9:4) even before they spoke them and even when he wasn't visibly near them (John 2:47–48).

You see me when I travel
and when I rest at home.
You know everything I do.
You know what I am going to say
even before I say it, LORD.

PSALM 139:3–4

Lord Jesus, remind me today that your eyes are always on me. And then help
me to see what you see. Amen.

DIFFERENCE MAKER

Realizing that God sees you, choose one positive action to accomplish today that you wouldn't have otherwise done. Then choose one negative habit to avoid.

GOD IS WITH YOU

If you could create a high-pressure diving suit and descend to the deepest underwater caves submerged several miles under the most remote surfaces of the ocean, you would still be as near to God as if you were at home asleep in your own bed. You are not alone. *Omnipresent* is the fancy word that smart people use to state a profound theological reality: God is everywhere.

If you feel alone, maybe this comforts you. Or, if you are trying to hide something, perhaps this gives you the shivers. Even if you rode a rocket past Pluto or if you ran away to the darkest recesses of your soul—still you would find God looking for you there because he is everywhere at all times. There is no place you can go to escape his presence. This is a profound and terrifying truth.

> I could ask the darkness to hide me
> and the light around me to become night—
> but even in darkness I cannot hide from you.
> To you the night shines as bright as day.
> Darkness and light are the same to you.
>
> PSALM 139:11–12

Lord Jesus, give me the sense to be aware of your presence today,
wherever I may be and in whatever I may be doing. Amen.

DIFFERENCE MAKER

Jesus goes to great lengths to reach you. Think of someone you know who either feels all alone or is trying to hide. Be bold and make the effort to let them know Jesus is there for them too.

GOD MADE YOU

It has been said that every stitch of a quilt is made with love. Actually, a quilt is made out of thread and fabric, with scissors and needles and sewing machines. But the sentiment is still there. The time and effort that, say, a grandmother puts into making a quilt for her new grandchild is evidence of love. Every stitch is another thought, another prayer, another action of care and compassion for the one she loves.

In the same way, the Lord took the time and effort to stitch you together. In the seclusion of your mother's womb, even before the day you gasped your first breath, the Lord's heart and hands were forming you. Every time he patiently wove a sinew or precisely measured a cell or miraculously gave beat to your heart, he thought about you, planned for you, and couldn't help but be consumed with love for you. Every fiber of your being was uniquely patterned and intimately sewn with God's hands. From before you were born, God committed himself to you and loved you.

> You made all the delicate, inner parts of my body
> and knit me together in my mother's womb.
> Thank you for making me so wonderfully complex!
> Your workmanship is marvelous—how well I know it.
>
> PSALM 139:13–14

Dear Jesus, thank you for investing so much in me. Keep creating my heart to beat with yours so that I will know how marvelous you truly are. Amen.

DIFFERENCE MAKER

Through a prayer, donation, or by volunteering, take a moment to support agencies that celebrate the precious created nature of each individual person (such as a crisis pregnancy center or an orphanage).

GOD PLANNED FOR YOU

You are not a mistake. God knew you would show up. You didn't surprise him. He was ready for you. And he was looking forward to your arrival. God also was looking forward to how you would live the life he has given to you. He has planned your days with purpose. He has things for you to do and people for you to reach.

Ephesians 2:10 says that you, along with others who follow God, are his masterpiece, created in Christ Jesus to do the good things he planned long ago. He shaped you with incredible attention to detail and with immeasurable value so that you could join him in his good work in this world. You are not a mistake—God made you into a beautiful masterpiece.

You watched me as I was being formed in utter seclusion,
as I was woven together in the dark of the womb.
You saw me before I was born.
Every day of my life was recorded in your book.
Every moment was laid out
before a single day had passed.
PSALM 139:15–16

Jesus, I am not an accident, but a treasure in your eyes. Let that thought filter what I do and how I interact with others today. Amen.

DIFFERENCE MAKER

What is something God created you to do? And what step can you take today to pursue that purpose?

GOD CHERISHES YOU

"The very hairs on your head are all numbered," Jesus said. "So don't be afraid" (Luke 12:7). Jesus wants you, just like his first followers, to be empowered by the fact that you are incredibly valuable to God. He wants you to stand with awe-inspiring confidence—a confidence that comes from learning how precious you are in his sight—and to declare with life-changing assurance that God loves you.

In other words, God puts your drawing on his fridge, not because it's perfect but because it came from you. His heart sparkles when you smile, sing, and serve. His hands clap when you create beauty and when you copy his character. His knees bend when you fall, his healing cleanses your wounds, and his power sets you on course to go and play again. He doesn't stop thinking about you—ever.

> How precious are your thoughts about me, O God.
> They cannot be numbered!
> I can't even count them;
> they outnumber the grains of sand!
> And when I wake up,
> you are still with me!
>
> PSALM 139:17-18

Lord Jesus, let me be bold in my steps today, knowing that you won't stop thinking about me. Amen.

DIFFERENCE MAKER

Think of a creative way that would bring joy to God's heart and let others know how much love he has for them.

GOD SEARCHES YOU

That cute little magnifying glass icon has tremendous power. Anything that is typed next to it is searched and, as long as it is connected to the Internet, returns millions of hits. The information transfer of the world is being driven by a little icon's algorithms.

Imagine now that the cute magnifying glass icon was ruled not by some little Internet search engine like Google, but instead was owned and operated by God. Then imagine typing your name next to it and hitting Enter. What would God's algorithms return on you? Are there any results that might worry you?

The good news about this search process is that Jesus celebrates everyone who comes to him with an open heart. He forgives and cleanses and heals and restores the life of those who seek him. Come to him today and let his cleansing take effect in your life.

Search me, O God, and know my heart;
test me and know my anxious thoughts.
Point out anything in me that offends you,
and lead me along the path of everlasting life.

PSALM 139:23–24

Jesus, you know me better than I know myself. Reveal those things in me that shouldn't be showing up but keep returning to the top of the list. Thank you for your forgiveness. Please lead me to walk with you through every result. Amen.

DIFFERENCE MAKER

Type your name in a search engine and pray this question:
Jesus, what results would you like to show up here?

GOD'S PATTERNS

Many people look at the commandments in the Bible as a negative list of don'ts—what they are not supposed to do. But God's patterns are more about living according to his original blueprint for life on this earth. Like a good parent trying to raise children for successful living, God's instructions provide the right framework for relationship with him, relationship with others, and responsibility on the earth.

It's as if God noticed his kids couldn't figure out how to build the coolest LEGO set ever (#483 Alpha-1 Rocket Base for those classic space LEGO fans out there!). God didn't want to derail the whole creative experiment called humanity, so he gave his children an instruction manual by which they were to live. And these commands are only tough for those who struggle with God.

> Loving God means keeping his commandments, and his commandments are not burdensome.
>
> 1 JOHN 5:3

Lord Jesus, teach me to love your commands. As I follow your ways, your Spirit will help me become more free to make this world the place you created it to be.
Amen.

DIFFERENCE MAKER

Read the Ten Commandments in Exodus 20:1–17, not from a mind-set of don'ts, but from a perspective of potential: What if people followed these commands? How would things improve? What damage could be avoided? What good could be done?

I LOST ON JEOPARDY

One of the great tortures of life is receiving grades on papers and tests. Sometimes those all-night cram sessions just don't cut it. Those practice questions and study groups might help a bit, but they don't solve every problem. The standard is 100 percent—and we all know that no one gets 100 percent all of the time.

Even Ken Jennings, the winningest contestant in *Jeopardy* game show history, eventually lost. Oh, he was pretty good. In fact, one could say he was amazing. For seventy-four *Jeopardy* shows in a row, Jennings outdueled other trivia wizards. But on appearance number seventy-five, he answered some important questions incorrectly and he lost.

The greatest achievements are not enough to sustain any human being forever. Eventually everyone succumbs to a less than perfect score. Often by mistake, and regularly even by deliberate choice, humans fail to measure up to God's pattern. We never hit the 100 percent mark.

For everyone has sinned;
we all fall short of God's glorious standard.
ROMANS 3:23

Lord Jesus, I am humbled in the face of your greatness.
Help me admit my failure to completely keep your commands.
Forgive me and restore me to your side. Amen.

DIFFERENCE MAKER

Any time some pride creeps into your judgment today, keep it in check.
A humble heart is an essential characteristic for a person God wants
to use to serve others.

EMERGENCY RESCUE EFFORT

God created humanity to walk with him in a close relationship. *Sin* is defined as anything that lets go of his hand and steps away from him. Sin is a "work" of our heart that leads us away from the life God created humans to have. Since God is the author of all life, the consequence of the refusal to walk with God is to miss out on God's life. We all get paid for our work. If the work is sin, however, then the paycheck is nasty.

Even after humans walked away and found themselves in serious peril, God went on a dramatic rescue mission. He sent his Son, Jesus, the greatest emergency response expert the world has ever seen, to save people who wandered away from life. He reaches out to those who got lost, extends his arms just as their lives hang in the balance, and urges them, *Grab my hand!*

For the wages of sin is death, but the free gift of God is
eternal life through Christ Jesus our Lord.
ROMANS 6:23

Lord Jesus, thank you for dying on the cross and saving me from my sin.
Please help me live the life you have given me. Amen.

DIFFERENCE MAKER

Accept the rescuing arms of Jesus Christ today. Accept his free gift of life
and reject sin. Restore yourself to a full walking relationship with God.

DON'T PRETEND

Have you unwrapped a present only to discover you didn't actually want it? Perhaps it was a hideous sweater or last year's trendy item or a gift card to a store you didn't like. When you unwrapped those sorts of presents (and I know you have), have you pretended to be thankful? Perhaps you said, "Oh, thank you! That was so thoughtful. I love it."

Many people have been hurt by others who say they love them but who actually are pretending, wishing for someone else to love. Jesus wants you to be honest, but not in a "Oh, I can't stand you" sort of way. He wants to reshape your heart so that you can receive people and truly say to them, "I am thankful for you in my life and I want to care for you." After all, he received you and rejoiced in the process.

> Don't just pretend to love others. Really love them. Hate what is wrong. Hold tightly to what is good.
>
> ROMANS 12:9

Lord Jesus, help me grow closer to you and become authentically true. As much as it might cost me, don't allow me to get away with being fake today. Help me to truly love people like you do. Amen.

DIFFERENCE MAKER

Think of someone you judge inappropriately and take a practical step to love them today.

BEAUTIFUL FEET

Feet can be really ugly. Bunions and calluses, hair and veins, nails and knobs—these things can combine to make feet look pretty gross. Add athlete's foot or some dank odor to the equation, and you might need some pretty strong spray to just get through the day.

There might be a chance even for the stinkiest, nastiest feet. The Bible mentions, both in the Old Testament and in the New Testament, that there is a way to make even the lowest part of a person's life look gorgeous. Feet look good when they are used for their proper purpose, which is to carry God's good message to this world. In other words, when you hear that Jesus saves people from sin through his work on the cross, you use your feet to run around and proclaim that good news. This has happened for thousands of years, and God wants you to be a part of his news team.

How beautiful on the mountains
are the feet of the messenger who brings good news,
the good news of peace and salvation,
the news that the God of Israel reigns!

ISAIAH 52:7

Lord Jesus, help me be so changed by your good news that I can't help but share it with others. Amen.

DIFFERENCE MAKER

In order to share the good news about what Jesus has done, where do your feet need to go today? (If you need ideas on how to share Jesus with others, go online and check out some ministries that share Jesus.)

TRANSPLANTED

Trees are meant to be rooted in fertile, well-watered soil. But many trees find themselves stuck in pots that are too small, too shallow, and too dry. What's needed is for someone to purchase that tree, bring it home, take it out of the pot, and replant it in ground where it can grow.

People need to be planted in a place where they can flourish. They don't need a restricted basin, superficial soil, or bare ground. The good news is that people who are stuck, who are struggling to grow, can be transplanted by Jesus to become strong and flourishing. This process is not always easy, and it most certainly costs the planter. But it also provides freedom for those with constrained hearts, release for the imprisoned, and beautiful joy for those who yearn for abundant life. It is a powerful message—and it takes root when those who were once stuck begin to find their freedom and identity in Christ.

> To all who mourn in Israel,
> he will give a crown of beauty for ashes,
> a joyous blessing instead of mourning,
> festive praise instead of despair.
> In their righteousness, they will be like great oaks
> that the LORD has planted for his own glory.

ISAIAH 61:3

Lord Jesus, let me become an oak replanted by you to flourish with your life. And, as a result, let me become a source of shade, oxygen, and seeds so that others can grow. Amen.

DIFFERENCE MAKER

Purchase a small plant in a pot. Place it in a window. Take care of it for a few months, making sure it gets adequate water and sunlight. Then, in the spring, plant it in fertile soil.

PAUSE

You must pause. Life has been running. Your breath has been flying and you need to catch it. The last few weeks have been incredibly rich—full of all the dramatic ups and downs that life has to offer—tragedies, victories, eateries, friendlies, and frenzies. You cannot complain about being bored, but at times you have been tempted to drift toward mind-numbing laziness. You have thought to yourself, *I'll just play one more round of this game…or maybe twenty more rounds.*

You know that a numbing of the mind leads to a dumbing of the mind, which then leads to a frustration of the soul. The effort you sometimes take to become an automaton is both surprising and exhausting. Between the busyness and the weariness, you are left to gasp on fumes, losing vitality, clarity, and aspiration. What you truly need is a rest. Not just sleep. You need a Sabbath. A restoration. A peace. A pause. A still. A capturing of time. A moment to shut your eyes and dream of what could be, what should be. A reflection of God's image at work and at rest within you. You must pause.

Then Jesus said, "Come to me, all of you who are weary and carry heavy burdens, and I will give you rest."

MATTHEW 11:28

Lord Jesus, let me rest—truly rest. Let me seek you, trust you, and take a… deep…breath. Amen.

DIFFERENCE MAKER

At a certain point today, put everything you have planned off to the side and take time off. Get away and get alone with God, letting him restore your soul with his peace and rest.

BE NEEDY

People need God. Every person needs a relationship with his or her Creator. People need the daily breath and long-term purpose that only God provides. When things fall apart, they cry out to the Lord because he is who they need during those time. And when people have God, they have everything they need.

But people have also been known to fail to recognize their need for God. Instead of finding their dependency in their Creator, they have tried to go at it alone. While independence from God might puff up the ego and build up a bank account, any get-rich-quick schemes or quick-fix solutions that avoid God are bound to end in ruin.

Being "poor of heart" is an important posture for humans to take. Pride is a false sense of having everything, while poverty is the desperation of not having enough. Those who realize they need God, that they are desperate without him, will be rewarded with the relationship and royal status only God can provide.

> "God blesses those who are poor
> and realize their need for him,
> for the Kingdom of Heaven is theirs. "
>
> MATTHEW 5:3

Lord Jesus, let me admit my need for you throughout the day.
Let me rely on you rather than myself. Amen.

DIFFERENCE MAKER

Think of something you have in your life that supplants your need for God and discard it.

BE SAD

One of the signs of a good heart is a sad heart. In other words, those who don't care don't mourn. But those who care are willing to feel the pain of loss. There is a remarkable amount of hurt in this world. And while it would be great to avoid pain, the only alternatives are to become abusive or to become numb to it. And, lest you're confused, neither of those are a good way to exist.

Jesus understands this. One of the shortest verses in the Bible, and one of the most significant, says this: "Jesus wept." At a funeral, Jesus mourned the loss of his friend and he carried the heartache of the situation, precisely because he was willing to love deeply. He didn't have to care. But he did. Jesus cries with his friends. He wears their burdens. He tends to their wounds. And then he raises them to life once again.

> "God blesses those who mourn,
> for they will be comforted."
>
> MATTHEW 5:4

Jesus, give me a heart big enough to mourn and a soul big enough to take the risk. Amen.

DIFFERENCE MAKER

Grab coffee with or write a note to someone you know who has recently experienced loss, expressing your sorrow.

BE HUMBLE

If anyone ever had a reason to brag, it was Jesus. After listening to some simpleton humans boast about conquering nations or building coliseums or inventing aqueducts, Jesus could have interrupted their grandiosity with a snap of his fingers. "Be still, morons! You don't know squat. Those nations you defeated—I made them. And you! You call those tiny buildings 'coliseums'? Ha! I made asteroids bigger than that. And what's so great about an aqueduct? So you can move a little bit of water from one place to the other. Have you ever heard of rivers? Seas? How about oceans? Oh, and have you ever noticed how your heart is beating right now? Yep, that's me. I sustain your life."

If he wanted to, Jesus could have put humans in their place pretty quickly. If he was tired of conceited humans claiming to be the greatest, he could have snuffed out their puffed-up arrogance with one breath. But instead he serves. He listens. He embraces. He heals. He saves. He treasures. All because he wants people to share with him all that he has made.

"God blesses those who are humble,
for they will inherit the whole earth."

MATTHEW 5:5

Jesus, you are greater than I realize, and yet you put my life ahead of your own. In humility, I fall to me knees and find that you already there serving me. Thank you, Jesus. Amen.

DIFFERENCE MAKER

Be humble like Jesus today. Try to make it through the entire day without using the word *I*. Instead of talking about yourself, take that effort to focus on others.

February

Jesus,

You have asked me to be like you.

Please lead me to be radically open handed.

Amen.

BE HUNGRY

Jesus wants you to make a difference in the community in which you live. It isn't enough just to feel like people shouldn't be treated unfairly, for instance, or to think that people shouldn't be oppressed. He actually wants you to figure out something to do that will help these people and address the terrible situations they are in.

Jesus hungered and thirsted for justice. He hated it when people were pushed down or overrun. His vision for the world did not include oppression and violence. In one of the most famous and countercultural messages the world has ever heard, Jesus' Sermon on the Mount, he made it clear that God values human life, and he expects people to fight for those whose life is being stolen. Does your heart break over the wrongs that are committed against the innocent? Does your soul cry for those whose voice has been taken from them? God's does.

> "God blesses those who hunger and thirst for justice,
> for they will be satisfied."
>
> MATTHEW 5:6

Lord Jesus, don't let me settle for a fast-food life. Let me be hungry for the nourishment and fulfillment that you have for this world. Amen.

DIFFERENCE MAKER

Connect with a local organization or church that seeks to defend those who are being wronged. Ask what kind of support they need, and choose a way to respond.

BE MERCIFUL

Martin Luther King Jr. was countercultural. In the face of hostility, he upheld mercy. He had every right to retaliate against those who hurled threats, insults, and physical harm. Yet he chose a different path, one that changed the trajectory of a powerful nation, not to mention the hearts of millions upon millions of people.

When you are in a position of power, when you are justified to dispense wrath, when you have the opportunity to absolutely let loose your fury, what would happen if you chose to withhold it? What if you extended a hand of grace and restoration instead? Mercy recognizes that God is in control, and it acknowledges that the person who deserves judgment is both a fellow child of God and in need of restoration.

Not everyone who is offered mercy accepts it or reorients to it. But someone else's response is not your responsibility. Mercy doesn't dictate a person's future; it simply opens it up.

> "God blesses those who are merciful,
> for they will be shown mercy."
>
> MATTHEW 5:7

*Lord Jesus, give me your authority to forgive and offer a hope
to those who need it. Amen.*

DIFFERENCE MAKER

Gut check. Whom do you judge too easily?
Who needs another chance today?

BE PURE

To "adulterate" a product is to add an inferior or polluted substance to what may have once been a spotless, good-hearted item. It is like secretly adding chemical ingredients to all-natural skin lotion, or adding an affair to a marriage.

Purity doesn't imply naiveté. To be pure doesn't mean you are inexperienced or ignorant. The world mocks purity because it doesn't understand it and doesn't believe it has survival power. Eventually, the world believes, purity has to be corrupted, right?

Jesus doesn't think so. He believes purity can be lived out practically. Jesus believes purity begins in the nature of a person's focus upon God, and then it extends into everyday action. He suggests that purity opens the eyes to see in ways that others cannot. In fact, purity actually expands the paradigm and adventure of life.

> "God blesses those whose hearts are pure,
> for they will see God."
>
> MATTHEW 5:8

Lord Jesus, re-create my heart to seek you in everything. Find anything impure in me, point it out, and begin the process to restore me to a pure vision for you. Amen.

DIFFERENCE MAKER

Pick a glaring struggle you have with impurity, then find a friend who struggles with the same issues so you can hold each other faithful in your pursuit of purity.

BE PEACEFUL

Peace is not passive. Where did that idea originate from anyway? Peace comes about through incredible strain and sacrifice. Ask the millions of people throughout history who have given their lives so that peace could stand.

There is a war in the world today against peace—ideologically, geographically, culturally, physically, emotionally, and spiritually. There are powers and movements whose goal is the disruption and deterioration and destruction of true peace. It is into this fray that Jesus jumps. Like a vigilante of justice, Jesus disarms evil. His effort costs him his life. But it is a cost he decided was worth the outcome.

Jesus is the "Prince of Peace" (Isaiah 9:6), and he exerts himself so that people can have "peace with God" (Romans 5:1). Jesus fought and died to give this world a powerful, proactive peace. When people embrace him, and when they choose to become peacemakers themselves, all of heaven celebrates.

"God blesses those who work for peace,
for they will be called the children of God."
MATTHEW 5:9

Lord Jesus, don't let me cheat the steps. Challenge me to become a peacemaker.
Amen.

DIFFERENCE MAKER

Take a moment to pray. Find something in your relationships or circumstances today, either big or small, that agitates you. Then ask God to show you what steps you need to take to fight for peace in that area of your life.

TREAT PEOPLE WELL

Imagine a religious dude entering the room, sweat beading down his brow, feverish "fainthood" (false + sainthood = fainthood) in his eyes, declaring dramatically in a dry, raspy voice, "Oh, I am so burdened because I am fasting for the Lord."

Well, isn't that special. God goes to great lengths in the Bible to make it clear that he doesn't want people to give up food in order to look more spiritual in the eyes of others. God doesn't think it's awesome for people to intentionally malnourish themselves in order to get attention. He actually looks away in disgust from that kind of theater.

God created you to live altruistically in the patterns of your life. If someone is wronged, give up your own interests to pursue freedom for them. If someone is working too hard on your behalf, take their extra burden upon yourself. If someone needs something that you have in abundance, then give it to them. The bottom line is that we are to treat people well because Jesus treated people well.

> "No, this is the kind of fasting I want:
> Free those who are wrongly imprisoned;
> lighten the burden of those who work for you.
> Let the oppressed go free,
> and remove the chains that bind people."
>
> ISAIAH 58:6

Jesus, show me what I can give up in order to give life to someone else. Amen.

DIFFERENCE MAKER

Think of somebody in one of the categories listed in Isaiah 58:6.
What can you give up today that would help their cause?

SHARE WITH OTHERS

What an amazing calling you and I have. You have been asked by the living God to tackle some of the biggest challenges this world has ever faced. In large scale, they are massive issues. But on a very personal scale, they are intimately and effectively addressed.

If you see someone who is hungry, do you think Jesus wants you to stuff your face and belch? If you see a family sleeping in a car, do you think Jesus wants you to judge them? If you see a kid who doesn't have clothes that fit, do you think Jesus wants you to do nothing? I'm guessing probably not.

> "Share your food with the hungry,
> and give shelter to the homeless.
> Give clothes to those who need them,
> and do not hide from relatives who need your help."

ISAIAH 58:7

Lord Jesus, use me in service for others today. Amen.

DIFFERENCE MAKER

You can give your lunch to someone who needs it more than you do; you can ask the local elementary school what size gym shoes they need donated; or you can send a family member a care package in the mail. Do something for someone else today.

FEED THE HUNGRY

Not here, really? Not now, right? Sure, I know there are problems around the world—out *there*—but not around me. Kids don't go hungry in *this* nation. People aren't cast aside *here*. Families have everything they need to be successful in my community, don't they?

Jesus is on mission. That means you had better be too. He listens for the cry of the hungry and leans into the mess of those who are in trouble. He looks for darkness and pierces it with his brilliance. He searches the rubble for signs of those who are trapped. He works with precision to remove the concrete and rebar and beams crushing them. He attends to wounds and orchestrates restoration efforts. He patiently heals and persistently rejoices when he sees people find life through his hands.

There is plenty of rescue work to do. What a privileged calling you and I have.

> "Feed the hungry,
> and help those in trouble.
> Then your light will shine out from the darkness,
> and the darkness around you will be as bright as noon."
>
> ISAIAH 58:10

Lord Jesus, thank you for blessing me in my needs. Please use me to share your blessing with others. Amen.

DIFFERENCE MAKER

Make arrangements for some friends to join you at a food-packing agency.

SABBATH

Followers of Jesus are asked to do a lot of good things, like treating people well, caring for those in need, and feeding those who are hungry. But there is one task that, at first glance, seems out of sync with the rest. Like the others, it's a task that requires great effort, but it is not an exertion of work. It is the pursuit of rest.

Rest is too often overlooked in this busy achievement-based culture of our time. Rest might be a neglected practice in your own life, as it is for many people around you. People make up for missing rest by binging on naps, hangovers, or laziness. That's not what God wants for us. God wants us to observe the Sabbath, a day set aside in the rhythm of each week, that focuses the heart and mind on God and others. The Sabbath is a type of restoration that reorients the soul to be ready to serve in the good work of following Jesus in the six days that follow.

> "Keep the Sabbath day holy.
> Don't pursue your own interests on that day,
> but enjoy the Sabbath
> and speak of it with delight as the LORD's holy day.
> Honor the Sabbath in everything you do on that day,
> and don't follow your own desires or talk idly."
>
> ISAIAH 58:13

Dear Jesus, help me rest in your interests instead of my own.
Amen.

DIFFERENCE MAKER

Ask God to reveal his interests for you and your community. As God shapes your heart, begin sketching plans to impact others the way God wants.

SING PRAISE

David didn't have Beats by Dre or an iPhone packed with the latest songs by Imagine Dragons. How did he even survive? Seriously, how did this guy function without the constant stimulation of media continually rewiring his brain?

Well, David spent some time alone (note: time = days, weeks, months) shepherding flocks in the countryside. To pass his hours he learned to write songs, play compact instruments, and talk to God. He had sheep. And they made only one genre of music. (Except when they ate too much grass, then they made a second genre of music. A symphonic movement, you could say.)

David wrote songs of praise—dozens, and perhaps hundreds, of them. Even while he sheered wool and killed bears that attacked his flock, he became an accomplished poet, theologian, musician, and composer. He used his growing skills to turn his heart, again and again, to the Lord.

Sing a new song to the Lord!
Let the whole earth sing to the Lord!
Sing to the Lord; praise his name.
Each day proclaim the good news that he saves.

PSALM 96:1–2

Lord Jesus, help my mind and heart sing for you. Amen.

DIFFERENCE MAKER

Either write a song of praise to God or listen to a song of praise to God. Get that song stuck in your heart and mind and refer back to it throughout the day.

REAPING

Sometimes the difference you make in this world is immediate. Perhaps you called someone on their birthday and they were greatly encouraged. Good job—you made a difference in their life. Quick response. Lives changed. Keep doing it! But other times the difference you make in this world isn't always immediately evident. Perhaps you have started getting rid of some bad habits in your life, but they keep rearing their ugly head and trying to drag you down. The battle is still there. It isn't fixed and it isn't clear if anything good is coming out of it.

But God's Word encourages us again and again to persist. Keep going. Don't give up pursuing Jesus and the life he has for you. Don't quit doing what he wants you to do. Don't stop changing the patterns of your life and the lives of those around you in the long-term direction of Jesus. You will reap a harvest if you don't give up.

> So let's not get tired of doing what is good. At just the right time we will reap a harvest of blessing if we don't give up.
>
> GALATIANS 6:9

Jesus, help me keep pressing on for those things you have asked me to do.
Amen.

DIFFERENCE MAKER

Write down five goals for your life that you would like to have accomplished five years from now. Put this somewhere that you will occasionally revisit to remind yourself to not give up.

PUBLISH

Let's say for a moment that in the future you discovered the permanent cure for cancer. But then, let's imagine, that instead of publishing that cure, instead of sharing it and making the cure known, you decided that you would keep it to yourself. Then, let's say, you were able to meet yourself in the future and have a blunt conversation. What would you say to yourself?

What if a group of people were to discover God? And what if they came to know about the great things God had done and the great things he had plans yet to do? What if they knew that God offered salvation and healing and peace and life for the world? And what if they kept all of that information to themselves? If you were able to meet these people and have a blunt conversation, what would you say to them?

The Psalms urge people who have discovered the good news about God to make him known to those around them. And this is what God has called each one of us to do as well—we are to publish what he has done to those around us.

Publish his glorious deeds among the nations.
Tell everyone about the amazing things he does.

PSALM 96:3

Dear Jesus, help me grow in my boldness for sharing what I know about you with others. Amen.

DIFFERENCE MAKER

Brainstorm for a moment: What do you personally know about Jesus? Do you know anyone who needs to know these things too?

WHAT IF?

What if for Valentine's Day a husband bought a card and some roses and gave them to his wife? What if he told his wife he loved her and that she was the only one for him? Nice, right? Well, what if that same husband didn't do much else for his wife for most of the rest of the year? What if he only spent effort on his wife on occasions like her birthday or a special holiday? What if he expected constant adoration and blessing from his wife in return? And what if he looked at other women from time to time, or spent time with pornography, or imagined being with another woman, or acted upon those desires secretively? He's not so nice now, right?

Now try this. What if on Sundays a person went to church and put some money in the offering plate? What if this person told God he or she loved him and that God was the only one for them? Nice, right? Well, what if that same person didn't do much else for God most the rest of the year? What if he or she only spent effort on God on special occasions like Christmas or tax season? What if she expected constant adoration and blessing from God? What if that same person looked at other objects from time to time, or spent time with other desires, or imagined being with another god, or acted upon those desires secretively? Not so nice now, right?

Come close to God, and God will come close to you. Wash
your hands, you sinners; purify your hearts, for your loyalty
is divided between God and the world.

JAMES 4:8

Lord Jesus, thank you for creating me to have relationship with you.
Turn my eyes from worthless things. Amen.

DIFFERENCE MAKER

Get rid of one thing that could compromise your commitment to God today.

UNFORTUNATE EVENTS

In the Lemony Snicket book series by Daniel Handler, a malevolent character named Count Olaf takes in three orphans—Violet, Klaus, and Sunny Baudelaire. In the process he disguises himself as a loving uncle, but it isn't long before the children realize that Olaf is a conniving, lying, twisted, and murderous criminal who is mercilessly trying to get his hands on the Baudelaire fortune. If it wasn't for the purity and determination of the children, their heartbreaking story would have been soul destroying as well.

Sadly, this "series of unfortunate events" is all too common in our world today. The Bible describes the presence of evil in this world, spurred on by Satan, to wreak havoc and destruction upon those whom God loves. One glance at a news site confirms that evil and unfortunate events seem to run rampant. And yet, in contrast to the evil that has invaded our world, Jesus rises to protect and to save.

> "The thief's purpose is to steal and kill and destroy. My
> purpose is to give them a rich and satisfying life."
>
> JOHN 10:10

Lord Jesus, you are so good. Let me live in the satisfaction and power
of your life. Let me be pure and determined to stand against evil,
in all of its varied forms. Amen.

DIFFERENCE MAKER

Take a sobering note today. What conniving events are at work to erode the life that God wants to give your community? Take time to pray for ways to help people be rescued by Jesus instead.

TRUE LOVE

Today is the big day of love, that fancy day where half-naked flying babies shoot people with arrows. Nothing says I love you like some kid sending projectiles into your backside in order to manipulate how you feel about someone else. Seriously, nothing says I love you like that. Some people treasure this day for the chocolaty-sugary romance, while other people can't wait until tomorrow.

At the risk of being sappy, perhaps this is a good day to remember how much Jesus loves you. He doesn't love you in some consumeristic way. He doesn't run to the store in a last-minute panic after realizing that he forgot to buy you a huge Power Ranger Valentine candy heart. No, Jesus actually loves you. He isn't fickle about it either. And he isn't cheap. He is in this relationship for good, and he wants his love for you to change the way you love others.

> "This is my commandment: Love each other in the same
> way I have loved you. There is no greater love than to lay
> down one's life for one's friends."
>
> JOHN 15:12–13

Lord Jesus, let it sink in how much you truly love me. And let that make a
difference in the way that I learn to love others. Amen.

DIFFERENCE MAKER

Because of what Jesus has done for you, what genuine action could you
take today to show your friends they are loved?

THE WRONG KIND OF DIFFERENCE

Jesus wants you to make a difference in the world. A good difference—not a mixed-up, mangled, messed-up difference. Unfortunately, all too often, people who say they follow Jesus end up making the wrong kind of difference in this world. Jesus said to his disciples that their love for each other would prove to the world that they were his followers (John 13:35).

So it would be a terrible thing if those who claimed to follow Jesus demonstrated tempers, idiocy, and conspiracy. People who are quick to anger inevitably do really stupid things, which in turn causes them to scheme and worm and twist things for their own protection and gain. It would be terrible for the reputation of Christians to suffer because people who claimed to follow Jesus failed to live with love. Christians are supposed to be a light to the world, reflecting Jesus into the darkness. They are not supposed to be dispensers of darkness themselves.

Don't make the wrong kind of difference.

Short-tempered people do foolish things,
and schemers are hated.
PROVERBS 14:17

Lord Jesus, don't let me mess up in anger today. Keep my heart cooled by your love. Amen.

DIFFERENCE MAKER

What do you see around the corner that is going to trigger your temper? How could you prepare yourself to respond in love?

WORTHMORE (THE OPPOSITE OF WORTHLESS)

Rare is the day when people are aware of what God wants them to do with their lives. Perhaps that is one of the underlying reasons for this devotional book, a simple reminder that God calls people to make a difference in this world every day they are alive.

People don't always check in with Jesus to get their daily assignments. As a result, they toil and labor, but their work is in vain when it's not something Jesus has set before them. People can play and laze, but their happiness is shallow and empty when it's not on God's radar.

Perhaps much of human dissatisfaction in life comes from not doing the work Jesus has assigned people to do. What would change in human hearts if people were to present themselves to Jesus ready for work? What if people checked in with him each morning and asked, "Sir, what do you want me to do today?" This world would be a much different place.

> "But my life is worth nothing to me unless I use it for finishing the work assigned me by the Lord Jesus—the work of telling others the Good News about the wonderful grace of God."
>
> ACTS 20:24

Lord Jesus, what do you want me to do today? Amen.

DIFFERENCE MAKER

Strive to align all of your actions today with the work that Jesus has called you to do.

HOT SEATS OF LOVE

Pop culture tries to trick you into thinking that love is often seated in your emotions: "How does that make you feel?" But what if it weren't true that love is seated in your emotions? Some people probably engage in their relationships this way and make some incredible mistakes of judgment. Emotional love without wisdom or a rooted foundation can get people into codependent situations or abusive influences or financial trouble or manic-panic roller-coaster rides of life.

It is really interesting that the apostle Paul refers to three seats of love in Philippians 1. First, Paul said that the Philippians held a special place in his *heart*. Second, he said that he loved the Philippians in the *bowels* of Christ Jesus, which is an awkward phrase nowadays, but it referred to the very core of his being. Third, Paul prays that their love would abound more and more in knowledge and depth of insight so that they would be able to discern what was best and be pure and blameless. In other words, he wants them to love with their *brain*. Each seat comes together to form a beautiful union—each distinct and yet each together—each encouraging and maturing and directing the other.

Paul's desire was for the Philippians to develop a smart, passionate, and, um, moving love.

> God knows how much I love you and long for you with the tender compassion of Christ Jesus.
>
> PHILIPPIANS 1:8

Lord Jesus, mature my ability to love others today. Amen.

DIFFERENCE MAKER

Which "seat" of love do you need to develop and practice more deeply? What can you do today to act upon this "seat" of love?

RESTLESS

Humans are restless creatures. They are busy carrying busy burdens and are afraid to stop, because, if they stop, they might have to think. And if they think, they might have to wrestle with their burdens and what is going on inside of them. And if they have to wrestle with their burdens, they might get tired. And if they get tired, they might need to rest.

Because of this, humans don't stop. Instead, they pride themselves in activity. They are the most productive least productive creatures in all of history. They overschedule, overcommit, and overextend themselves and then wish they had time to enjoy themselves. Even God stopped the activity of creation to pause and rest. But not humans. No. They are so over that pattern. Instead they choose pace over peace. They are restless creatures. But Jesus, the Lord of the Sabbath, is restful. He asks us to stop our scurry long enough to sit down at the table together for a meal.

> Then Jesus said, "Let's go off by ourselves to a quiet place and rest awhile." He said this because there were so many people coming and going that Jesus and his apostles didn't even have time to eat.

MARK 6:31

Lord Jesus, help me rest today. Amen.

DIFFERENCE MAKER

Schedule time today to rest. Do something that will rejuvenate your soul. Invite along others who will be refreshing for you. And be sure to enjoy God's presence as you pause your pace.

PROVOCATIVE

You were created to live a radical life. You were made to be deeply alive, to be stretched to your fullest, and to be passionately involved in this world. So it is no wonder you are attracted to the provocative.

Provocative simply means to "call forward." It recognizes your God-created thirst for activity and purpose. You were created to be called and called to be creative. You were formed so that you could step forward in the shaping of how life is lived on this planet. Jesus didn't make you to squander your days; rather, he made you to live them.

Both Jesus and Satan employ the provocative. But let your ninja-like reflexes be aware that Satan calls you forward, but his is an enticement to eat from a cornucopia of carnage, scheming plans to use you for his own self-serving survival. On the other hand, Jesus calls you forward, and his is an invitation to dinner, shared with friends, empowering you as his partner to give life to others.

Jesus says, "Look! I stand at the door and knock. If you hear my voice and open the door, I will come in, and we will share a meal together as friends."

REVELATION 3:20

Jesus, help me reject the alluring trap of evil and respond to your life-giving call.
Amen.

DIFFERENCE MAKER

Pray for someone who could use a positive nudge. Then call that person on the phone. Invite them to take a step forward in life with you today.

WHATEVER

Do you have a love-hate relationship with your snooze button? Without your alarm you might wake up in a panic because you missed the beginning of the *Phineas and Ferb* all-day marathon. And yet those nine extra minutes of sleep sure would be nice. But do those 540 seconds actually help your grumpy attitude? Some people claim to be even crankier after each smack of their snooze button.

What if, instead of the next time you hit the snooze button, you stopped to pray? Knowing that you have nine more minutes to ask Jesus to get you into the right frame of mind could transform everything about your day. Perhaps that extra slumber could be used to reorient your entire way of thinking. Instead of letting the problems of the world, including your own flaws, failings, and festering worries, muck your mind, choose in those snooze minutes to see whatever is good. Choose to trust God enough to consider, to pursue, and to place your hope in whatever is true.

> Since you have been raised to new life with Christ, set your sights on the realities of heaven, where Christ sits in the place of honor at God's right hand. Think about the things of heaven, not the things of earth.
>
> COLOSSIANS 3:1–2

Lord Jesus, let me take every opportunity today to fix my thoughts on what is right in your eyes. Amen.

DIFFERENCE MAKER

Seriously, try this out: The next time you hit your snooze button, or get some other kind of extra time, focus your thoughts on good things and see what happens.

SPRING IS COMING

Winter can be a cold, harsh drag. But spring is coming.

Near the back of the Bible is a little book named Jude. This little book, which is only twenty-five verses, has an underlying intensity of hope. It begins in love and joy, addresses a frigid concern, and then springs back to love and joy at the end.

The last couple verses of Jude thaw the cold and blooms freshness into the soul. Arms once huddled close to the chest are suddenly spread wide open! God's Word sings hope. When the season seems most somber, the eternal song of Jesus brings out the Bermuda shorts and points to the refreshing life that is to come.

Now all glory to God, who is able to keep you from falling away and will bring you with great joy into his glorious presence without a single fault. All glory to him who alone is God, our Savior through Jesus Christ our Lord. All glory, majesty, power, and authority are his before all time, and in the present, and beyond all time! Amen.

JUDE 24–25

Dear Jesus, let me see the new life that you have for me just ahead. Embolden my faith and keep my heart warm. Amen.

DIFFERENCE MAKER

Do something whimsical that will give you, and others around you, a glimpse of hope.

PROVERB

The book of Proverbs is all about wisdom, but not just the sort of wisdom that helps you do well on a test. This wisdom is proactive, or maybe better said, it is pro-action. Stationary, nondescript living is not an acceptable posture for this type of wisdom. Proverbs does not allow for generic living, or just going with the flow, or being what culture says you should be, or limiting yourself because someone placed a ceiling on you.

This book is not called Pronouns. It is called Proverbs. As you read this book, you are the subject who acts with the wisdom that you learn through its teachings. Wisdom is not slothful, lazy, inactive, or dead. Wisdom is productive. Wisdom flashes like Usain Bolt. In the right moment, it makes its way through the race and realigns things to the way God patterned.

My child, listen to what I say,
and treasure my commands.
Tune your ears to wisdom,
and concentrate on understanding.
Cry out for insight,
and ask for understanding.
Search for them as you would for silver;
seek them like hidden treasures.
Then you will understand what it means to fear the Lord,
and you will gain knowledge of God.

PROVERBS 2:1–5

Lord Jesus, kick my mind into gear. Give me wisdom that will be relevant and active for everything I will face today. Amen.

DIFFERENCE MAKER

Practice one of the action steps in Proverbs 2:1–5 again and again today: listen, treasure, tune, concentrate, cry out, and search.

POCKET PROTECTORS

People can be a lot like pocket protectors. They can be tight-fisted, tight-minded tightwads. Even if they were to see another person in need, they might seize the grip on their wallets, their time, their appearance, their performance, and their stuff. They can desperately keep for themselves whatever precious item they have treasured in their pockets. To let their guard down would be to relinquish control—so without thinking they might find themselves standing defensively against others who simply need the smallest helping hand.

But Jesus lives with wide-open arms. He shares his life, kingdom, mercy, and salvation. He offers himself sacrificially, generously, and even scandalously in concern. He reaches his hands out in an invitation for the poor and downcast to join him in communion. People were never meant to be stingy, stuffy, or stuck. They were created to treasure Jesus, and, as a result, to generously treasure others.

> "Wherever your treasure is, there the desires of your heart
> will also be."
> MATTHEW 6:21

Lord Jesus, you have asked me to be like you, radically committed to open-handedness. Lead me to an opportunity to practice generous living today.
Amen.

DIFFERENCE MAKER

Offer to buy something for someone in need, or leave a larger tip than normal, or send a donation to a charity, or go get your hands dirty at a soup kitchen. Do something generous today that loosens up your comfort zone.

ROT

Three thousand years ago there was a chart-topping pop song that must have gotten stuck in King Saul's mind and driven him mad. The lyrics weren't too deep really, just regular boy-band type of stuff. But they must have irritated Saul over and over and over again. The words from 1 Samuel 18 went like this: "Saul has killed his thousands, and David his tens thousands." Saul didn't like that song.

King Saul began to envy this young warrior named David. What David had (faith, fame, adoration, potential, promise, good looks, magazine covers?), Saul once had, but had lost. And so Saul thought, *Well, if I can't have it, then David can't have it anymore either.*

In fact, the Bible says that the song was "bad in the eyes of Saul." He looked at the song, he looked at David, and he looked at himself, and his eyes made his heart malignant. Jealousy, not God, took control of the way he looked at his life, and so he "kept a jealous eye on David."

A peaceful heart leads to a healthy body;
jealousy is like cancer in the bones.

PROVERBS 14:30

Lord Jesus, rid my heart of jealousy today. Let me find my peace in you alone.
Amen.

DIFFERENCE MAKER

Choose something that you have acquired out of jealousy and figure out a way to give it up.

TAKE A DEEP BREATH

Take a deep breath. You really should do this more often. It's cleansing. Oxygen refreshes your brain and strengthens your heart, not to mention all of your other organs as well. Pause. Breathe in. Hold. Breathe out. Right now, before tackling any more work, or before allowing yourself to fall into an endless loop of laziness, remember to breathe. It is what makes you alive.

A new creation. That's what you are in Jesus.

Take a moment to breathe. Remember what makes you alive. Don't try to manipulate the events of your life. It was God who first breathed life into you. He now gives you the ability to do the same. With deep yearning, find the rhythm God composed for you. Give all of the rises and falls, the notes and beats, the crescendos and melodies of your life to him.

> Be still in the presence of the LORD,
> and wait patiently for him to act.
> Don't worry about evil people who prosper
> or fret about their wicked schemes.

PSALM 37:7

Dear Jesus, don't let the wind get knocked out of me today. Teach me to breathe in rhythm with your breath. Amen.

DIFFERENCE MAKER

Commit yourself to silence for at least ten minutes. During that time lay out your thoughts to God. Then, shut up for a while, take a deep breath, and just try to be still before God.

THE FRESH MAKER

God's breath is fresh. Always fresh. It's like he has a constant eternal supply of Mentos, those mints with cheesy commercials and a great slogan. God is like the ultimate "Fresh Maker" of heaven and earth. Everything he breathes upon flourishes with life. When he starts the day, his breath is not like yours after a night of snoring. When you wake up and breathe, things wilt and coil back. But when God breathes, everything draws closer and opens up for even more. God's breath gives abundant life and incredible power.

When he created Adam, he stood there as a lump of molded sinew, until God breathed into him the breath of life. Then he blossomed with relationship and had a lively time naming things like the platypus and the manatee. When God gave Ezekiel a vision of dry bones, they stood there as lumps of reformed sinew until God breathed on them the breath of life. Then they lived again. When Jesus commissioned his followers, they stood there as speechless lumps of confused sinew, until he breathed on them and gave them the Holy Spirit, the breath of God. Then they ran through the world changing the air of history.

Then he breathed on them and said,
"Receive the Holy Spirit."

JOHN 20:22

Lord Jesus, breathe in me today, this unworthy soul. Take this lump of sinew and breathe in me, expand my lungs and revive my soul. Amen.

DIFFERENCE MAKER

Brush your teeth, chew some Mentos, and go around breathing on people all day, but be ready to tell them why you're doing it.

SKUBALA

You could say it is "dog dung," or maybe you would rather call it "garbage," or, if you're British, perhaps you'd like to call it "rubbish." And maybe you have a more profane word for it. Literally, when he wrote it in Greek, the word the apostle Paul used is σκύβαλα, or written in English it looks like *skubala*. It means "excrement." Did you just read that correctly? Yep. Paul wrote it. It's in the Bible. Offal. Dookie. Cow pies thrown on the top of a dump. *Skubala*. That's what Paul wrote.

Why did he drop the boys off at the pool like this? Well, he came to a point in his life where the things that he once held as most important he now considered *skubala*. All of his ambitions and work, all of his pride and achievements, all of it he says was worth a pile of poop when compared to the surpassing greatness of knowing Jesus. Compared to knowing Jesus, everything else is *skubala*.

> Yes, everything else is worthless when compared with the
> infinite value of knowing Christ Jesus my Lord. For his sake
> I have discarded everything else, counting it all as garbage,
> so that I could gain Christ.
>
> PHILIPPIANS 3:8

Dear Jesus, help me get my priorities straight. Amen.

DIFFERENCE MAKER

The next time you go to the bathroom, think about those things that have more value in your life than Jesus, and, in manner of speaking, flush them down the toilet.

ADVOCATE

There are situations, unfortunately, where people do wrong, stupid things. Sometimes these people realize what they have done, feel terrible, and strive to turn their lives around. But the problem is that they have still committed harmful mistakes. Eventually, those foolish acts come around to haunt them and they stand judged.

In that moment, they could try to plead their own case. They could pour out their heart with apologies and ask the court to compassion. But the judge, as benevolent and caring as he might be, is in a no-win situation. That stupid thing still happened, damage was done, and someone still needs to pay for it and restore it.

At the end of their life, people will appear before God. They will plead and pour out. The Judge will want to forgive. He will want to grant mercy. But who then will pay for the damage that has been done? That's when Jesus will stand up, look at his Father, and declare, "I will take the punishment. I will pay for the damage. I will stand in judgment in this person's place."

> My dear children, I am writing this to you so that you will not sin. But if anyone does sin, we have an advocate who pleads our case before the Father. He is Jesus Christ, the one who is truly righteous.
>
> 1 JOHN 2:1

Jesus, I need you. You are my advocate. Thank you for standing for me and taking the consequences for me. How could I ever repay you? Amen.

DIFFERENCE MAKER

The biggest difference you could ever make is to accept Jesus Christ as your Savior. With a sense of overwhelmed gratitude, receive what he has done on your behalf.

March

Jesus,

Strengthen me to stand tall in you.

Amen.

ORPHANS BROUGHT HOME

One the places on this planet where God can most be understood is in a loving orphanage. The sickness of the world has left too many children alone. But there are places—homes—where orphaned babies are bathed in water, wrapped in blankets, nourished to health, sung to sleep, and cherished as precious people with a great destiny.

The Love of Christ orphanage, also known as TLC, is a place like this. Babies in South Africa who have been left to fend for themselves, because of conditions like HIV/AIDS, are lovingly accepted in a home like TLC. It's not easy for those who dedicate their lives to this work. It is a nonstop restorative mission. But those who care for orphans are living in the heartbeat of God himself.

Those who care for orphans are reflections of God's heart. He is a God who rescues. Jesus came to this earth just so that people could be brought home into the family of God.

> God decided in advance to adopt us into his own family by
> bringing us to himself through Jesus Christ. This is what he
> wanted to do, and it gave him great pleasure.
>
> EPHESIANS 1:5

Dear Jesus, thank you for treasuring me and giving me a home with you. Amen.

DIFFERENCE MAKER

How could you use your career to support an orphanage
or adoption ministry?

KINDNESS

What makes you feel the best about *you*? What is it that gives you hope about the direction of your life? What is it that fills you with confidence? What makes you laugh without worry? What helps you look in the mirror and see someone who has something good to offer?

One thing that most certainly impacts how anyone feels about themselves is how they treat others. Ironically, by focusing on treating others with kindness, people usually feel built up within themselves. Kindness causes people to stop turning inward and to start living outward. It expands their freedom, their creativity, their joy, and their optimism.

The opposite is also a reality. Cruel treatment of others echoes back to the attacker. Heated anger thrown at another burns more than one person. Hurtful words, despicable harm, shameful acts—they ricochet like shrapnel, rend the hearts of those nearby, and poison the soul of the aggressor. The world hesitates at this thought, but the truth is that kindness has the power to change the world for good.

> Your kindness will reward you,
> but your cruelty will destroy you.
>
> PROVERBS 11:17

Lord Jesus, let your kindness change me. Let me overflow with kind action for others today. Amen.

DIFFERENCE MAKER

Do as many random acts of kindness for others today as you can possibly think of doing. Then rest with confidence and a smile at the end of the day.

WILLINGLY

Have you ever been asked to do a job that you didn't want to do? Of course you have. Perhaps it was mowing the lawn while your friends played outside. Perhaps it was finishing your homework while your favorite show was on. Or perhaps it was cleaning up someone else's mess, or picking up your clothes, or acting polite when you were actually seething with frustration inside.

Whatever it was that you had to do, it didn't kill you. (You're reading this right now today because you are probably still alive.) It may have bugged you and made you feel a wee bit justified in letting whoever told you to do it that you were just a wee bit upset with them. Perhaps you huffed and puffed, perhaps you grumbled and complained, or perhaps you devised ways to get even. Unless the person or job was evil, the work you were asked to do was likely some sort of responsible service in one way or another. It probably served a purpose, even if mundane or routine, or unknown to you. It is God's desire that we work willingly, as if we are working for God, not for people.

> Work willingly at whatever you do, as though you were
> working for the Lord rather than for people.
>
> COLOSSIANS 3:23

Lord Jesus, give me a bigger capacity to serve than I have been known to show in the past. Let me see the work that I do, whatever it may be, as a service to you. Amen.

DIFFERENCE MAKER

Stretch yourself. Find something to do today that will be helpful for somebody else, but that will give you no glory.

MOTIVATE GOOD

Jesus celebrates when we spur one another on to do things he wants us to do. When you give a sudden display of kindness to someone, others notice and eventually do likewise. Your good works can "pay it forward" to someone else.

And when you are creative about your good deeds, your impact increases even more. Your creativity in serving others shows your commitment to love others. It shows that you are thinking of the unique needs and personalities of other people. When you take the time to care uniquely for someone, you display God's love by treasuring and cherishing who they are. Keep doing good. Keep making a difference. Keep blessing this world with the blessing of Jesus.

Let us think of ways to motivate one another to acts of love and good works.

HEBREWS 10:24

Jesus, help me to keep serving you by serving others. Surround me with a group of people who will sustain and motivate me to be a source of life. Amen.

DIFFERENCE MAKER

Think of two new "acts of love" or "good works." Practice one of these ways yourself and encourage someone else to practice the other. Then be sure to connect in the next twenty-four hours to celebrate what happened.

WHAT TO DO

Do you know what to do today? Did you know that God has already told you? He's already told everybody, in fact. Actually, he's made it pretty clear. God has let the world know what he believes is good. And not good as in "I guess that's cool," but good as in "God looked at all he had made and he saw that it was good" kind of good. Got that?

Well, what is good in God's eyes? He tells us to do what is right, love mercy, and walk humbly with him. That's pretty simple, huh? There's nothing confusing about that. This was why God created people. Oh man, how far from "good" has humanity fallen? What would happen if people set their efforts on restoring these patterns to the earth once again? Since God has already told you what to do, then I'd encourage you to start doing it.

> No, O people, the LORD has told you what is good,
> and this is what he requires of you:
> to do what is right, to love mercy,
> and to walk humbly with your God.
>
> MICAH 6:8

Dear Jesus, today, challenge me to make the right moves, to love being merciful to others, and to walk with your arm wrapped around my shoulders. Amen.

DIFFERENCE MAKER

Which of the three "requirements" do you most need to focus on today? What is one action you can take to pursue that focus?

CREATED TO PRAY

Three thousand years ago King Solomon was finishing one of the wonders of the world. The temple in Jerusalem was an architectural masterpiece. People would travel from around the world to visit this structure and worship the God of Israel. As it was being completed, the Lord wanted to put things into perspective for King Solomon and the people of Israel. As great as the building was, he knew that they would struggle to keep their focus on him. God told them that he would do certain things (or, better said, withhold from doing things) to get back their attention. And if they turned their eyes once again to him, he promised to restore their grandeur. When you find yourself losing focus on God, do not forget that he will try to get your attention. And when he does, turn your eyes to him.

"Then if my people who are called by my name will humble themselves and pray and seek my face and turn from their wicked ways, I will hear from heaven and will forgive their sins and restore their land."

2 CHRONICLES 7:14

Lord Jesus, turn my eyes to you today. I pray that you will not hide your face from me, but let me see you clearly working in my life. Amen.

DIFFERENCE MAKER

Attend to God. Pray to him today. Repent, asking him to forgive your sins.

SO

If you had all the power in the world, what would you do with it? Would you make life comfortable for yourself, hire people to bring you a burrito whenever you felt hungry, or try to become pals with someone famous? The Bible says that Jesus had all the power in the world. But he didn't use his power to serve himself. In fact, right before he was betrayed and arrested, right before he was beaten and ridiculed, right before he had nails driven into his hands and feet, Jesus did something that you wouldn't expect from the most powerful being on earth. John, in his eye-witness account, describes the moment like this:

> Jesus knew that the Father had given him authority over everything and that he had come from God and would return to God. So he got up from the table, took off his robe, wrapped a towel around his waist, and poured water into a basin. Then he began to wash the disciples' feet, drying them with the towel he had around him.
>
> JOHN 13:3–5

Dear Jesus, I'm so thankful that it is you, and not someone else, who has all the power. Thank you for serving me, even though I should be the one serving you.
Amen.

DIFFERENCE MAKER

Think of a way to bless someone
with whatever authority God has blessed you.

WALK

Considering that humans were created to walk with God, they have sure spent a lot of time and energy trying to blaze trails without him. It's remarkable that people are so quick to step off the path that God is on. Like people who rely on GPS for direction, when they walk away from God they inevitably get disoriented and lost.

But what's even more astonishing, perhaps, is that if these lost people were to stop and listen, they would see God's steps and hear his voice. If they had the sense to look for him, they would discover that God had followed them down that rough trail and had been calling out their name. God leaves his stroll in the garden in order to save people from the minefield they wandered into.

Thomas, a worried wanderer, once asked Jesus, "How can we know the way, Lord?" Jesus, preparing to save the lost who had walked away, replied:

"I am the way, the truth, and the life. No one can come to
the Father except through me."

JOHN 14:6

*Jesus, I want to walk with you today. Thank you for coming to find me. Thank
you for the chance to take steps with you. Amen.*

DIFFERENCE MAKER

Go for a walk. With each step, talk to Jesus about your life, your passions, your goals, and your worries. Confide yourself in him and he will direct your path to the Father.

BENIGN NEGLECT

Are you one of the growing number of people who need a swift kick in the backside to get you going today? There is a mentality in society today known as "benign neglect." Basically, it means that people feel like they can put the normal responsibilities of life off until some other time in the future. They feel like they can extend their adolescence for years, even into their thirties or forties, and that "real life" begins later when they feel more ready.

It is "benign" because it doesn't "feel" bad (at first), but over time it can be neglectful of a person's potential and gifts and calling in life. Now is not the time to put off doing what you need to do. Don't fall into the pit of this off-putting chronic illness. Don't give in to "benign neglect." Rather, work hard to prove that God has made you alive by his Spirit.

So, dear brothers and sisters, work hard to prove that you really are among those God has called and chosen. Do these things, and you will never fall away.

2 PETER 1:10

Dear Jesus, give me the guts to get rid of any benign neglect. What you have called me to do, motivate me to do it. Amen.

DIFFERENCE MAKER

What is something that you should strive to accomplish, but have been putting off? What do you need to do to get going once again?

FOR HE GAVE

If you could buy anything, what would it be? A sports car? Wireless Beats headphones? College tuition? Good grades? Love? Respect? What you would buy?

Jesus had the same question posed to him. His answer? "Well, here's what I'd buy: freedom for people enslaved to sin. That's what I'd want to purchase." And so he did. But not with money. He gave over all that he had to purchase freedom for humanity. He gave over his status, his glory, and his very blood to purchase freedom for the very people who took his life from him.

If you want, Jesus will free you from your bondage to sin, for he gave himself to forgive people of their sin.

> For he has rescued us from the kingdom of darkness and transferred us into the Kingdom of his dear Son, who purchased our freedom and forgave our sins.
>
> COLOSSIANS 1:13–14

Lord Jesus, I don't deserve what you have done for me. Thank you for your forgiveness. Let me live in the freedom you have purchased for me today. Amen.

DIFFERENCE MAKER

Do you know anybody stuck in a pattern of sin or weighed down by the effects of sin? Buy them a coffee, a card, or a creative gift. Find a way to encourage them with the freedom that comes only through Jesus.

RUN

Life is a lot like a marathon. Learning how to run over a long distance is the key to finishing well. You can't just wake up one day and go out and run a marathon—you need stamina for long-distance running. You need training and discipline to stay focused on the big picture, especially while being tempted to grab a dozen caramel-glazed, chocolate-filled donuts.

Many runners have gotten derailed over the years. Sadly, they have missed the opportunity to pursue their full potential. They have missed the chance to change people's lives, to give hope where it was needed, and to rejoice at the finish line with others who have faithfully put one foot ahead of the next for an entire lifetime. Jesus created you to run the marathon of life. So run as if it was the only thing you had to do. Run from the things that mess you up, and run toward the things that build you up.

Run from anything that stimulates youthful lusts. Instead,
pursue righteous living, faithfulness, love, and peace.
Enjoy the companionship of those who call on the Lord
with pure hearts.
2 TIMOTHY 2:22

Dear Jesus, I don't always feel like exercising my faith, but I pray that you will push me like my trainer today so that I can learn to run for you. Amen.

DIFFERENCE MAKER

Go for a run today. Find others who will celebrate the steps that you are taking in your life.

INSTEAD

Worry creeps everywhere. What I mean is that it gets around. When the future is unknown or circumstances are fearful, worry tosses people around. Instead of giving worry power and letting stress steal life from you, twist the intent of worry to your advantage. Every time apprehension hits your heart, take the opportunity to deflect it over to God. He created you to depend upon him. So use your anxiousness to help you trust Jesus more and more today.

The more worry tries to tear you down, lift it up to God. The more you worry, the more opportunity you have to ask him for help. Take the energy that your anxiety is taking from you and focus it on prayer. The sweat and sleeplessness, the panic and pace, dedicate it all to Jesus. Give it to him today. And thank him when he lifts it off your shoulders.

Don't worry about anything; instead, pray about everything.
Tell God what you need, and thank him for all he has done.
Then you will experience God's peace, which exceeds
anything we can understand. His peace will guard your
hearts and minds as you live in Christ Jesus.

PHILIPPIANS 4:6-7

Lord Jesus, I lift my worries to you today. Thank you for guarding me. Amen.

DIFFERENCE MAKER

Write the verses for today on a piece of paper and tape it somewhere you'll see throughout the day. Try to commit it to memory. Each time worry comes after you, pray about it and entrust it to Jesus.

PERSEVERE

Perseverance. What a terrible word. *Per* means "through," while *severance* means "to get cut off." So perseverance means going through a time of getting cut off. Those who have had to persevere through terrible circumstances understand the near-devastating process of longsuffering, especially when the suffering is caused by someone else, or, perhaps, especially when it means saying no to a tempting desire or cheap escape.

The first Christians were persecuted for simply following Jesus. They had to learn to persevere through some terrible treatment, some harsh realities. They had to face fear and threat and loss and pain. It must have been tempting at times to wonder about giving up and pursuing a path that would help them fit in better with the world around them. And yet they endured. Their trials proved their perseverance, displaying miraculous character that changed the world.

Perseverance for following Jesus does not come from a mild commitment to faith. It comes only from a daily practice of deep devotion, of learning how to live for Christ.

God blesses those who patiently endure testing and
temptation. Afterward they will receive the crown of life that
God has promised to those who love him.

JAMES 1:12

Lord Jesus, I don't have the strength in me, unless you enable it. Please give me the motivation to never quit. Amen.

DIFFERENCE MAKER

What testing or temptation do you need to patiently endure today?

EXTRAORDINARY

Jesus thinks people are extraordinary. Even those who feel like their lives are far from glorious, Jesus thinks they're remarkable. Even those who feel like they could never get close to the glamourous grandeur of stardom, Jesus lifts them up on his shoulders and cheers them on. Even those who dream of hanging out with somebody famous, Jesus longs to hang out with them.

The truth is that Jesus came to those who didn't feel like they had a shot at glory. He came to walk with them in the ordinary moments of their lives; he came to sit in their homes, eat dinner with them, talk politics and religion, and laugh at their jokes. Jesus came to cry with them in times of loss and encourage them to do greater things than they could have ever imagined. He came to heal their wounds and their hearts. He came to challenge their despair and their cynicism. He came because he thought ordinary people were worth far more than they could ever realize.

No one is more amazing than Jesus. And yet he came to be with you.

So the Word became human and made his home among us.
He was full of unfailing love and faithfulness. And we have
seen his glory, the glory of the Father's one and only Son.

JOHN 1:14

Dear Jesus, you are the living God, and yet you came to me. Thank you for wanting me to be in the presence of your glory. Amen.

DIFFERENCE MAKER

See the extraordinary in someone you would dismiss as ordinary today. Jesus thinks they are worth his attention, so perhaps they should be worth yours too.

MUSTACHE MARCH

This is the middle of Mustache March. Maybe you have already been braiding your lip hair for the last two weeks, or maybe you haven't…but you certainly cannot deny the countercultural power of the mustache. People simply look at it and are changed by its mesmerizing audacity.

Jesus has called you to be a radical person. He wants to empower you to stand rooted in him against the winds of culture that try to make everybody look the same. Too many people conform to the patterns of this world, giving in to pursuits that are not good for them. Jesus wants you to be an example of a more audacious path.

The apostle Paul told a young leader this very same thing a long time ago. While culture expected him to conform, Paul challenged him to rise to the occasion and make a difference with the people around him.

> Don't let anyone think less of you because you are young.
> Be an example to all believers in what you say, in the way
> you live, in your love, your faith, and your purity.
>
> 1 TIMOTHY 4:12

Dear Jesus, strengthen me to stand tall in you today. Amen.

DIFFERENCE MAKER

What kind of a role model could you be for those around you? What could you do as an example of countercultural living that would encourage others to make the right decisions too?

TREASURE

It is in your broken heart where God has room to walk around and restore. It is in the midst of your weakness that God's light and strength and power can do its glorious work. When you embrace the treasure of Jesus in your life, you quickly recognize that you cannot contain him. You are much too fragile to be the living container of Almighty God. And yet in you is precisely where Jesus wants to live. He wants to take up residence in your life and use you to bring his light to others.

True followers of Jesus admit that their power does not come from their own stature of greatness. Rather, those who invite Jesus to live within them are the first to say that they don't deserve such marvelous company. The church, where fragile people are being empowered through Jesus, is a community where real people with real concerns will find real restoration.

We now have this light shining in our hearts, but we ourselves are like fragile clay jars containing this great treasure. This makes it clear that our great power is from God, not from ourselves.

2 CORINTHIANS 4:7

Dear Jesus, what I have to offer is not perfect,
but please make yourself at home in me. Amen.

DIFFERENCE MAKER

Find a church community that displays a humble gratitude for what Jesus has done, and a resilient and confident strength that comes from knowing Jesus.

DO GOOD

God enjoys people who do what he created them to do. In fact, God wired people with the desire and ability to do what is good. That means, in a world that has rejected God, and as a result is struggling with so much bad, people who do what God created them to do become world changers. People who do what God wants them to do are people who change the world with God's authority and God's ability.

Look around. What problems do you see? What did Jesus do about them? Now ask Jesus to look at you. What potential does he see in you, his follower? What does he want you to do? God rejoices when his people participate in his restorative work for this world. Practice the patterns that God initiated to rescue people from the devastation that is all around them.

"Learn to do good.
Seek justice.
Help the oppressed.
Defend the cause of orphans.
Fight for the rights of widows."

ISAIAH 1:17

Jesus, I have a lot of opportunity to do what you'd like for me to do.
Thank you for inviting me into your line of work. Amen.

DIFFERENCE MAKER

Of the five lines of Isaiah 1:17, which one can you do something about today? What can you do toward that cause? Take immediate action: write it down or tell someone to hold you accountable to do it.

TAKE HEART

If you decide to live for Jesus today, then take heart. It is not easy to decide to go against the flow of the culture, to stand for truth, to rally around those who are outcast, to speak up for those who cannot defend themselves, and to do it with humility and integrity. Following Jesus means not following the patterns in society that are self-serving or peer pressured or garbage grabbing. Following Jesus means making a difference in a world that needs a difference to be made.

And that is not easy. But, then again, Jesus didn't say it would be easy. He said he would give us peace and strength and that he would fight on our behalf. He said he would empower and embolden us and that he would be with us as we stand for the truth. He said he would enable us to love the unlovable and to fight the good fight of faith.

Jesus wants to change this world. And he wants you to change it with him.

> "I have told you all this so that you may have peace in me.
> Here on earth you will have many trials and sorrows. But
> take heart, because I have overcome the world."
>
> JOHN 16:33

Lord Jesus, I'm all in. I will take heart because you are changing this world,
and you are doing it through me. Amen.

DIFFERENCE MAKER

Stand up for Jesus with an emboldened heart today,
trusting him for the outcome.

SEE CLEARLY

In a way that would impress any good redneck, Jesus spit. He hocked a loogie. That wasn't even the gross part of it. His spit was directed straight into a man's eyes. Yes, that's right—Jesus spit into a man's eyes. But the man didn't get mad. In fact, he let Jesus do it. He trusted Jesus. He let Jesus form and create and spit on him. He let Jesus ask him questions and put his hands on his eyes. He didn't rub out the spit, because he knew that Jesus cared for him. Jesus might not always do things for you in the way that makes you feel comfortable. Now and then he enjoys doing things that are a little messy in order to focus your eyes and bring about healing within you.

> Then Jesus placed his hands on the man's eyes again, and
> his eyes were opened. His sight was completely restored,
> and he could see everything clearly.
>
> MARK 8:25

Dear Jesus, someone needs to do the dirty work in my life. Heal me so that I can see everything clearly. Amen.

DIFFERENCE MAKER

Be ready to get messy today. Even if it means doing something that is uncomfortable, don't miss an opportunity to help someone see life clearly.

PLANKINEYETIS

Plankineyetis is a debilitating condition that distorts the way people see reality. It diminishes their ability to see themselves with clarity. Plankineyetis attacks the soul through the eyes, and it evidences itself when a person sees a splinter in someone else's eye and announces with pride that he or she will help clean it out. This is a monstrous proclamation, because what they fail to realize, but what everybody else can easily see, is that the person's judgment is affected by the fact that there is an entire log jammed into their own eye socket.

Chaos ensues as the diseased patient moves around. People have to duck out of the way. Family and friends begin to avoid eye contact with the one who has contracted plankineyetis. It ruins relationships, leads to blindness of heart, and needs to be cured. Luckily, Jesus tells us the cure.

> "And why worry about a speck in your friend's eye when you have a log in your own? How can you think of saying to your friend, 'Let me help you get rid of that speck in your eye,' when you can't see past the log in your own eye? Hypocrite! First get rid of the log in your own eye; then you will see well enough to deal with the speck in your friend's eye."
>
> MATTHEW 7:3–5

Lord Jesus, forgive my judgmental attitude. Heal my condition. Help me see clearly again. Amen.

DIFFERENCE MAKER

Try to catch yourself every time you have a judgmental thought about someone today. When you do have a judgmental thought, cover one eye for one minute.

JESUS...

Jesus seeks after the lost and searches for runaways.
Jesus finds the hidden and heals the broken.
Jesus gives footing to the lame.
Jesus opens the ears of the deaf.
Jesus restores sight to the blind.
Jesus frees the prisoner.
Jesus has coffee with the prostitute.
Jesus loves the sinner and forgives the repentant.
Jesus strengthens the weak.
Jesus fills the empty and dwells with the lonely.
Jesus weeps with the sad, the hurting, and the grieved.
Jesus comforts the mourner.
Jesus breathes into the lifeless.
Jesus lifts up the trampled and gathers the displaced.
Jesus feeds the hungry and quenches the thirsty.
Jesus puts the last at the front.
Jesus eats with the unsanitary and dines with the despised.
Jesus carries the world's sins and burdens.
Jesus dies for his enemies and bleeds for his friends.
Jesus stretches out his arms to welcome you home.

Jesus also did many other things. If they were all written
down, I suppose the whole world could not contain the
books that would be written.

JOHN 21:25

Dear Jesus, you have done so much. Thank you! Amen.

DIFFERENCE MAKER

Jesus asks you to do a lot. What is one thing that he has done that you
should put into action today?

SERVE

As he was preparing for the day ahead, Jesus said something startling. "Normally," he said, "the master sits at the table and is served by his servants. But not here! I am your servant." Jesus could have demanded their allegiance. He could have instructed them to bring him some sandals and iced tea (with a lemon slice and one of those little paper umbrellas). He could have called down his angels and waylaid everyone in his path, especially Judas—the guy who was about to betray him. But instead, he attended to their needs, he washed their feet, and he served them food and drink. Jesus turned the tables upside down.

> "But among you it will be different. Those who are the greatest among you should take the lowest rank, and the leader should be like a servant."
>
> LUKE 22:26

Dear Jesus, I don't deserve to have you serve me. I am humbled to be loved by you so much. Let me be changed by this truth in everything I do today. Amen.

DIFFERENCE MAKER

Serve someone today. Wash the dishes, pay for gas in their car, buy them lunch, leave them a note, or find some other creative way to do something that shows how much you value them.

GAWKING

Crowds gathered at the scene of the horror. They just stood there, entranced at the violence and injustice, hypnotized by the spectacle of it all. When Jesus went to the cross, people just watched—afraid and captivated by the awfulness of the moment. People were ignorant and angry at Jesus. Some were shouting at him while others were silently condemning him to die. Everyone was unable to avert their eyes, and yet they were unwilling to truly see what was going on. The cross of Jesus was hideous—so horrific that people couldn't help but stare.

Jesus, in that very moment, as he hung crucified, was looking back at the crowd. He had eyes on the very people that were watching him die. But instead of a look of revenge, Jesus had compassion in his sight. He wanted those gawkers to make eye contact with him so that he could peer into their souls and overcome their judgment and fear with his forgiveness and hope.

The crowd watched and the leaders scoffed. "He saved others," they said, "let him save himself if he is really God's Messiah, the Chosen One."

LUKE 23:35

Jesus, thank you for dying on the cross for me. Let me look to the cross and look you in the eyes, allowing your gaze to brighten my frightened soul. Amen.

DIFFERENCE MAKER

Draw a cross on something that you will see again and again throughout the day. Let it remind you to look Jesus in the eyes.

THE GARDEN

After Judas had betrayed Jesus, and just before soldiers came to arrest him, Jesus and his disciples went to the Mount of Olives, to the garden of Gethsemane. He warned his disciples to avoid temptation and sin, but in their emotionally exhausted condition they chose instead to sleep. But Jesus walked "about a stone's throw away," knelt down, and prayed. It was in a garden that humans first tasted sin; it was in a garden that Jesus wrestled with it.

His time of prayer was intense. Sin was not going to die easily. Jesus prayed so fervently, with such agony of spirit, that his sweat became mixed with great drops of blood. This condition is known as hematidrosis, which occurs when someone is experiencing extreme stress. While the disciples slept through it, Jesus took it upon himself to do the very thing the disciples were unwilling or unable to do.

> Father, if you are willing, please take this cup of suffering away from me. Yet I want your will to be done, not mine.
>
> LUKE 22:42

Dear Jesus, what can I say? You wrestled against what I have so easily been beaten by. Thank you for what you have done. Amen.

DIFFERENCE MAKER

After he prayed, Jesus told the disciples to get up and pray so that temptation didn't overpower them. Why not take his words to heart? If possible, find a garden to walk through and pray about overcoming sin through Jesus.

QUAKE

The tomb that held Jesus didn't know what hit it! It was a new tomb, a respectful burial spot offered by a wealthy man near a garden. A peaceful place. Then the earthquake hit. The entrance to the tomb, a huge stone chiseled round, was rolled aside. The new tomb, which had been used, was once again available for rent. Jesus had risen from the dead.

The first people on the scene were guards who had been stationed there to keep things from getting shook up. But the tremor, not to mention the angel of the Lord who seemed to be casually sitting on the stone, made the guards quake in their boots. The second group of people on the scene were women who were close followers of Jesus. They actually spoke to the angel, who informed them that Jesus had been raised from the dead just as he said would happen. Instead of fainting like the guards, they turned their fear into great joy and ran to tell others the good news that Jesus had risen.

> Suddenly there was a great earthquake! For an angel of the
> Lord came down from heaven, rolled aside the stone, and
> sat on it.
>
> MATTHEW 28:2

Lord Jesus, not even death could stop you from walking on this earth. Thank you for conquering everything that stood in the way of life. Amen.

DIFFERENCE MAKER

In terms of your awareness of Jesus, do you, or the people around you, need a quake to shake you up a bit? Use this question as a filter throughout your day.

FLASHLIGHT

You know that moment when you've been in a dark room for a while and somebody suddenly flicks on the light switch? Your eyes recoil, your face winces and squints, and you inevitably shield your head from the glare of the bright beams. But even with your eyes closed, somehow behind those eyelids of yours, you can see the image of the light burned into your retinas. Jesus is like that light. And when he shines into the darkness of someone's actions, or the gloom of someone's soul, the glare can be painfully intense. But the light of Jesus is so very good too. It was his light that illuminated the earth at creation. It was his light that led God's people to freedom from slavery. It was his light that represented the greatness and love of God throughout the entire Bible. Jesus created you to walk in his light.

Adjust your eyes to the light of Jesus today. You were made to see his glory, the beauty of his creation, and the worth he gave to every person. Don't recoil back into a shadow of who you were made to be.

"All who do evil hate the light and refuse to go near it for fear their sins will be exposed. But those who do what is right come to the light so others can see that they are doing what God wants."

JOHN 3:20–21

Dear Jesus, help me to stop groping around in the darkness. Call me to walk in your light. Amen.

DIFFERENCE MAKER

Grab a small flashlight and carry it around with you all day. If you find yourself shrinking back into darkness, shine that light in your eyes.

STUPID THINGS

People need Jesus because they make so many frustratingly foolish choices. It's almost like humans can't stop acting out their inner idiocy. Like dogs that return to their own vomit, some people knowingly hurt themselves by pursuing pleasures that interest them in the moment but revolt them in the long run. Like vultures that hunt their prey, some even knowingly hurt others by taking advantage of weaknesses for their own selfish gain. Like sheep that wander, some people simply make wrong choices that end up hurting everyone in their circle of influence.

God did not create people to do stupid things. And yet people continually stray from God's patterns, either intentionally or unintentionally. People constantly find themselves humiliated and trapped by the lure of sin's idiocy. But Jesus overcame humanity's corrupt absurdity by pursuing the cross, where all the stupidity of sin is collected and destroyed. There, the life-giving wisdom and heart-empowering joy of Jesus is offered in exchange. And in this way, the cross of Christ dumbfounds foolish pursuits.

Those who belong to Christ Jesus have nailed the passions
and desires of their sinful nature to his cross and crucified
them there.

GALATIANS 5:24

Dear Jesus, don't let me do stupid things today. Get them out of my life.
Let them hang on the cross. And let me follow you. Amen.

DIFFERENCE MAKER

Don't do something today that you will regret doing. Choose to do something else instead.

TURNED BACKS

If you had been in the crowd that day, what would you have done? Would you have yelled at him? Would you have denied the miracles your own eyes had seen him do? Would you have looked at the open slices across his back, and would you have patronized him or felt a ping of pity? When somebody spit on him, would you have laughed or would you have watched it unfold? When he collapsed under the weight of the cross, would you have stepped out of the crowd to help him lift it back up? Or perhaps you wouldn't have participated in any of it at all. Maybe you would have fled town, overcome with fear and grief. Afraid or unwilling to honestly confront the rejection absorbed by the Savior, people still turn their backs on Jesus to this day. But, ironically, that's why he carried the cross through the crowd.

> He was despised and rejected—
> a man of sorrows, acquainted with deepest grief.
> We turned our backs on him and looked the other way.
> He was despised, and we did not care.
>
> ISAIAH 53:3

Lord Jesus, how did you put up with this? How did you forgive? You took the brunt of all hatred and agony and rejection. Your love overwhelms me. Amen.

DIFFERENCE MAKER

Jesus carried your sorrow. What sorrow can you carry for someone today?

MISJUDGED

Susan Boyle walked out on the stage in front of a theater full of people ready to dismiss her. The judges and the crowd struggled to imagine what she could be doing there. The moment they saw her meek appearance, most concluded that she would be just another *Britain's Got Talent* contestant laughed off the stage. And then she sang. And before she could finish her first phrase to the song, people were overwhelmed, standing on their feet in amazement.

When people looked at Jesus, they dismissed him too. He wasn't what they expected. They thought he was just another Messiah contestant who would be booed off the stage of history. Even worse, they looked at him and thought he deserved the ridicule and punishment he received. Humans don't have a great track record of judging, do they?

> Yet it was our weaknesses he carried;
> it was our sorrows that weighed him down.
> And we thought his troubles were a punishment from God,
> a punishment for his own sins!

ISAIAH 53:4

Dear Jesus, you took my sins upon yourself while I pointed and laughed. And then you sang your song of sorrow, and I became dumbfounded and ashamed. Forgive me. Amen.

DIFFERENCE MAKER

Go to YouTube and watch Susan Boyle's first appearance on *Britain's Got Talent*. As you watch, realize that Jesus never dismissed you. Don't dismiss others today.

BEAUTY MARKS

The wounds of Jesus are beauty marks. After his resurrection, Jesus presented himself to one of his followers, a man named Thomas, a man who doubted whether or not the resurrection had actually happened. To prove who he was, though, Jesus showed him the nail scars in his hands and feet, and the spear wound in his side. Not pretty. Certainly terrible. But definitely beautiful.

Even in his resurrected state, Jesus chose to keep his scars. They mean everything to him. His wounds show his story, a story that is woven with more love and intentionality than the world had ever understood before. The Creator of the Universe, the one who had been rejected, was crushed to bring life. His scars are evidence of this good news.

> But he was pierced for our rebellion,
> crushed for our sins.
> He was beaten so we could be whole.
> He was whipped so we could be healed.
>
> ISAIAH 53:5

Lord Jesus, forgive my sin and heal my wounds. Turn the scars of life into beauty marks that will tell the story of what you have done in my life. Amen.

DIFFERENCE MAKER

What wounds do you carry today? What healing do you need from Jesus? How can Jesus use your story to reveal the good news of what he can do?

SHEEP

When people chart their own path, they crisscross and crush one another and create a chaotic, cacophonous confusion to life. God made life so much more simple than that. "Follow me," he said. "Here's how: Listen to my voice. Stay close. If you do that, I'll feed you and take care of you. I'll defend you and give you a home." But nope. People just feel a magnetic pull to *baaaah* their way around boulders and into thickets and wander into the jaws of lions. Thankfully Jesus is the Good Shepherd who knows that his sheep are prone to wander and who is willing to lay down his own life to save them.

> All of us, like sheep, have strayed away.
> We have left God's paths to follow our own.
> Yet the Lᴏʀᴅ laid on him
> the sins of us all.
> ISAIAH 53:6

Dear Jesus, thank you for bearing my wandering soul on your shoulders.
Lead me in your path today. Amen.

DIFFERENCE MAKER

Simplify your life. Get rid of things that complicate your direction or distract you from following Jesus.

April

Jesus,

Let me be a part of an unflinching movement

of world changers.

Amen.

QUIET POSTURE

Jesus could have talked back, but he didn't. He didn't retaliate when he was accused of blasphemy and evil. He just took it when he was whipped and beaten, and when he was mockingly forced to wear a robe and crown (which was crudely made out of thorns and pressed down on his head). He even carried the cross down the road on the way to his own execution.

Why didn't he defend himself? He knew where their anger and hatred was leading. He knew it meant his torture and eventual death. He knew they were about to make him a spectacle of shame. His accusers even mocked him for his quiet posture. "Who hit you?" they screamed. "Why don't you call down your angels to save you?"

Had Jesus reacted in revenge against their rejection, the world would not have been saved. No false accuser would withstand the unrestrained power of Almighty God. So Jesus, in order to defend and rescue humanity, chose a quiet posture and said nothing.

> He was oppressed and treated harshly,
> yet he never said a word.
> He was led like a lamb to the slaughter.
> And as a sheep is silent before the shearers,
> he did not open his mouth.
>
> ISAIAH 53:7

Lord Jesus, thank you for not retaliating. My rescue depended on it. Amen.

DIFFERENCE MAKER

Who will you see in the next twenty-four hours who could be helped by your quiet restraint?

UNCOMPROMISED

Just because you do what is right doesn't mean you will be treated fairly. In fact, some of the best people in history were mistreated *because* they were doing what was right. So how committed are you to doing right? If the right road gets tough, will you keep on going?

In the future, when people talk about you, will they be inspired by your example? Will your story encourage them to live with integrity in the face of opposition? It takes tremendous courage to continue to do what is right in the face of adversity. But the world needs uncompromised people who stand for what is right, no matter what.

Jesus pursued the right path and paid a severe price. But the world is forever grateful he didn't join the wrong march, but chose to walk to the cross. Imagine how pessimistic this devotional book would be if he had compromised himself and not gone to the cross!

> He had done no wrong
> and had never deceived anyone.
> But he was buried like a criminal;
> he was put in a rich man's grave.
>
> ISAIAH 53:9

Jesus, I don't know if I have the courage to live and die like you did. In the face of adversity, give me the strength to do no wrong. Amen.

DIFFERENCE MAKER

Anticipate what difficult situations you might be in today. Pray that Jesus will give you the integrity to do what is right.

GOOD PLAN

One of the most startling lines in the Bible is found in Isaiah 53:10. It says that everything that happened to God's "Suffering Servant"—all the crushing and grieving, the accusations and execution, the carrying of humanity's sin and disdain—was all a part of the Lord's "good plan" for his Son. How is someone—someone innocent, I might add—being betrayed, arrested, falsely accused, tortured, and executed a "good plan"? That certainly sounds like a very bad idea, right?

The "good" in the plan, however, is the key. God created everything "good," but because death was brought to creation through sin, Jesus took it all upon himself through the cross so that he could offer forgiveness and new life. In other words, God's rescue blueprint called for the terrible things that happened to Jesus in order to restore "good" to this earth. As a result of what Jesus did, the day of crucifixion became known as "Good Friday," and the day of resurrection would prove victory over death.

> But it was the LORD's good plan to crush him
> and cause him grief.
> Yet when his life is made an offering for sin,
> he will have many descendants.
> He will enjoy a long life,
> and the LORD's good plan will prosper in his hands.
>
> ISAIAH 53:10

Jesus, your idea of "good" is so much better than mine.
Thank you for being so good. Amen.

DIFFERENCE MAKER

On a piece of paper, brainstorm all that is "good" that Jesus offers through the cross. Which of these things would be life changing for someone you know?

SPEAK OUT

Talk about someone who made a difference—the world was changed by Martin Luther King Jr. He painted grand scenes of unity with words like freedom, justice, and hope. He provided a vision for the future through creative patience, resolve, and forgiveness. People loved him for his voice, and callous people hated him for his impact.

He spoke about the example of Jesus, who gave voice to the voiceless and ushered people to the seat of God's justice. King was especially impacted by the way Jesus offered mercy instead of retribution, even as the forces of hatred closed in around him. When given a chance to fight back or run away, Jesus demanded of his closest follower, "Put away your sword."

Martin Luther King Jr., a champion of the dignity for every person, was assassinated by a narrow-minded bullet on April 4, 1968. It was a very bleak day. But the world's attention had already been caught and the climate had already been changed. Even death cannot hold back the powerful ring of freedom.

Speak up for those who cannot speak for themselves;
ensure justice for those being crushed.

PROVERBS 31:8

Jesus, give me the inner motivation to speak with your voice for those who need an advocate. Amen.

DIFFERENCE MAKER

Read about Martin Luther King Jr.'s story. Who could use your voice today?

SPEND ENERGY

Have you ever felt like you wasted your energy on something before? Have you been frustrated about something you were working on and asked with disgust, "What's the use?" Perhaps the commute is driving you crazy. Maybe the last seven hours of your Netflix binge didn't really improve your life after all. Maybe the effort you put into grocery shopping didn't produce the sort of fruit you had hoped. (Get it? Grocery? Produce? Fruit? Just roll with it.)

Jesus doesn't want you to waste your energy. He doesn't want you to regret how you spent even one minute of your life. What gives purpose and meaning to all that you do, he says, is himself. Pursuit of him, and the life he gives, is worth every effort. You will know you are spending your energy wisely when you are seeking after Jesus and filtering all you do through him. Everything in your life will begin to fall into its proper place as you find your priority in Jesus.

> "But don't be so concerned about perishable things like food. Spend your energy seeking the eternal life that the Son of Man can give you. For God the Father has given me the seal of his approval."
>
> JOHN 6:27

Dear Jesus, help me match my priorities with yours. Amen.

DIFFERENCE MAKER

This devotional time was a great start. How else could you spend your energy searching for the life Jesus offers today?

BELIEVE IN JESUS

It would be wrong, in a book all about making a difference in this world, to give the impression that somehow your good works are what God ultimately wants from you. God actually wants only one thing from you; he has only one requirement. At the end of your life, as you look back over the years, it would be nice to remember the good things you accomplished or ways you were kind. But whether or not you believed in Jesus will be what God ultimately cares about the most. After all, if you believe in Jesus, the good works will come—they will follow. Good deeds are simply a natural overflow of Jesus being alive within you. There is nothing in life that makes more of a difference than this one thing: Believe in the Lord Jesus Christ.

Jesus told them, "This is the only work God wants from you:
Believe in the one he has sent."

JOHN 6:29

Jesus, I believe in you. I believe you died for me and you want me to follow you. I believe you want to use me to impact this world with your good news. Jesus, place my life in your hands. I believe in you. Amen.

DIFFERENCE MAKER

What would belief in Jesus look like practically today?
What would need to change? What would stay the same?
How would belief in Jesus impact the way you treat others,
approach a tough situation, or prepare you for a meeting?

NOWHERE ELSE

Many people leave the church simply because they can, feeling like they have a choice in the matter. They don't feel compelled to stay. For whatever reason, many just slip away through the crowd.

There was a time when many people left the crowd that was following Jesus too. They deserted him because they couldn't stomach Jesus' calling on their lives. What Jesus was asking them to do was too radical. And once a few people started wandering away, many others took the easy route too.

As a result of this, Jesus turned to his closest followers and asked, "Are you going to leave too?" That's when Peter, the roller-coaster adrenaline disciple, declared that he couldn't imagine anywhere else they would rather be. Jesus was too startlingly compelling, too earth-shatteringly true, too eternally good.

> Simon Peter replied, "Lord, to whom would we go? You have
> the words that give eternal life."
>
> JOHN 6:68

Dear Jesus, grab ahold of my heart and squeeze tight. Grab ahold of those around me too. Let me be a part of an unflinching movement of world changers. Amen.

DIFFERENCE MAKER

Think of someone you know who has given up on God. Don't let that person walk away from Jesus. How can you invite them to join you in making Jesus the center, not an addition, to life?

NO-ZOMBIE ZONE

Resurrection means to "raise from the dead." To be undead is all the rage nowadays. It could get you your own TV or movie series. But it wasn't always cool to be undead. Two thousand years ago a man named Lazarus had gotten sick and died. A funeral full of wailing was well underway—that is, until Jesus decided to try out this undead thing on his recently deceased friend. He yelled into the tomb, "Lazarus, I want to hang out, bro!" (or something to that effect). So, as anybody would do when Jesus speaks life, Lazarus came out of the tomb walking, much to the astonishment of everyone (except for Jesus, who played it all very cool).

A little later, after of course people unwrapped Lazarus' burial cloths, they ate dinner together—for Jesus, this was just another day of work. Raising people to life is what he does for a living. People didn't know what to think about this situation. They had never seen an undead person before. And even though he was no zombie, Lazarus scared them. And this of course made them scared of Jesus too. The people were challenged to either accept the life-giving power of Jesus or to run away.

> Jesus told her, "I am the resurrection and the life. Anyone who believes in me will live, even after dying."
>
> JOHN 11:25

Jesus, let me hear your voice calling me to life today. Amen.

DIFFERENCE MAKER

Imagine the conversation people had with Lazarus and Jesus at dinner that evening. Why don't you invite some friends out for dinner and bring this story up? See where the conversation takes you.

SEEK

Finding Big Foot has become an obsession for some people. They'll go to great lengths to find the creature, even spending thousands of dollars on camo gear, tracking devices, and all-night surveillance equipment. Some will travel around the continent pursuing alleged sightings.

Tracking Big Foot certainly isn't a lifestyle that's right for everyone, but pursuing God certainly is. What if we had that much passion in our pursuit of God? God has established a kingdom that offers hope, guidance, restoration, and freedom for anyone who wants to be a part of it. What might we find if we spent our energy seeking God's kingdom? What if we kept a vigilant eye open for God's reign throughout each day? What if we began to expect to find him rummaging in our life? And what if we anticipated spotting him in the community around us?

Perhaps we often miss what God is doing because we are often not looking. What people seek defines their lives. It's time to ask ourselves what we seek today.

> "Seek the Kingdom of God above all else, and live
> righteously, and he will give you everything you need."
> MATTHEW 6:33

Lord Jesus, keep me watchful for your kingdom today. Help me find you at work in circumstances I hadn't considered before. Amen.

DIFFERENCE MAKER

Seek God's kingdom throughout your day today. Saturate your thoughts with a search for God's reign in creation, in timing, and in interactions.

LEAN

How do you handle a choice that will dramatically shape your future? Do you get stuck with worry that you might make the wrong decision? When you are at an important juncture in your life, how do you select which way to go? What leads you or guides you in that place?

The Bible encourages you to make a decision based upon what God wants for your life. If you get into the habit of walking with God, then the choices become much clearer. Following God naturally improves your confidence in the direction of your life. Your goal in any decision should be to align yourself with God's will. You should not trust yourself more than God for the future of your life. If you seek God's input, then God will give you the ability and the freedom to make good choices that have a positive impact on your future.

Trust in the LORD with all your heart;
do not depend on your own understanding.
Seek his will in all you do,
and he will show you which path to take.

PROVERBS 3:5–6

Jesus, guide me in the choices I make today. Let the steps I take be in step with you. Help me see clearly what I need to do and where I need to go. Amen.

DIFFERENCE MAKER

Lean on something, like a stool or a wall or a desk. As you trust this object to support you, lean on God in prayer for a few minutes. Ask him for his wisdom in any decision you need to make.

THINK THANKS

If you could be with anyone you are not currently with, who would that person be? What is it about that person that makes you long to see them again?

When Paul wrote his letter to some friends in a city called Philippi, he couldn't help but to gush all over the papyrus. He absolutely loved these people. If he could have hopped on a jet and had dinner with them that evening, he would have spent any amount of money to get there. He felt at home, he felt like he could be himself, and he felt like life was more enjoyable when he was with them. Whenever he thought of his Philippian friends, Paul gave thanks to God. He also prayed for them. He was so grateful for these life-giving partners who were also making a difference for Jesus.

Every time I think of you, I give thanks to my God. Whenever I pray, I make my requests for all of you with joy, for you have been my partners in spreading the Good News about Christ from the time you first heard it until now.

PHILIPPIANS 1:3-5

Lord Jesus, thank you for the people in my life who inspire and encourage me. Help me be that way for them as well. Amen.

DIFFERENCE MAKER

Make a connection with someone far away that fills you with joy. Before, after, or during your chat, give thanks to God for that person, and stop to pray for them.

OPEN DOOR

Have you ever walked into a sliding glass door? You thought it was open but it actually wasn't. *Bam!* It took you a moment to figure out that there was a door there, and that the door was closed. And the worst part was probably that all your friends or family were laughing at you. You just had to roll with it. So you smiled and maybe chuckled a bit. But *ouch*, your face hurt!

To find the open door, you must use all the resources God has given to you—sight, hearing, and senses. You must search for it. Ask God to lead you. Listen for his Spirit's guidance and ask for wisdom. Stay close to Jesus so that you aren't led the wrong way. He wouldn't lead you the wrong way. Jesus wouldn't trick you and laugh at you when you smash into a closed door.

The apostle Paul wrote about a wide-open door God had opened for him as well. He didn't assume everything would be easy or perfect because the door was open, but he knew God was giving him an opportunity to make a big impact in the world in which he lived.

There is a wide-open door for a great work here, although
many oppose me.

1 CORINTHIANS 16:9

Dear Jesus, lead me to the right opportunities, the ones you want me to go through. Amen.

DIFFERENCE MAKER

Every time you walk through a door today, remember to look for opportunities God is giving you to serve him and others.

BOAST

What would happen today if you boasted about Jesus? What if, instead of bragging about your own accomplishments or calling attention to your own problems, you spoke boldly and favorably about what Jesus did on the cross? What would you even say if you chose to do this? Why would you even do that? People don't want to hear you talk about that, do they?

Well, many of your friends or family are glad to hear you talk about what's important to you, right? What if forgiveness from Jesus through his death on the cross were important to you? Proud parents put their kid's picture on the fridge because they celebrate their child. A good husband buys flowers because he is honored to be married to his wife. A caring teacher displays a student's artwork because she loves what was created. None of these people are worried about what others might think. They just feel the need to share and rejoice.

> As for me, may I never boast about anything except the cross of our Lord Jesus Christ. Because of that cross, my interest in this world has been crucified, and the world's interest in me has also died.
>
> GALATIANS 6:14

Lord Jesus, thank you for dying on the cross to save me from sin. Let your forgiveness sink to the very core of who I am. Let it overwhelm me today. And let me brag about you a bit. Amen.

DIFFERENCE MAKER

In some way today, boast about Jesus.

IN BETWEEN

On a scale from 1 to 10, how antsy do you get when you have to wait? How good are you at waiting? And I don't mean waiting for a couple of minutes, but I mean really waiting—like days, weeks, or even months? When is your patience most easily worn out?

If you want to make a difference in your life or in this world, you might discover that sometimes you'll need to be patient. Everything impactful is not immediate. Some changes take long investment, persistent attention, consistent behavior, and dedicated evidence of your faithfulness. Perhaps you'd like to only do one action, as if you only had to make one motion of your magic wand in order to make everything around you appear better. However, circumventing true process can produce undesirable side effects.

Some things just take time. Making a difference is an everyday endeavor. Your daily commitment to cultivate your heart will harvest huge rewards as time goes on.

> Wait patiently for the LORD.
> Be brave and courageous.
> Yes, wait patiently for the LORD.
>
> PSALM 27:14

Lord Jesus, give me the resilience to work with confident patience today. Let me trust you for the long-term impact of my actions. Amen.

DIFFERENCE MAKER

As an illustration of God's long-term work, and even though you won't see the impact for quite a while, put some money in your savings account today. (Or put some money in someone else's savings!)

RESURRECTION

The cross and empty tomb go together—it is a double event. The cross demonstrated God's verdict against sin, a punishment that Jesus took in our place, while the empty tomb proclaimed hope after judgment, the power of death rolled away by the life and authority of Jesus. We need both. We need the cross because on it Jesus takes our sin to its grave, but we need the empty tomb because from it Jesus offers us life after death.

This is the central truth of Christianity. Without it, everything churchy is just good (or bad) religion that actually offers false hope. All of the Bible points to the crux of history in Jesus. He came to bring God's wrath against humanity for its sin and to also offer forgiveness. Jesus came as a human, took the wrath upon himself, and offered new life that gracefully dances upon the ashes of judgment.

> He was buried, and he was raised from the dead on the third day, just as the Scriptures said.
>
> 1 CORINTHIANS 15:4

Lord Jesus, the most life-changing truth I can ever hold is this: Though I did nothing to deserve it, you died for my sin and offered me new life. Amen.

DIFFERENCE MAKER

How can you live practically in the double event of the cross and the empty tomb? How will forgiveness and new life in Jesus impact the way you interact with others today?

ASK GOD ABOUT HIS DAY

Have you ever had a one-sided relationship with someone who talked all of the time? It's difficult and exhausting. But you love the person so you put up with him or her, just hoping for the day when the friendship becomes a bit more reciprocal, mutual, or friend-like. The truth is that God wants to chat with you. But like everyone else, you can be preoccupied to actually have a conversation with him, too loud to commune. Oh, you probably "pray," but you can be tempted to do all of the talking, using God like a paid psychologist or a call-in radio talk show host.

If you feel like prayer has been too much of a one-sided conversation, try paying attention to God. Ask him what's going on with him. Ask God how he's doing. Silence your life long enough and open your soul wide enough to hear what's on God's heart at that particular moment. In other words, be a friend to God. He's been one to you. It's not that he needs your friendship; rather, it's that he wants it. Perhaps he has something he'd like to say to his friend.

> "My sheep listen to my voice; I know them,
> and they follow me. "
>
> JOHN 10:27

Lord Jesus, what's going on? What would you like to do with me today?

DIFFERENCE MAKER

Stop everything, be still, and listen for God today.

HELPLESS

We often can't help ourselves. We see something tempting and we can't resist it. We hunger for something and we must consume it. Our diagnosis is this: The more we gain, the less we feel like we actually have. This sickness only fuels our thirst for even more. It is a perpetually spiraling cycle: craving and conquest and loss, craving and conquest and loss, craving and conquest and loss. When we live loopy like this, our emptiness is emphasized.

The pursuit of our own happiness leaves us disappointed in our own futility. "No matter how much we see, we are never satisfied," Solomon reminds us (Ecclesiastes 1:8). The fleeting pleasures we have sought cannot satisfy our deep thirst for wholeness. But Jesus can help us. He is able to give us what we cannot grasp by our own power and strength. Christ alone can give us the fulfillment we were created to have.

> When we were utterly helpless, Christ came at just the right
> time and died for us sinners.
>
> ROMANS 5:6

Jesus, why do I keep trying in vain to grab things I don't ultimately need? What I need is you. Only you can help me overcome the looping repetitions of my life.
Amen.

DIFFERENCE MAKER

Instead of buying something new today, get rid of something you already have. Simplify your attachments so that you can be more ready to receive satisfaction in Jesus alone.

GARBAGE COMPACTOR

R2-D2 was the only one who could save them. Luke, Leia, and Han Solo were all trapped in the Death Star's garbage compactor. (Yes, this is a geeky but awesome illustration!) The walls started compacting, ready to squish everyone inside. It looked like all was lost—that is, until R2-D2 disabled the detention cell's garbage compactors and the heroes were able to escape.

Sometimes life feels a lot like this. Pressures close in on us like a trash compactor on the Death Star. No matter what creative options we devise to wrangle free, no amount of personal effort could offer rescue forever. But Jesus is freedom. He didn't need to use a cool digital arm with decoding software or a bunch of beeps and boops. Instead, he used the resource at his disposal: his abundant life. Even in overwhelming circumstances, Jesus enables people to escape from being crushed so they can keep on fighting. Stand confidently today by finding freedom in Jesus' everlasting ability to rescue.

We are pressed on every side by troubles, but we are not crushed. We are perplexed, but not driven to despair.

2 CORINTHIANS 4:8

Dear Jesus, in those moments where I become overwhelmed today, give me the hope of your life. Amen.

DIFFERENCE MAKER

Throughout the day, press your fingers together hard for thirty seconds and then release them. Each time you do this, be mindful of the pressing struggles people have, and that Jesus offers rescue.

HYPOCRITE PROOF

Be real today. If you say you are a follower of Jesus, then follow him. Don't be all show. Be substance. Have integrity. Act on your words. If you are a follower Jesus, then do what Jesus is doing.

Faith involves actually putting yourself in action. Faith is risky because it takes proactive effort. You put one foot ahead of the next, trusting that each step is leading you where you should go next. Faith is not lazy. It does not sit around bored, just hoping something good might happen. It is not worried. Faith does not panic at what might occur. Faith is doing what you believe is true. If your faith is in Jesus today, then you will naturally act upon what Jesus is leading you to do.

> What good is it, dear brothers and sisters, if you say you
> have faith but don't show it by your actions? Can that kind
> of faith save anyone?
>
> JAMES 2:14

Dear Jesus, let my words and actions match yours. Amen.

DIFFERENCE MAKER

Pick one of these actions to follow through with today (and if you are asked, be ready to share the reason why you are doing it): Tell the truth, help someone, work hard, choose purity, defend someone, listen to a friend, and be calm in a stressful situation.

TEACH KIDS

One of the greatest differences you could make is to help the next generation to follow Jesus. God wants us to be intentional about sharing faith with kids in every circumstance of our lives. Whether you have kids of your own, you have a niece or a nephew, or you are just around kids at church, the call to share faith with children is given to everyone.

Following Jesus is not just a Sunday-morning activity. We follow him and demonstrate our faith to younger people when we are hanging out at home, commuting to work, praying before bedtime, or eating breakfast in the morning. Everything we do and everywhere we are is an opportunity to grow in Jesus and inspire younger people to do the same.

And you must commit yourselves wholeheartedly to these commands that I am giving you today. Repeat them again and again to your children. Talk about them when you are at home and when you are on the road, when you are going to bed and when you are getting up. Tie them to your hands and wear them on your forehead as reminders. Write them on the doorposts of your house and on your gates.

DEUTERONOMY 6:6–9

Dear Jesus, help me figure out how I could share with some kids what it means to follow you. Connect me with a local ministry that teaches children about you. Amen.

DIFFERENCE MAKER

Tie a string around your wrist (loosely, of course—don't cut off your circulation!) to remind yourself to help kids (maybe in a local church ministry?) learn about Jesus.

GIFTED ON PURPOSE

You are uniquely gifted by God on purpose. He gave you specific talents, experiences, and passions so that you can make a difference in the world in which you live. Your unique set of gifts can help others live according to their God-given giftedness too. God has planned to use you to do good things in this world.

Remember that God has gifted other people on purpose as well. You aren't the only one who has been uniquely gifted by the Lord. He also exceptionally wired others so that they could encourage and equip people like you to do what you have been called to do. God has put everyone on the same playing field. Each person is a recipient of this radical generosity so that each person can serve the Lord with his or her whole heart.

Search your own talents and desires today, considering how God might want you to use them for the good of others. At the same time, seek out others who will build you up and help you develop the gifts God has given you.

> However, he has given each one of us a special gift through the generosity of Christ.
>
> EPHESIANS 4:7

Lord Jesus, thank you for gifting me to make a difference in this world. Help me to commit to using my gifts to serve you. Amen.

DIFFERENCE MAKER

Pick a talent God has given to you, and then combine it together with some passion God has given you. Practice putting your gift and passion in action today.

WORK FOR EVERYONE

People have assumed it is the pastor's job to visit a sick person in the hospital, to pray before a meal, or to do the Bible teaching for Wednesday Bible study. After all, it's what he was hired for, right? It is what we pay him to do. This is true to a degree, but just to a degree. Ultimately, the pastor's job is to shepherd people (*pastor* means "shepherd") to a closer relationship with Jesus so that Jesus can empower them to do good work. In other words, the pastor is not the only person who is supposed to be doing ministry. He is simply supposed to equip people to work for Jesus.

The truth is that it is everyone's calling to do work. There is no shortage of good things to do in this earth, so God has called you to use your gifts to do work that builds others up. Walk in your gifting today, knowing you are making a difference in this world.

> Now these are the gifts Christ gave to the church: the apostles, the prophets, the evangelists, and the pastors and teachers. Their responsibility is to equip God's people to do his work and build up the church, the body of Christ.
>
> EPHESIANS 4:11–12

Lord Jesus, help me work for you. Don't allow me to let others do my work for me. Amen.

DIFFERENCE MAKER

Pick one of these ministry "jobs" to accomplish today: Visit someone who is sick, pray out loud before dinner, do a house project for an older person, or volunteer for a ministry role in church this weekend.

WORK TOGETHER

Your ability to work with others to make a difference is much like the hand and the mouth working together. When the hand and mouth refuse to bless one another as a team, eating dinner is really dysfunctional! But when the hand uses its gift to grab onto that Chipotle carnitas burrito, and when the mouth uses its giftedness to open up wide and take a gargantuan bite, the whole of the body benefits and praises the Lord.

The church is an amazing team of great people who are uniquely gifted and uniquely flawed, and who are ready to work together to bring good to this world through faith in Jesus. Practically, this means your life should be lived within a network of others who are striving to follow Jesus and impact this world too. While you use your gifts to bless others, others use their gifts to bless you. No one has a monopoly on God's calling.

The one who plants and the one who waters work together
with the same purpose. And both will be rewarded for their
own hard work.

1 CORINTHIANS 3:8

Lord Jesus, surround me with others who want to impact this world so that I can be encouraged to become even more effective for you. Amen.

DIFFERENCE MAKER

If you are not involved already in a vibrant church or ministry group, start taking the risk to do so. If you already are involved, then invite others in your group so that they could be built up too.

EAGLE EGGS

There is a scene in the movie *Nacho Libre* where Nacho (a wrestler played by Jack Black) was extremely frustrated with his friend for telling him that drinking the yoke from eagle eggs would give him special fighting skills. After climbing a cliff, finding a nest, cracking open an egg, and guzzling, he went on to embarrassingly lose his next wrestling match. Later, he rebuked his friend, saying, "Those eggs were a lie, Steven! A lie! They give me no eagle powers. They give me no nutrients!"

Lies, even ridiculous ones, mislead and set people up for heartache. Lies sell a twisted lotion that applies to itchy ears, but in reality only serves to make the problems worse. Lies erode trust, cause confusion, and get people into all kinds of convoluted messes. But in Jesus there is transparency and truth. He is refreshing to a world that is oversaturated with untruths. What Jesus says is what is. He isn't selling anything or trying to gain from manipulation. Jesus is genuine, authentic, and confident with his words.

> Don't lie to each other, for you have stripped off your old
> sinful nature and all its wicked deeds. Put on your new
> nature, and be renewed as you learn to know your Creator
> and become like him.
>
> COLOSSIANS 3:9–10

Lord Jesus, shape me into an honest person. If I start a lie today, stop me from completing it. Help me speak the truth. Amen.

DIFFERENCE MAKER

Speak honestly today. No tricks. No cover-ups. Only tell the truth.

FINISH

Jesus is so committed to you that he will not give up with you. In fact, he is going to finish what he began in you. As an artist, he might choose to add more texture and lighting. As a sculptor, he might just chisel away some rough edges. And as a gardener, he might decide to prune some dead branches. And then there's his carpentry skills, in which case he might measure and cut and hammer and sand for a while—sometimes a long while. Whatever he needs to do, he is going to continue creating in you until he is finished with his work.

Creating a masterpiece is one of his favorite things to do. You, together with everyone else he is working on, have captured his vision. He wants to pour his heart into his most treasured work. He would never let himself get distracted from his attention to your every detail. And he won't give up until he can step back and look at all he has made and say, "Very good!"

And I am certain that God, who began the good work within you, will continue his work until it is finally finished on the day when Christ Jesus returns.

PHILIPPIANS 1:6

Jesus, don't stop working on me. Form me into who you want me to be. Amen.

DIFFERENCE MAKER

Think of a project that has been hanging over your head.
Finish it today. Get it done. And as you do,
remember God's determination to work on your behalf.

BE YOURSELF

If we truly believed in Jesus, then we wouldn't struggle so much with our identity as individuals. If we trusted him fully, we would embrace our unique self-makeup and triumph in the way we have been wired together.

Imagine waking up in the morning knowing that God loves you and believes in you—that he is there for you and has some pretty great ideas for your day. Imagine living in such a way that you seek to please him rather than seeking to please others. Imagine finding the firmest footing for your feet in the midst of tempting whirls all around you because you are rooted in the firmest foundation (Jesus). Imagine being able to speak the truth in love because you aren't tempted to fold to the ears of others. Imagine having the courage to face your shortcomings because God empowers you. Imagine having the guts to spill your guts because Jesus wants to restore his authority and blessing in you. Imagine being so secure in God that you are able to love your family, your friends, and your coworkers with a love beyond yourself. And imagine finding your identity in God so that no matter what turmoil happens you will not be able to lose yourself.

This means that anyone who belongs to Christ has become
a new person. The old life is gone; a new life has begun!

2 CORINTHIANS 5:17

Dear Jesus, let me find my identity in you so that I can be who you want me to be for others. Amen.

DIFFERENCE MAKER

Because you know that God has a purpose for you, do something bold today that you would not otherwise have done.

CLOTHE YOURSELF

Look at yourself in front of a mirror. What are you wearing? Did you have trouble deciding what to put on this morning? How do you feel about how you look? Are you happy with the fashion option you chose? Isn't it hard to stand in front of the mirror day after day and think that what you are wearing is perfect? Some people change multiple times before heading out of their room. To avoid the wear and tear of deciding what to wear, Steve Jobs, the founder of Apple, famously decided to use only one style of clothing.

In this culture, what you wear reflects who you are in many ways. So that wrinkle in the shirt or that out-of-style fashion pattern can feel annoying. But there is one set of clothes that never fades, never looks bad, and never makes you feel below average. When you put on Jesus you feel like a million bucks—or more. Jesus may not always be "in style," but he always looks great on you.

Instead, clothe yourself with the presence of the Lord Jesus
Christ. And don't let yourself think about ways to indulge
your evil desires.

ROMANS 13:14

Lord Jesus, when people see me, let them notice your characteristics. Amen.

DIFFERENCE MAKER

If you were to wear Jesus, what sort of "clothing" would you put on? How can you motivate yourself to put him on and keep him on all day long?

PEACE RULES

Does anxiety get the best of you at moments throughout your day? Remember that you are called to let peace get the better of you. For who, by worrying, can solve the unresolvable? No one thinks, "Maybe if I worry enough everything will get better." No, if you let it, worry will play a mad king over your heart.

Peace, not worry, is to reign in your heart. But how? You've learned you cannot attain peace on your own. If you try to grab it without help from anyone, you'll simply snag more stress. It is important to recognize that peace comes from Jesus. And he loves to give it to people who once were separated from him. You see, peace is the restoration of relationship. Peace does not look like you, by yourself, trying to hold it all together. Rather, it looks like you and others learning to entrust your lives together in Jesus.

> And let the peace that comes from Christ rule in your hearts.
> For as members of one body you are called to live in peace.
> And always be thankful.
>
> COLOSSIANS 3:15

Jesus, let your peace have ownership of my heart. Let me be thankful for all that you have done and are going to do. Amen.

DIFFERENCE MAKER

Connect with someone you know who is anxious.
Creatively and personally share Christ's peace with them.

MESSAGE SPILL

If you received a memo straight from heaven, what do you think would be written on it? Perhaps, *We need to talk. Or, Will you be mine? Or, Dinner tonight. RSVP. Bring guests.* No matter what that memo would have on it, the message would certainly be good. It might not be an easy message; it could even be convicting or alarming. But it would be grace filled and trustworthy. I'm almost certain the memo would include an invitation to a significant celebration. It would be what you needed to know just at that very moment.

Jesus, the Word of God, wants to communicate with you on a regular basis. His message is this: He has come to fill you with overflowing life. He loves you and wants you to know it in the depths of your being.

> Let the message about Christ, in all its richness, fill your lives.
> Teach and counsel each other with all the wisdom he gives.
> Sing psalms and hymns and spiritual songs to God with
> thankful hearts.
>
> COLOSSIANS 3:16

Dear Jesus, overwhelm me with your message of hope today. Catch me off guard with your wisdom and let me spill over with joy. Amen.

DIFFERENCE MAKER

Sing praise to the Lord! It doesn't matter where—the shower, the car, the bus, the sidewalk, the hallway, the elevator, the bike, the dinner table, or the church group. Just sing songs of praise somewhere today.

REPRESENT

Look back on your last twenty-four hours. Would you say that your words reflected Jesus? Did your conversations suggest someone who is letting Jesus make a difference? Don't worry, everyone is guilty of messing up with our mouths. People often have a shoe-shaped hole in the bottom of their face because they keep putting their foot where their mouth is. Everyone allows wrong things past their lips more than they'd like to admit: coarse language, poisonous jabs, vengeful attacks, perverted jokes, abusive yelling, God's name in vain, insults, lies, excuses, and gossip. The mouth can spit venom.

This world needs you to set a different pattern with the words that come out of your mouth. One simple way to make a dramatic difference would be to use your words to express gratitude. "Thank you" is one of those phrases that the world does not hear nearly enough. It is a freeing phrase. In fact, those two words help people feel good about themselves.

And whatever you do or say, do it as a representative of the
Lord Jesus, giving thanks through him to God the Father.

COLOSSIANS 3:17

*Jesus, thank you for doing all you have done for me. Help me speak as if I
actually realize it. Amen.*

DIFFERENCE MAKER

Speak well today. Say thank you more than you ever have before. Watch the
change that happens in your heart and in the people around you.

May

Jesus,

Let me learn you.

And let me invite others to learn alongside me.

Amen.

PACED

A busy life is often a stressed life. A life paced around prayer, however, is often filled with thankfulness and peace. On one hand, when people are hurried, they are worried about what might happen or what they might miss. When people are paced by prayer, on the other hand, they develop a growing sense of gratitude because they become increasingly aware of all Jesus is doing in them and around them.

People are often tempted to think they don't have time for prayer. There is just too much going on, too many things to get done. But prayer forms an alert mind and cultivates a thankful heart. It provides wisdom for decisions, reassurance for apprehension, strength for trials, and unity with God's plans.

This is one of the reasons Jesus prayed so much. He surprised people by how often he would withdraw from busy moments to spend time with the Father. At the height of his popularity, he would withdraw from the crowds and spend time in prayer. In the midst of his darkest moments, he would pray. When alone and tempted, he would pray. Before gathering with others, he would pray. His life was paced by prayer, not hectic activity.

Devote yourselves to prayer with an alert mind and a
thankful heart.
COLOSSIANS 4:2

Dear Jesus, thank you for wanting to spend time with me. Cultivate a more prayerful mind and heart within me. Amen.

DIFFERENCE MAKER

At least twice today, set aside several minutes to pray.

MAKE DISCIPLES

The word *disciple* means "learner," so a disciple of Jesus is a learner of Jesus. No matter how young or old someone is, being a learner of Jesus is the goal of that person's life. A Christian is never be a know-it-all; rather, a follower of Jesus is in a continual process of absorbing and practicing the teachings of Rabbi Jesus.

One of the most important things a disciple of Jesus learns is this: Disciples make disciples. Learners of Jesus produce more learners of Jesus. This calling, to make other disciples, has come to be known as the Great Commission. It is the greatest difference-making, history-changing, boundary-breaking strategy this world has ever known. People at all stages of learning have discovered that knowing Jesus is the best thing anyone could possibly do. So from generation to generation and geography to geography, people have come to learn Jesus.

"Therefore, go and make disciples of all the nations,
baptizing them in the name of the Father and the Son and
the Holy Spirit. Teach these new disciples to obey all the
commands I have given you. And be sure of this: I am with
you always, even to the end of the age."

MATTHEW 28:19–20

Jesus, let me learn you. And let me invite others to learn alongside me. Amen.

DIFFERENCE MAKER

Be bold. As a learner of Jesus, whom should you influence
toward Jesus today?

YOU WILL BE

A witness of a crime possesses valuable information to an investigation. A witness of an accident provides important testimony for an insurance company. A witness to a marriage signs a document declaring that the union truly occurred. It is easy to see from these examples that a witness is someone who has seen something and confirms that they actually saw it take place, giving accurate details for those who are interested.

The early followers of Jesus saw him perform miracles, teach crowds, die on a cross, and rise again to life. Then they confirmed what they had seen by telling people about it everywhere they went. Today, followers of Jesus do the same thing. The way that Jesus works in our lives becomes the foundation for what we share with others everywhere we go. Our testimonies speak of what Jesus has done and what he is still doing in our lives. We are witnesses of Jesus Christ.

> But you will receive power when the Holy Spirit comes upon you. And you will be my witnesses, telling people about me everywhere—in Jerusalem, throughout Judea, in Samaria, and to the ends of the earth."
>
> ACTS 1:8

Lord Jesus, let it be this simple: Let me share what I have seen you do in my own life. Amen.

DIFFERENCE MAKER

Sit down in a coffee shop or restaurant today. Grab a napkin and a pen. At the top write, *What I have seen Jesus do*, jot down what you have seen Jesus do in your life, and then give your napkin to someone else before you leave.

NEVER LEAVE

If you follow Jesus, then you won't have only the Son of God defending your back, you'll also have God the Father and the Holy Spirit too. You're covered. In a world where abandonment is such a big problem, this is indeed good news. But there is a key concept embedded here that should not be missed. It is true that God won't ditch you, but he also longs for you to not give up on him either. He asks you to love him and, in your love, to obey what he has asked you to do.

To *obey* simply means to "listen." Jesus states the obvious: If you love him then you'll listen to him. And if you listen to him, then you might just hear him asking the Father to give you his Spirit, who will come to your aid, comfort you, empower you, and stand up for you in every circumstance at any given moment.

> "If you love me, obey my commandments. And I will ask the Father, and he will give you another Advocate, who will never leave you."
>
> JOHN 14:15–16

Jesus, just as you promise to be with me, I want to be with you too. Thank you for your attention and care. I love you and will be listening to you today. Amen.

DIFFERENCE MAKER

Name something you should do in obedience to Jesus today. As you follow through with this, listen for the Spirit's presence in your life.

PENTECOST

It would be wrong to say that the first followers of Jesus—you know, the ones who changed the entire course of human history—had a great plan. They didn't sit around large conference-room tables with the best minds in the industry or the most brilliant political strategists checking popular opinion polls every few minutes.

The truth is that they really didn't know what to do. Jesus had given them instructions after his resurrection to wait for him to send the Holy Spirit who would empower them to be his witnesses to the ends of the earth. So they waited according to his word. They spent time praying. And they spent time going about their daily routines. They would gather together often and eat and talk about all they had seen Jesus do and all they had heard him say. And they waited. And then God showed up.

On the day of Pentecost all the believers were meeting together in one place. Suddenly, there was a sound from heaven like the roaring of a mighty windstorm, and it filled the house where they were sitting.

ACTS 2:1-2

Dear Jesus, show up in my life today. Let your Spirit move me. Let your Spirit move among my friends. Impact our lives deeply today. Amen.

DIFFERENCE MAKER

Gather some other followers of Jesus to wait with you for God to move. Pray and expect him to do something in your lives.

ADDED TO THE CHURCH

We live in an era when people are walking away from church in droves. Some feel church isn't relevant or cool, while others feel church isn't trustworthy. And others just don't see the point of it all. But ultimately people leave church because they can. They don't feel compelled to stay. They simply aren't finding in church what they need to find. When "church" began 2,000 years ago, the feeling was just the opposite. People left behind everything else in their lives because they had to be a part of the church. The reason for this is simple: They needed Jesus, and church was were they could find him.

Church means "gathering" or "assembly." The church is a gathering of people who are compelled to find Jesus and be forever changed by him. Church changes the world because Jesus changes those in the church. It is a light and shelter and rock for communities, in any moment, for all seasons. It is a gathering where individuals discover they are a part of something greater together. Church is where people find Jesus and learn to live with him and for him.

> Those who believed what Peter said were baptized and
> added to the church that day—about 3,000 in all.
>
> ACTS 2:41

Dear Jesus, don't let me leave church. Help me find you in a gathering of people.
Amen.

DIFFERENCE MAKER

Change the trends. If you are not already a part of a good church or ministry group, find one. And grab some others to join you.

DEVOTED

One of the great losses of our current society is the gathering around the table to share a meal. Mealtimes used to be regular daily moments where people would set aside their busy schedules and spend time together. Now for many people, meals can often be on the go, last minute, and eaten alone.

But a new generation of Jesus followers seems to be discovering the blessing of having meals together. The lost art of the meal is being revived once again. We are relearning that there is a sacredness to eating with others. It's called "fellowship," that moment in the practice of everyday life when people who intentionally follow Jesus gather together to share life. In fellowship there is a great reminder that we have been drawn together by Jesus. It can be, if we remember, a worshipful experience.

All the believers devoted themselves to the apostles'
teaching, and to fellowship, and to sharing in meals
(including the Lord's Supper), and to prayer.

ACTS 2:42

Lord Jesus, let me be devoted to you, to your followers, and to prayer. Amen.

DIFFERENCE MAKER

Invite some people close to you to share a meal today. During the meal, make sure to give thanks, to break bread, and to drink the cup in remembrance of what Jesus did on the cross for each of you. Try to make this a tradition whenever you gather with other followers of Jesus.

SHARE

"That's mine!" Did you ever yell these words to some kid in your preschool? (Hopefully this only happened when you were five, and not when you were volunteering last week!) Those words, and more so the attitude those words reveal, are a sorry revelation of how even the most pure-hearted among us struggles with humanity's tendency toward selfishness. With all those kids fighting for their preferred toy, preschool play time can look like the Cornucopia in *The Hunger Games*. Life is much more fun for preschoolers when an attitude of sharing prevails. "Here, would you like to play?" sounds so much more freeing than "You can't have that!" or "Get your own!"

The early church was amazing at playtime. They shared. And then they shared some more. There was so much sharing going on that everyone had everything they needed. Jesus had gotten such a hold of their lives that they felt they didn't need to hold onto anything else. The presence of God's grace in our hearts causes us to be a people who share what has so freely been given to us.

> And all the believers met together in one place and
> shared everything they had. They sold their property and
> possessions and shared the money with those in need.
>
> ACTS 2:44–45

Lord Jesus, make me more generous today. Help me fight the urge to possess and then to possess more. Amen.

DIFFERENCE MAKER

Take your extra clothes to a thrift store or homeless shelter today.

SEVEN DAYS A WEEK

The Christian faith was never supposed to be limited to Sunday mornings. Neither was it considered to be just singing and sermons. Those are good, but they are just part of following Jesus. Christianity, in its truest form, involves followers of Jesus gathering to worship God every day of the week, gathering in homes to share meals and communion, and living respectfully and supportively in society.

This sort of lifestyle, saturated in the very way people live, naturally encourages others to want to be a part of church. The difference maker in this pattern of faith is not the weekly service or the seasonal outreach event. The difference maker in this pattern is the everyday practice of following Jesus. It simply works in the ordinary routines of life.

> They worshiped together at the Temple each day, met in homes for the Lord's Supper, and shared their meals with great joy and generosity—all the while praising God and enjoying the goodwill of all the people. And each day the Lord added to their fellowship those who were being saved.
>
> ACTS 2:46–47

Lord Jesus, be alive in me today and every day this next week. Amen.

DIFFERENCE MAKER

On a scale of 1 to 7, how many days a week are you a follower of Jesus? Which of the characteristics mentioned above can you put into action today?

SLOW AND RICH

The world is still here, isn't it? God is a patient, loving God. He initiates and reinitiates love again and again and again. Even though people have repeatedly turned against him, God still desires that no one would perish apart from him. He longs to restore relationship with those he has made. He loves the world so much that he died for every single person. He did that even while they were doing the very things that rejected him. What causes a normal person to react in anger and retaliation causes God to respond with another outburst of grace. If anyone else offered us this much latitude, this much time, this much empathy and support, we would have no excuse but to accept their kindness. How could any of us say no to such an amazing friend?

The LORD is merciful and compassionate,
slow to get angry and filled with unfailing love.
The LORD is good to everyone.
He showers compassion on all his creation.

PSALM 145:8–9

*Dear Jesus, thank you for your patient forgiveness. You keep helping me along.
Thank you for never giving up on me. Amen.*

DIFFERENCE MAKER

Who can benefit from you being gracious and compassionate today? How can you express a slowness in anger and a richness in love toward them?

LET IT SHINE

The one who created the light when there was nothing but darkness is shining his light into your heart today. If the vast darkness before time could be dissipated by his brilliance, imagine how brightly Jesus could shine in you. Against the glare of his light, icy exteriors melt, dark shadows flee, and murky thoughts clear up. God's light reveals his truth in the midst of confusion and gives knowledge of his glory in the midst of fog.

Jesus is called the Light of the World. The Bible teaches that darkness just doesn't understand the light—it misunderstands it, to be more precise. Darkness thinks it knows how Jesus works but is totally blindsided by his brilliance again and again. Darkness tries to hide but quickly discovers it can't. So let there be light in your heart today, and allow Jesus to reflect his light through you.

For God, who said, "Let there be light in the darkness," has made this light shine in our hearts so we could know the glory of God that is seen in the face of Jesus Christ.

2 CORINTHIANS 4:6

Dear Jesus, shine brightly in me and through me today. Amen.

DIFFERENCE MAKER

Find the sun today. If it's cloudy, find a bright and warm lamp. Go sit under it. Close your eyes. Run this verse through your heart until it sinks in.

HIDE IT UNDER A BUSHEL

The old kids' song went like this: "This little light of mine, I'm gonna to let it shine… / Hide it under a bushel? No! / I'm gonna let it shine / Let it shine, let it shine, let it shine." What is a bushel? A bushel is a form of measurement equal to eight gallons of dry goods. Sometimes the basket, holding a bushel of grain, for instance, was also called a bushel. The idea of the song is simply that no one can hide a candle under a bushel basket. *Why would anyone do that?* you may be thinking. It might as well not be lit. Jesus, the Light of the World, wants to brighten the world through you. Don't hide today.

> "You are the light of the world—like a city on a hilltop that cannot be hidden. No one lights a lamp and then puts it under a basket. Instead, a lamp is placed on a stand, where it gives light to everyone in the house. In the same way, let your good deeds shine out for all to see, so that everyone will praise your heavenly Father."
>
> MATTHEW 5:14–16

Lord Jesus, let the same light that you have flooded into my soul overflow into others. Amen.

DIFFERENCE MAKER

Light a candle (maybe a scented one to make your room smell better), then put a bowl over it (not a flammable bowl!). Notice how ridiculous that is. Then relight the candle and let it shine as a reminder of what you were created to do.

LIFE PRESERVER

Out of his loving-kindness the Lord saved us. We had fallen off the boat into the raging sea because we didn't listen to his commands to stay off the deck during the storm. We thought that was unfair. After yelling at him for being too constrictive, we pounded up the stairs to play outside on the poop deck. It wasn't long before we slipped off. But God, always keeping a loving eye on us, called out our name, jumped in the torrent with a life preserver, put it around us, and pulled us back into the cabin of the boat. It was his kindness that saved us, not because of what we have done, but only because of his great mercy.

When God our Savior revealed his kindness and love, he
saved us, not because of the righteous things we had done,
but because of his mercy.

TITUS 3:4–5

Lord Jesus, how could I ever tire of saying thank you? Even when the trouble
was my fault, you saved me anyways. Thank you. Your kindness rescues me.
Your love warms me. Your mercy simply saves me. Thank you. Amen.

DIFFERENCE MAKER

Do you know anyone who's in the middle of a storm and needs their name
called and a life preserver thrown out to them?
Reach out to that person today.

CALLED NEAR

No matter who you are or where you are or what you are with or without today, the Lord is near to you. Whoever you are, call on him today. If you're cool or awkward, just say, "Jesus, I need you." If you're rich or wrecked, just lift up his name and say, "Jesus." Wherever you are, call on him today. If you're lost or found, just reach out and say, "Jesus, will you stand with me?" If you're at home or far away, just speak his name. "Jesus." And whatever you have, call on him. If you have plenty or little, just ask, "Jesus, could you give what I truly need?" If you have a broken heart or a full one, just whisper, "Jesus." In each circumstance, he will hear you and he will do what needs to be done for you. Just be honest about who you are, where you are, and what you have. Don't try to impress, don't try to trick. Just be yourself and call his name.

> The LORD is close to all who call on him,
> yes, to all who call on him in truth.

PSALM 145:18

Lord Jesus, I call on your name. Be near to me now in the reality of my life.
Amen.

DIFFERENCE MAKER

Take a moment to pray about who you are, where you are, and what you have. Ask Jesus to be close to you in each of these areas of your life.

IN STEP

Have you ever tried to get to the store without actually going there? Or tried to brush your teeth without using a toothbrush—or toothpaste for that matter? Or have you ever tried to make baked ziti without turning on the oven, or using ziti? Any of those would be just plain stupid.

So why try to live today without using the Spirit for your every step and breath? If you want an abundant life, why not walk with the one who gives abundant life? If you need direction for major decisions in your life today, why not walk with the one who provides all wisdom and truth? If you need hope in a time of despair, why not take the effort to walk with the one who gives comfort and counsel?

It can be tempting to complicate something so simple. But if you want to truly live, then walk in step with the Spirit. You were created to walk with God. Do what you were created to do, and see how everything else works out from there.

Since we are living by the Spirit, let us follow the Spirit's
leading in every part of our lives.
GALATIANS 5:25

*Lord Jesus, don't let my feet trip. Don't let me wander off. Instead, let me walk in
step with you today. Amen.*

DIFFERENCE MAKER

Go for a walk with someone. Allow your strides to fall into rhythm together,
then talk about how we are to walk with God just like that.

WORK FOR JESUS

Even as our bodies and minds grow tired, and as our emotions need a rest from stress causers (like people and jobs), we should not let up on our responsibilities to the Lord. We are to serve him enduringly, forever, with fervor.

It would be so much easier to play another thirty minutes on Clash of Clans. It would be so much more relaxing to binge watch for the rest of the afternoon. "Me time" is very alluring, especially when responsibilities hang over the head, stresses keep beckoning, and needy people wait out in the real world ready to suck the life out of us.

Do you have something you should do today? Do you have something you could do for someone today? Do you have something someone asked you to do? What if you just did it? Like, right now? And what if, when you did it, you did it really well? And what if you kept in your mind that you were doing it for Jesus?

Never be lazy, but work hard and serve the Lord enthusiastically.

ROMANS 12:11

Lord Jesus, help get me off my butt today. Motivate me to do hard work that helps someone in some way. Mostly, inspire me to focus my heart's work on serving you. Amen.

DIFFERENCE MAKER

Write Romans 12:11 on a piece of paper and tape it where it will serve as a reminder throughout the day.

PROUD OF THE TANK ENGINE

Little kids try to hide bad things from their parents because they feel embarrassed. But no little kid has ever tried to hide something good from his or her parents. When kids have something that is joyful and fulfilling, they run to their parents and tell them loud and fast all about it. If a little boy sees on a video that Thomas the Tank Engine fell off his railroad tracks into the water, he might worry. But if he then saw Thomas' friend James come along and pull him out and get him "back on track" (so to speak), that little boy just might run around with excitement and tell everyone about the good news. If he didn't share, he'd burst.

For some reason, though, the world tricks us into thinking we cannot, or should not, feel the same way about Jesus. If we see God doing something great, it's as if we're conditioned to suppress our wonder or make our faith a private matter. But this is ridiculous. Jesus dying on the cross for our sins to give us abundant life, and get us back on track (so to speak), is better than anything. Let it be known today what God has done in and through you.

For I am not ashamed of this Good News about Christ. It is the power of God at work, saving everyone who believes.

ROMANS 1:16

Dear Jesus, don't let me feel embarrassed because I know you. There is nothing greater in my life than to follow you with my whole heart. Why should I be ashamed? Amen.

DIFFERENCE MAKER

When the opportunity arises today, be proud that you know Jesus.

BEAUTIFUL

We see a glimpse of it often. The brilliance of millions of stars. The intricate dance of leaves in the wind. The sparkle of wonder in someone's eye. The deep pausing breath of a treasured moment. The hopeful spring of a child's step. This is how the world was created to be. Beautiful. But often we also see the exact opposite. Stars obscured. Creation spoiled. The snarled brow of anger. The mourning of loss. The shattering of innocence. This is how many people perceive the world. Contaminated. What we need today is Jesus because he is the one who created this world to be beautiful. Even though it got messed up, he is ready to re-create it again. And he wants to begin his re-creative work in us.

Instead, let the Spirit renew your thoughts and attitudes.
Put on your new nature, created to be like God—truly
righteous and holy.

EPHESIANS 4:23–24

*Jesus, don't stop working on me until I am entirely yours. Continue your re-creative work in my life. Spur others I know to be renewed by your Spirit too.
Amen.*

DIFFERENCE MAKER

Invite some people to look at the world with fresh eyes today. Take a moment together to notice the beauty that is inherent in creation. Then imagine what the world would be like if people fully followed God's patterns. Take time to pray, asking God to re-create hearts in this world.

UNICORNS AND GRACE

Wishful thinking. That's how we treat grace. Almost like we treat unicorns. Unicorns are magical and pretty. They can fly and roast marshmallows from their horns. They seem so nice. Did you know that a group of unicorns is even called a "blessing"? But for real, if someone said to you, "Blessings on you," would that be a good thing? What if a stampeding herd of unicorns descended down upon you as these words left their mouth? They could trample you, hee-haw with terror, skewer you, and leave you covered in burnt sparkly marshmallows or something like that.

Thankfully, the difference between unicorns and grace is that grace is real. Don't ever treat grace as wishful thinking, like it is a pretend thing that would be nice to have but is elusive and mythical. No, grace has the power to change lives for real. So accept the power of grace through Jesus in your life. Be graceful and give a dramatic blessing of grace to others.

> Each time he said, "My grace is all you need.
> My power works best in weakness." So now
> I am glad to boast about my weaknesses,
> so that the power of Christ can work through me.
>
> 2 CORINTHIANS 12:9

Dear Jesus, your grace is all I need. Help me believe and live in that truth today.
Amen.

DIFFERENCE MAKER

Remind someone who feels weak of the reality of God's grace through an act of extreme kindness.

EXTRAVAGANT GRACE

We don't think we can handle this. People in droves rejected Jesus because he was different, or maybe, more accurately, he was more than what they had imagined. They probably tried to go back to their regular patterns, numbing themselves to apathy. *We need grace*, they must have admitted, *but Jesus is too good; he's too much. He would change our lives.*

The only way to truly live according to grace is to be changed by Jesus. But that means giving up control of our lives. Grace doesn't give us the power to do what we want. Rather, grace empowers us to do what Jesus does.

When we receive God's grace, we let ourselves be overwhelmed and we let Jesus use us to make a difference in others—not just in times of catastrophe, but in everything. When we accept Jesus, we start to stand and to overflow with grace toward others. Grace isn't what we deserve; it's what we need. And it's even more than what we need. That might be overwhelming to think about. But this is what followers of Jesus do—they receive and offer extravagant grace.

> Stephen, a man full of God's grace and power, performed amazing miracles and signs among the people.
>
> ACTS 6:8

Jesus, help me to walk gracefully today. Amen.

DIFFERENCE MAKER

The next time you pay for a meal, leave an extravagant tip.

BAPTISM

Baptism is a lot like taking a bath. It is a symbol of cleansing. As we go under the water, it's as if our sin is washed away and Jesus presents us spotless before God. Baptism is also a lot like dying. It is a visual declaration that we have committed our sins and selfish pursuits to Jesus. It's as if we are being buried and agreeing with Jesus to leave our sin in the grave.

Baptism is also a lot like resurrection. It is a picture of receiving new life in Jesus. As we are lifted from the depths of the water, it's as if our old life is gone and a new life has come. It is also like a big step, but it's also a simple one. It gives everyone who wants to follow Jesus a visual opportunity to show faith in Jesus in front of friends, family, and fellow followers of Jesus.

Peter replied, "Each of you must repent of your sins and turn to God, and be baptized in the name of Jesus Christ for the forgiveness of your sins. Then you will receive the gift of the Holy Spirit."

ACTS 2:38

Lord Jesus, thank you for washing me clean of my sins. Let me live a baptized life today. Amen.

DIFFERENCE MAKER

Encourage people you know to take the step of baptism. If you have not been baptized, go and talk to your pastor or ministry leader about it.

CONTINUE

Jesus is the greatest difference maker of all time. The fact that you are reading this book shows that you understand this truth in one way or another. That's great! Keep challenging yourself to be changed by him every day for the rest of your life. Don't ever stop this pursuit.

At some point in your life, you recognized your need for him and received him as your Lord and Savior. You've probably had some ups and downs in your walk with Jesus since then, but today you know he needs to be the primary focus of your life. Just as you received him already, keep receiving him. Treat every day as a new opportunity to give your life to Jesus afresh. Continue to bring the things of your life to him. Continue to discover who he is and what he wants for you. Continue to learn about what he has done and what he is doing for you. And continue to look for him and call out to him and follow him.

> And now, just as you accepted Christ Jesus as your Lord, you must continue to follow him.
> COLOSSIANS 2:6

Lord Jesus, thank you for making such a difference in my life.
Keep doing that today. Amen.

DIFFERENCE MAKER

Think for a moment. Because of your commitment to Jesus, what will you do differently today?

ROOTED

You've been told you're supposed to be an adult. What a ridiculous pressure that is. Society is already too full of grown-ups. Many of them, who rushed to become adults without grounding themselves in Jesus, are more childish than the most tantrum-crazed kids. "Mine!" or "I need this!" or "I deserve this!" are common mantras for today's adults.

People who keep adding other things to their lives in pursuit of fulfillment are never satisfied. That's why the Bible suggests a different way to grow: down in Jesus. People don't need to pursue anything more, unless it is more of him. So instead of growing up and standing on your own, try growing down into Jesus. Root yourself in him. Build your life in him. Draw from him all the nourishment you'll need for each day. Overflow with gratitude for his abundance within you.

> Let your roots grow down into him, and let your lives be built on him. Then your faith will grow strong in the truth you were taught, and you will overflow with thankfulness.
>
> COLOSSIANS 2:7

Lord Jesus, today I place all of who I am in you. Amen.

DIFFERENCE MAKER

What have you added to your life that doesn't fit with a life rooted in Jesus?

UNLIMITED

If you could do anything to influence this world, what would it be? What is it you would like to see changed? When you look out at the world, what causes you the most angst? If you could, would you change it? "I understand what you're doing here," you might say. "You're trying to make me think about being heroic or something. But really, who am I to do anything about it?"

Who are you? I'm glad you asked. You are child of the King of Heaven. You are an heir of the kingdom of God. You have a seat at the table with the Creator of the World. The King is inviting you to the chance to make a difference in the world he has placed you. He only wants you to know where your heart is in line with his own.

> I pray that from his glorious, unlimited resources he will
> empower you with inner strength through his Spirit.
>
> EPHESIANS 3:16

Lord Jesus, you created this world, and you want to empower me to do extraordinary things in it. Let me take that seriously today. Amen.

DIFFERENCE MAKER

Take your answers to the questions above and offer them to the King.
Ask him to empower you to do something about it.

ROOTED DEEP

Jesus just showed up with his moving truck. He motions for you to come help him unload. "Today's the day!" he says. "Thanks for welcoming me in. This is going to be good." You panic when you realize you haven't gotten things ready. You do a quick scan of your heart and realize that there is moldy pasta in the fridge, toenail clippings on the carpet, and chips in the cracks of the couch. And (gross) you haven't cleaned the toilette.

Yes, Jesus is moving in. Will he feel at home right away, or will he have some cleaning to do and some furniture to rearrange? Think quick: What would Jesus need to do to make your heart his home? Having Jesus make himself comfortable in your life might not be such a comforting thought. But it is the best possible scenario. It might mean some disruption for your old habits and routines, but those didn't bring you confidence or peace anyways. The new daily routines with Jesus are going to be so much more fulfilling than what you have been doing.

> Then Christ will make his home in your hearts as you trust
> in him. Your roots will grow down into God's love and keep
> you strong.
>
> EPHESIANS 3:17

Lord Jesus, I'm so glad you are here. Please, make yourself at home within me.
Amen.

DIFFERENCE MAKER

What is one thing you can do to show Jesus he is welcome
in your heart today?

LOVE IS

Have you ever jumped into a pool and allowed yourself to float under the surface in the expanse of the water? In any direction that you waved your arms, there was only water. If you extended right or left, in front of you or behind you, there was only water. If you reached down, water. If you stretched upward, water. Your whole self was immersed in this new understanding.

Now imagine being submerged in an endless pool—no, not one of those pools that spills over the sides and overlooks a valley (though that sounds really nice)—more like a pool with no edges at all. You could swim in any direction (down, up, left, right, forward, back) and still not be any closer to edge than you were before. Overwhelming? Frightening? This is what it is like to be immersed in the love of Jesus.

> And may you have the power to understand, as all God's people should, how wide, how long, how high, and how deep his love is.
>
> EPHESIANS 3:18

Lord Jesus, I'm not sure if I want to be completely overwhelmed by your love. It might be too much for me. But I pray that you will give me the power to understand how much your love covers me. Amen.

DIFFERENCE MAKER

If God's love covers you so much, then shouldn't you live a life surrounded with love? In what ways can you show God's great love to those you will see today?

EXPERIENCE

Do you remember the first time you gave a speech? Did your knees shake and your voice quiver? Did your words get jumbled up? The truth is that you probably are better at giving speeches now than when you were nine years old, though you could still improve with more experience. When you practice something over and over again, you get more comfortable and learn subtleties and rhythms. The more you rehearse something, the more it embeds into who you are.

Growing in your love of Jesus is similar. Gaining experience helps you improve as a person and to know God better. At first, his love was exhilarating, and maybe even nerve racking. But over time, and with daily practice, you began to understand the expectations and rhythms of what it means to know God's love. Keep experiencing Jesus today. Don't ever give up. Pick up his love every day and learn the nuances and empowerment that only comes from experience with him.

May you experience the love of Christ, though it is too great
to understand fully. Then you will be made complete with
all the fullness of life and power that comes from God.

EPHESIANS 3:19

Lord Jesus, I look forward to experiencing you more today. Amen.

DIFFERENCE MAKER

Practice the love of Jesus. Take a chance experiencing his love in a new way that might make you nervous or stretch you a bit. What could you do?

INFINITY

Infinity is impossible to measure. We know infinity is huge, but its never-ending limits are beyond our scope. It leaves us in awe. We can capture enough of the concept to comprehend the idea of "boundless," but never enough to fully grasp it. The greatest imaginations of our mind could never control infinity.

This is how the apostle Paul describes how much God can accomplish when he works through us. Take the greatest thoughts, the greatest dreams, the most inventive requests that any of us could conjure up, lift them up to God, and even that wouldn't scratch the depths of what God is able to do. This reveals God's glory. The beauty, wonder, and power of his action is absolutely boundless. It is why creatures like us fall to his feet in awe. So why would we not expand our understanding of what is possible with God?

Now all glory to God, who is able, through his mighty power
at work within us, to accomplish infinitely more than we
might ask or think.

EPHESIANS 3:20

Lord Jesus, may your glory be seen through your work in my life today. Amen.

DIFFERENCE MAKER

Think your greatest thought and lift up your greatest question to God.
Be inventive in the ways that God works in you. Expand your idea of what
God is able to do through you today.

ROOTED STRONG

Take a moment and look outside at a tree. The reason you can see that tree right now is because it is seriously grounded below the surface. The root system of that tree, which you can't see (unless some of the stronger roots are breaking through the ground), are equipping that tree to stand tall and flourish. The effort and focus of a tree's growth is downward. The roots supply the nutrition and resources that it needs to thrive.

Likewise, a life rooted into Jesus focuses not on the outward appearance, on what people can see with their eyes, but on the inward growth in Jesus. As a result, though, what people end up seeing is a person standing tall through the winds and trends of culture, a person overflowing with abundant life.

> But they delight in the law of the LORD,
> meditating on it day and night.
> They are like trees planted along the riverbank,
> bearing fruit each season.
> Their leaves never wither,
> and they prosper in all they do.
>
> PSALM 1:2–3

Lord Jesus, I choose to delight in you today. Let my actions be fruit providing for others. Let me prosper in all I do today because I put you first. Amen.

DIFFERENCE MAKER

Find a big tree, sit underneath it, and contemplate the roots beneath you, the trunk standing by you, and the branches and leaves (or springing buds) above you. How could this visual make a difference in your Christian life?

THRIVE

Even though it is small in size, the olive tree has made a tremendous impact throughout history. It is an evergreen tree that can flower and bear fruit for centuries to come. Its leafy branches are a symbol of abundance and peace, often extended after a violent war between enemies. Olive oil is a useful cooking resource, and it is used symbolically as a sign of blessing in many religious ceremonies and rites of passage around the world.

The olive tree is a metaphor for those who follow God's ways and live daily in his love. Though the world may look upon them as insignificant at first, their lasting impact cannot be disputed. They give shade and refuge in every season of life. The difference they make can be evidenced for generations to come. They supply this world with a source of abundant life and offer the stability of peace. They provide regular daily care for people and also blessing for the major events of life. In other words, followers of Jesus make an incredible difference in this world.

But I am like an olive tree, thriving in the house of God.
I will always trust in God's unfailing love.

PSALM 52:8

Lord Jesus, let me thrive in life by trusting in your love every day. Amen.

DIFFERENCE MAKER

Which aspect of the olive tree illustration can you put into action for the people around you today?

FLOURISH

Palm trees in Israel are known as date palms, flourishing for at least 5,000 years. They are a symbol of refuge for travelers and an abundant economic resource for fruit, syrups, grains, fibers, and timber. Their leaves were used to celebrate victory, such as when Jesus entered Jerusalem on what has come to be known as Palm Sunday.

Cedar trees were once abundant in Lebanon. They were tall (sometimes a 120 feet) and strongly rooted. Their wood was world renowned for its beautiful red color, for its lightweight yet resilient strength, and for being resistant to decay and repellant to insects. When people choose to root themselves in the patterns of God, they flourish and bless the world like these two types of trees.

> But the godly will flourish like palm trees
> and grow strong like the cedars of Lebanon.
> For they are transplanted to the LORD's own house.
> They flourish in the courts of our God.
> Even in old age they will still produce fruit;
> they will remain vital and green.

PSALM 92:12–14

Lord Jesus, let me live a life rooted deeply into you so that I may be used to bless others. Amen.

DIFFERENCE MAKER

Do one of the following today: Sit under a palm tree and enjoy life with God (if you are too far north, look at a picture and drool), or make something with cedar wood, remembering the richness of God at work in your life.

June

Jesus,

Don't let me treat you like an add-on to my life.

You are the center of my life.

Amen.

LISTEN QUICKLY

One of the best quotes from the classic 1980s movie *Ghostbusters* occurs when Dan Akroyd's nervous character poses the following question: "Listen! Do you smell something?" We are a very distracted people. We struggle to listen without being flooded by all kinds of other stimulation that stirs all of our other senses. Our challenge today is to be radically different than the preoccupied culture around us.

Listen carefully. Don't speak quickly. Listen quickly. Don't get angry quickly. This is wise advice in a world that can be just the opposite: flare up the temper, vomit the verbal output, and, sorry, what were you saying? While hotheaded and loose-mouthed reactions can be signs of uncaring attitudes, the skill of listening to others shows a heart that cares for people. Listening to someone shows a person they are valued, important, and worth the time. This could simply be life changing.

Understand this, my dear brothers and sisters: You must all
be quick to listen, slow to speak, and slow to get angry.

JAMES 1:19

Lord Jesus, let my words be few and my ears be wide open. Amen.

DIFFERENCE MAKER

Go a whole day without talking about yourself (unless you absolutely must, like if you get pulled over for speeding and the officer asks you questions). As much as possible, ask friends and family open-ended questions. (And by the way, if this challenge makes you angry, then you need to read this devotional entry one more time.)

PURE RELIGION

When Christianity is at its best, it is undeniably beneficial for the world. The irony, however, is that Christianity is as its best is when it is countercultural. Spending yourself on behalf of people who cannot pay you back goes against the give-and-receive culture in which we live. If you give money, you get something in return. If you invest your time or energy, you deserve some kind of return on your investment. The world operates this way on a daily basis.

But imagine if you did not have much to give or were unable to invest. Imagine if you lived at the mercy of others, in a mode of complete dependency. Imagine if your parents died while you were a child. And imagine if your spouse passed away while you were elderly and poor. Your opportunity to survive according to the world's standards would be diminished. It is into this reality that the followers of Jesus enter, radically uplifting those society belittles as "the least of these."

Pure and genuine religion in the sight of God the Father
means caring for orphans and widows in their distress and
refusing to let the world corrupt you.

JAMES 1:27

Lord Jesus, make me undeniably radical. Amen.

DIFFERENCE MAKER

Contact a nursing home or an orphanage today. Tell them you would like to invest in caring for those in need, asking them if you can visit to see what opportunities they have.

DISCRIMINATION

In 1955, Rosa Parks was told to give up her seat in the "colored" section of the bus to a white person, even though it would mean she would no longer have a place to sit herself. When she refused, she was arrested. Her bold action drew national attention to the blatant discrimination that prevailed in the (dys)functional order of the country. The society around her favored one type of person over another, the privileged over the oppressed, the rich in status over the poor.

The human heart is full of so much potential. It was made to reflect the love that God has for every person, and yet in its corruption are the ingredients for all kinds of hatred and cruelty. The person who discriminates against people incriminates against himself in twisted, self-regarding ambitions. Each person, no matter their life circumstance, is valuable in the eyes of God. Jesus is calling you to restore the way people are treated to a godly pattern.

> If you give special attention and a good seat to the rich person,
> but you say to the poor one, "You can stand over there, or else
> sit on the floor"—well, doesn't this discrimination show that
> your judgments are guided by evil motives?
>
> JAMES 2:3–4

Lord Jesus, let me see everyone through your eyes. Amen.

DIFFERENCE MAKER

To remind yourself of these verses, whenever you have the opportunity, give dignity ("the seat of honor") to someone society doesn't readily recognize as being worthy.

FAVORITISM

Let's pretend for a moment and say you were a sheep. And then let's say that for some reason the shepherd empowered you with the task of inviting any sheep you see into the safety and fellowship of the sheep pen. And then let's say that you saw two sheep outside the sheep pen. One of the sheep was a famous celebrity ewe with a golden fleece, while the other was some chump of a lamb with a crusty flannel wool shirt. Which of these two sheep would you choose to invite into the sheep pen?

Hold on, you didn't say neither, did you? Good. Just checking. Maybe you said the golden sheep because your popularity would go up among the other lambs? Or maybe, out of the pity of your heart, you even said the crusty sheep because you knew that was the right answer. But in humility, for the shepherd's offering, did you say "both"?

Yes indeed, it is good when you obey the royal law as found in the Scriptures: "Love your neighbor as yourself." But if you favor some people over others, you are committing a sin. You are guilty of breaking the law.

JAMES 2:8–9

Lord Jesus, your heart desires that all people would know your favor. Help me to act justly, to love mercy, and to walk humbly with you, my Shepherd. Amen.

DIFFERENCE MAKER

Challenge yourself to equally open doors, be polite, say thank you, give your time, make eye contact, or smile whenever you encounter someone today.

SUPPOSE YOU SEE

We've all seen them. Men and women huddled up on benches with a piece of cardboard or some newspaper. Asleep. Or drunk. Or sick. Or stoned. Whatever. But there is a lot we haven't been willing to see. We haven't seen the families sleeping in cars. We haven't seen the malnourished boy skip gym class because he can't afford running shoes. We haven't seen the runaway daughter trapped in an industry that wants to sell her to the highest bidder. We haven't seen the despair and death in the alley. Oh, we've seen some problems. We know they're there. But we haven't seen the people. And that means we haven't noticed Jesus with them.

Suppose you see a brother or sister who has no food or clothing, and you say, "Good-bye and have a good day; stay warm and eat well"—but then you don't give that person any food or clothing. What good does that do?

JAMES 2:15-16

Lord Jesus, what a miserable wretch I can be. I know you love the "least of these." Quicken the link between my eyes and my soul so that I will care for a neighbor in need. Amen.

DIFFERENCE MAKER

Contact a homeless shelter or food pantry. Ask them when they could use some help and how many people they could use. Then organize a team of people to go and serve.

SATURATE

Summer adventures are just around the corner. How do you plan to spend your days? Earning as much money as possible through work? Bike rides? Sunburns? Iced coffees? Picnics and bonfires? Baseball games? How about a mission project? Or helping at a camp? Or a Vacation Bible School? Mentoring younger students? Summer prayer group? Volunteering at a local youth drop-in center? Food-packing events?

Did you know you have permission to put your faith into action this summer? True adventure happens when all of your activities become saturated with Jesus. Your bike rides become more exhilarating because every aspect of creation you see produces praise from your heart. Your summer employment becomes more rewarding because you practice faithfulness and integrity while saving for your future expenses. Your intentional ministry projects become more fulfilling because they become regular features to your weekly routines.

Don't segregate your faith from your practical life this summer. Faith doesn't live that way and life doesn't truly work that way either. Saturate faith and life with one another, for then you'll see your life reflecting Jesus in this world.

So you see, faith by itself isn't enough. Unless it produces
good deeds, it is dead and useless.

JAMES 2:17

Lord Jesus, don't let me treat you like an add-on to my life.
You are the center of my life. Amen.

DIFFERENCE MAKER

Do something adventurous today that is influenced by James 2:17.

WALKING DEAD

Lifeless. No pulse. DOA (dead on arrival). That's how the Bible describes faith that fails to evidence any vital signs. It's a dramatic statement, but the point is valid. Faith inhales and then exhales the very breath of God. So a faith with no indication of dynamic activity is no faith at all. Don't let the coroner be called out to comment on your faith: "Well, what we have here is a depletion of oxygen." No, be alive with Jesus. Let him kick-start your heart and motivate your hands to action in this world. Let others see a living faith, pulsating with the life of the Creator of the Universe.

At the same time, don't let others confuse good works with faith. No one earns a way to salvation or gets badges on their heavenly robes for doing good things. Good "works" are simply the natural outflow of a living and vital faith. Because Jesus loves you, you can't help but share his love with others. Because Jesus forgives, you forgive. Because Jesus gives you security, you offer peace and confidence to your community. You overflow with the life he has given you. Don't be another person counted among the walking dead. Be alive today!

> Just as the body is dead without breath, so also faith is dead without good works.
>
> JAMES 2:26

Lord Jesus, make me alive in all that I do today. Amen.

DIFFERENCE MAKER

As a reminder throughout the day, notice your breathing. Each time you inhale and exhale, think about what a living, breathing relationship with Jesus would look like in that moment.

TAME

We have figured out how to train elephants to stand on buckets—we somehow thought that would be a good idea, so we did it. Also, for some reason, we have persuaded lions to let us stick our heads between their open jaws. We have figured out how to make seals clap, dolphins wave, and killer whales belly flop, all on command. We have even convinced snakes to dance to music, tigers to jump through hoops, and bears to wear tutus and tiaras. And yet none of us has yet to figure out how to control that little muscle in our mouths. Our tongues praise God and then scorch the earth. Our tongues are unbridled beasts that pretend to be housebroken but stain the carpet when the master lets down his or her guard.

People can tame all kinds of animals, birds, reptiles, and fish, but no one can tame the tongue. It is restless and evil, full of deadly poison. Sometimes it praises our Lord and Father, and sometimes it curses those who have been made in the image of God.

JAMES 3:7–9

Lord Jesus, let my tongue offer you praise and speak your truth today. Amen.

DIFFERENCE MAKER

Draw a small smiley face (on your hand or arm) and write James 3 next to it. Keep looking at this as a reminder to speak well all day long.

HUMILITY WORKS

To truly make a difference during your lifetime, it might mean that you don't get the glory for much of what you actually accomplish in your life. Humanity does not need any more egomaniacs drawing attention to themselves. But it does need more people who are willing to do things for the benefit of others.

A rudder on a ship makes what seems like a small impact at first. Of all the impressive parts that make up a great ship, the rudder is small and doesn't get the attention it deserves. But over time, the constant influence of that rudder changes the entire course of direction for that massive ship. Though people don't normally think about the rudder, they do notice where the massive ship goes—the direction it takes.

Those who live a consistent life of integrity, who make wise choices and follow God's patterns, can make an impact that lasts for several lifetimes. But such a way of living takes humility—a terribly selfless word that puts God and others in the position of priority in one's heart.

If you are wise and understand God's ways, prove it by living an honorable life, doing good works with the humility that comes from wisdom.

JAMES 3:13

Lord Jesus, let the good things I do bring you more praise than they bring me. Amen.

DIFFERENCE MAKER

Do something really good for someone today, but don't let them find out it was you.

CLOUDY WITH A CHANCE OF FRUIT

In the movie *Cloudy with a Chance of Meatballs*, an inventor named Flint Lockwood creates a machine that turns clouds into food. Any kind of food. *Zap*. It's done quicker than in the microwave and falls from the sky above. This machine is a blessing, as long as they don't allow selfish ambition to abuse the abundance of food it provides.

God wants to produce an abundance of good works through you. This "fruit from above," so to speak, comes from the inventiveness of your heart and mind as you learn how to walk with Jesus. When you live appropriately in his patterns, God uses your actions to provide precisely what others need at just the right times. His abundance can rain down on anyone, regardless of circumstances in life. Jesus delights in delighting others through you.

> But the wisdom from above is first of all pure. It is also peace loving, gentle at all times, and willing to yield to others. It is full of mercy and the fruit of good deeds. It shows no favoritism and is always sincere.
>
> JAMES 3:17

Lord Jesus, help me follow your patterns so that you can bless others through me. Amen.

DIFFERENCE MAKER

In the wisdom God is growing within you, choose someone you could bless by doing something unexpectedly encouraging today.

PLANT PEACE

Clashes create chaos. One side pitted against the other. Flagrant fouls fueling frustrations. Places where people argue and fight around the world inevitably become riddled with landmines and disturbed by displacement. This is true for wars between nations and even disputes within a family.

There is too much quarrel in our world today. When people who say they are followers of God throw grenades into the mix, the world stumbles even further into battle. No one needs Christians to add to the agitation that already exists. Retribution and followers of Jesus do not make a redeeming recipe for the world. What is needed are individuals, armed with kernels from Jesus, who will patiently but confidently sow peace among those in conflict. Become a person who seeds peace today. Resolve to be a refreshing presence in the midst of the strife.

And those who are peacemakers will plant seeds of peace
and reap a harvest of righteousness.

JAMES 3:18

Lord Jesus, let your peace reign in my heart so that I can bring calming assurance to others. Amen.

DIFFERENCE MAKER

Have you offended or hurt anyone recently? Think of a way to humbly approach them, ask for forgiveness, and make peace with them today.

HUMBLED

Humility is such an elusive, ironic beauty. The moment we think we have it, haven't we lost it? Could anyone ever accurately say, "I am humble"? Yes. Someone could. Jesus could. But he's the only one who was qualified to do so. Jesus is the ultimate King and he is the ultimate Servant. Although he is greater than the greatest greatness that could ever be, he humbled himself to the point of dying on a cross for our sake. He voluntarily gave up all of his glory so that we could live. No one can ever be as truly great as Jesus or as truly humble as Jesus. And that fact should humble us even further.

Humble yourselves before the Lord,
and he will lift you up in honor.

JAMES 4:10

Lord Jesus, thank you. Thank you. Thank you. I can do nothing else but bow before you. I am not worthy to be called yours, and yet that is exactly what you call me. Let me respond to you with the honor you deserve from me today.
Amen.

DIFFERENCE MAKER

Today, don't ask God to honor your plans or to do something for you. Instead, consider how you might honor the Lord through your words and actions today.

POUNCING PROSECUTORS

What if lawyers could make the judgment in a case? Instead of pleading or prosecuting, what if they just jumped to their own conclusions of freedom or condemnation? Or what if the witnesses in the case could declare innocence or guilt based not on what they had seen but on their one-sided perceptions? In either of these scenarios, the justice system would absolutely crumble. There is only one person who is ultimately allowed to make the final judgment, and that is the judge. The judge might use a jury occasionally, but even the jury relents to the rules established by the judge.

So when people are judgmental against or in favor of someone, justice is skewed. Pouncing prosecutors and drooling defenders are unreliable in their accusations and discernment. Ultimately, judgmental attitudes themselves will be tried and sentenced. Every person will appear before the Judge one day, and those who took the Lord's responsibility upon themselves will have some pretty tricky explaining to do.

> God alone, who gave the law, is the Judge. He alone has the power to save or to destroy. So what right do you have to judge your neighbor?
>
> JAMES 4:12

Lord Jesus, make me slow to judge others and quick to place myself before the mercy of your court. Amen.

DIFFERENCE MAKER

Prosecute yourself. Make a case against your sin. Then read Romans 5:8 a few times. Consider how the generosity of the Judge should be reflected in your treatment of others today.

OMISSION

It's wrong to hit your little brother when your mom isn't looking, right? We know it's a sin to do bad things. Bad behavior leads to bad consequences. It's a transaction that we have learned does in fact take place. But if sin was just about not doing bad things, then someone could conceivably lock themselves up and never do anything bad to anyone. This, of course, would be ridiculous, but at least that person wouldn't sin against others. Or would they?

Well, what if sin also involved *not* doing good things? If your little brother got his hand stuck in the refrigerator ice-making machine and started crying for your help, it would be wrong to just walk away and do nothing for him. You didn't put his hand in the ice maker—check. You didn't hit him while his hand was stuck in the ice maker—check (how kind of you!). But you didn't help him either. There is a lot going on in this world where people are stuck. Don't just walk away.

> Remember, it is sin to know what you ought to do
> and then not do it.
>
> JAMES 4:17

Lord Jesus, don't let me be like the jerks who walked by the man stuck on the side of the road. Let me be like the Samaritan, doing what is good in your eyes. Amen.

DIFFERENCE MAKER

Today be on the lookout for people who could use your help, in a big or small way. Then actually help.

GRUMBLE

There is a lot to complain about, isn't there? Maybe your day has been disrupted by a friend's grumpiness. Maybe your to-do list is getting longer because your boss keeps giving you more and more to do. Maybe someone cut you off while driving to work this morning. Maybe somebody let you down. Maybe you didn't get something you thought you should have gotten from your friend. Or maybe you got something you didn't think you should get from someone.

Complaining about someone else is our bratty way of venting our frustrations with others. Being frustrated with friends or family or bosses is not necessarily a bad feeling to have; in fact, it is quite normal to be frustrated with others. But turning that frustration into a kind of venting gossip or passive-aggressive attack displays a sour heart.

There is a better way of handling your angst with others. Pray about it. Take a deep breath. Realize that someone else's rudeness reflects upon them, so don't let it echo off of you. A heart that grumbles is a heart that is empty. Fill your heart with Jesus instead.

> Don't grumble about each other, brothers and sisters, or you
> will be judged. For look—the Judge is standing at the door!
>
> JAMES 5:9

Lord Jesus, change my grumbling heart into a fulfilled one. Amen.

DIFFERENCE MAKER

Stop at a bank and get a pile of one-dollar bills. Every time you catch yourself complaining today, put one-dollar in a jar. Then donate that money to your church.

ACCOUNTABILITY

When you mess up, simply admit it. Don't let the mess fester. Free yourself from the self-imposed shackles of your sin. Let if off your heart. Share it with someone you can trust and who will help you take the next steps toward freedom. This is especially true if you have a recurring mess that you keep stepping into.

It would be good to find someone to hold you accountable—a friend who will follow up with you and encourage you and watch where you step, a friend who will pray for your healing and change. The goal isn't to find someone who will haunt you every time you sin. You don't need more guilt heaped on you. You don't need more oppression. You've already given yourself enough constriction as it is. What you need is freedom. The goal, ultimately, is to walk toward faithfulness with Jesus. Fidelity, not accountability, is what you truly need. But accountability might just help get you there.

> Confess your sins to each other and pray for each other so that you may be healed. The earnest prayer of a righteous person has great power and produces wonderful results.
>
> JAMES 5:16

Lord Jesus, forgive me for my sin. Let me trust my steps to another person so that I can find the support I need to be faithful to you. Amen.

DIFFERENCE MAKER

If you haven't already done so, ask someone you trust to be an accountability partner for you.

REACH OUT

One of the most gut-wrenching things in life is a friend who wanders away from relationship with God and with you. This can be especially difficult when the person has sung with you during worship or served alongside you in helping others. It is much harder when he has laughed with you during times of joy, or she has supported you through your struggles.

Don't give up on your friend. Reach out. Extend a loving invitation back into relationship. Organize people in your church community to show love and acceptance, forgiveness and joy. Don't try to push or trick your friend. Simply and vigilantly, just as the father ran to embrace his lost son (Luke 15:11–32), keep watch for the moment of restoration.

My dear brothers and sisters, if someone among you wanders away from the truth and is brought back, you can be sure that whoever brings the sinner back from wandering will save that person from death and bring about the forgiveness of many sins.

JAMES 5:19–20

Lord Jesus, use me to help restore others to relationship with you and with your church. Amen.

DIFFERENCE MAKER

Think of a friend you have not seen for a while who has slowly wandered away. Contact them. Let them know you are thinking of them. Invite them to grab a coffee or to hang out sometime.

B = S + C

Be strong and courageous. Notice the command here. Don't just be strong and don't just be courageous. But be strong *and* courageous. This is what the Lord told Joshua as he was about to take a huge leadership role. The responsibility must have been overwhelming. Moses, Mister Miracle Man, who had effectively led Israel for forty years, had passed the baton on to Joshua. Everyone must have wondered, *Are we going to be okay? Will Joshua be able to lead us like Moses did?*

The Lord can enable anyone he wants, to do anything he wants them to do. Joshua had proven himself to be a consistent, dedicated person who put God's interests above his own. So when the grand moment came, the Lord was ready to empower him and use him. "Don't listen to everyone's fears. Don't be led astray by your own anxiety. Trust me."

God is calling you to make a difference in the world. Trust him to work through you today. He is with you when you are following his lead in your life.

> "So be strong and courageous! Do not be afraid and do not panic before them. For the LORD your God will personally go ahead of you. He will neither fail you nor abandon you."
>
> DEUTERONOMY 31:6

Lord Jesus, empower me to do what you want me to do today. Amen.

DIFFERENCE MAKER

What do you believe God has called you to do, but you have struggled to take the initiative to get started? Apply this verse to your life today.

SELAH

Stop whatever else is in your mind right now except for this very moment with God. Halt any distraction. Press pause. This moment right now is an interlude in your life. Let the activities prior to this moment be still. Let the activities that will come after this moment wait. You'll get to them soon enough. They don't need you for the next few minutes. Stop. Quiet your soul. And listen.

Selah is a Hebrew word used dozens of times throughout the Psalms. Scholars think it means something like "interval" or "quiet break." It seems to be a moment in the activity of a song where everything pauses. In the vacuum of words and sound, people are encouraged to give reflection to God's mighty work. So take all of your to-do lists and hanging-over-the-head worries and put them aside for a moment. Reflect on this passage from Psalm 46 and then *selah* for a moment.

> God is our refuge and strength,
> always ready to help in times of trouble.
> So we will not fear when earthquakes come
> and the mountains crumble into the sea.
> Let the oceans roar and foam.
> Let the mountains tremble as the waters surge!
> *Interlude* [Selah]

PSALM 46:1–3

Lord Jesus, let me pause my life in you for this moment. Amen.

DIFFERENCE MAKER

Make a quiet break with God a regular pattern in the hectic activity of your life today.

SPIRIT OF POWER

Look ahead a few years into your life. For this moment right now, as you envision the potential God has for you, don't let yourself worry about things that are out of your control. Instead, think about the type of person Jesus wants you to be. Consider the sorts of things he is preparing you to do. As the picture takes shape in your mind, ask yourself: Between now and then, what would Jesus want me to do today to get ready for tomorrow?

Contemplating your future can be both overwhelming and exciting. God's long-term goals for you can seem too far away or even too blurry. Yet, at the very same time, as Jesus brings clarity to your steps, they could send your heart racing in anticipation for what is ahead. Just like an expectant mom who is waiting to hold her child in her arms, treat each day with the confidence, love, and self-discipline that you need to bring about God's plans in your life.

> For God has not given us a spirit of fear and timidity, but of power, love, and self-discipline.
>
> 2 TIMOTHY 1:7

Lord Jesus, overcome my hesitations to do what you want me to do. Give me a new boldness of heart and hands today. Amen.

DIFFERENCE MAKER

What is the next step you can take today toward what God has called you to do?

TO GOD

Imagine your heart and mind being squashed by a bus. Or two buses! How about three? And the buses that are squeezing you are rusty yellow hulks of metal belching out smoke and overflowing with sugar-crazed middle school kids screaming for your attention! The driver just keeps turning the radio up louder and louder in a futile attempt to drown out the cacophony of noise, and the station just keeps playing the same annoying pop song that always gets stuck in your head on repeat. Repeat. Repeat. Repeat. Aaahhh!

Life can feel like this sometimes. Pressing. Heavy. Anxious and crushing. Loads of concern piled on hectic demands shrieking for your immediate attention. Your burdens need to be lifted off of you somehow, or else your heart will struggle to beat. The cares need to be taken off of you sometime, or your mind will struggle to think. But who is able to lift your burdens for you? Peter gives us a pretty good hint.

Give all your worries and cares to God, for he cares about you.

1 PETER 5:7

Dear Jesus, I lift up my concerns to you now. Take them. They're yours. Amen.

DIFFERENCE MAKER

Write down your concerns on a piece of paper. Once your list is complete, on the top of the paper write, Jesus can have these now. Pray. Then crumple up the paper and throw it in the trash.

YOUR PLANS

If you wanted to rob a bank, and you committed this plan to the Lord, would you succeed? Of course not! The whole robbing-the-bank part wouldn't work out because God wouldn't support it. He'd probably hand you back your blueprints and tell you to get a life.

To commit your plans to God means to hand them over, let him look them over, and work them over until they match his will. He'd be glad to work with you on any necessary changes (instead of "robbing" he might suggest "investing"). If you accept God's revised plans and act on them, then you have shown that your plans are committed to the Lord. Once this is true, your plans will succeed. In other words, do what God wants you to do today. Make your plan of action in line with God's plan of action and all will go according to plan.

> Commit your actions to the Lord,
> and your plans will succeed.
>
> PROVERBS 16:3

Lord Jesus, I have big things in the seasons ahead. Please guide the goals that I have and the steps I take. Amen.

DIFFERENCE MAKER

Work on your résumé (or scholarship applications for the fall), and practice interviewing for the opportunities God has for you in the future. As you do, ask yourself this question: Do God's plans for me match my plans for me?

BUT...

During their last meal together, tensions were high. Jesus spoke about being killed, and Judas got up and left after being marked as the betrayer. Jesus had washed their feet, served bread and wine as symbols of his death, and spoke about going away for a little while. Jesus told his disciples, "Love each other." But his disciples thought of everything else but love.

Their heads were spinning and their hearts were flooded with worry. Instead of loving, they stressed, "What's happening here?" Peter blurted out, "Lord, where are you going?" Thomas anxiously cried, "Lord, we have no idea where you are going." They grew exhausted from apprehension and began to drift apart. By the end of the night, overwhelmed by their fear, most of them denied Jesus and ran away from each other.

"Love each other." But Lord, I have a big test. But Lord, I have so much going on in my life right now. Lord, I am really tired today. Lord, that guy drives me crazy. "Love each other." Lord, I don't like the style of music they play. Lord, he literally stinks. Lord, I'm busy. Lord, I'm worried. Lord, I don't feel in control of things. "Love each other."

> "So now I am giving you a new commandment: Love each other. Just as I have loved you, you should love each other. "
>
> JOHN 13:34

Lord Jesus, with everything happening right now, help me to love my friends and family. Amen.

DIFFERENCE MAKER

Think of the three closest people you have in your life. Find a practical way today to show each of them that you love them.

OOPS

"Oops. Didn't know I was supposed to do that." Picture saying that to your boss after missing an important deadline. Then imagine hearing yourself say, "Uh, yeah, it's not really my fault because I didn't even know about it. So…no big deal." Yeah, right. That project was assigned to you and was supposed to get done. Sorry, but you're going to be looking for a new job pretty soon.

At the end of your life, imagine feeling pretty fine about all the good stuff that you did, but then Jesus informs you that you missed several significant projects. There were some people you passed by whom you could have helped. There were times when you didn't defend someone who was being hurt. There were kind words you could have said, doors you could have held open, and patience you could have given. Oh, and then there was all the time you could have spent praying for people, but you played Candy Crush instead.

> And he will answer, "I tell you the truth, when you refused to help the least of these my brothers and sisters, you were refusing to help me."
>
> MATTHEW 25:45

Jesus, I have missed so many things that I should have done. Poke my heart today when I begin to miss the work you have for me. Amen.

DIFFERENCE MAKER

Be attentive to what you can do for others today.

GENERATION →?

Why are we so easily drawn away from God and toward things that hurt us? Why are we so attracted to detrimental people or activities? And why do we secretly adore things that leave us empty, unfulfilled, and worse off? Why do we look for empty pleasures? And why do we like immediacy more than we like patience? Why do we think that selfishness is justified?

Those questions are the sad story of the book of Judges. A people who once experienced God in spectacular, personal ways became a people far from God, not knowing his presence, not following his patterns. Generation after generation grew more disgusting, more degrading, and more depraved than the one before it. People grew more and more removed from God, less and less aware of right and wrong, more confused and less secure, and more shallow and less happy.

One of the most significant things we can do today is to pray for our generation to have the courage to turn from darkness and to walk toward the light of Jesus.

> After that generation died, another generation grew up
> who did not acknowledge the LORD or remember the mighty
> things he had done for Israel.
>
> JUDGES 2:10

Lord Jesus, my heart breaks for my generation. Don't let us walk away from you.
Restore us to relationship with you. Amen.

DIFFERENCE MAKER

Grab some friends and set aside time to pray for your generation today.

IMPOSSIBLE INSTRUCTIONS?

Two thousand years ago, the apostle Paul encouraged a church to "always rejoice" and to "pray without ceasing." He also told them to "give thanks always," no matter what they were going through. This, Paul said, was God's will for their very lives.

But are these instructions practical? Is it realistic to think that anyone could truly "always rejoice"? Is it actually possible to "pray without ceasing"? Or what if life absolutely stinks (absolutely, repulsively, horribly stinks)—is it thinkable to "give thanks always" in those situations? Are these instructions from Paul just pleasant "Christianese" phrases similar to "keep your chin up" or "it'll all be okay"? Or can people actually live these commands out?

These must be more than just empty commands. Perhaps in our fallen human strength these are mission impossible, but perhaps in the power of Jesus there is potential to actually live these out. Perhaps in Jesus people can be captured by joy, be caught up in conversation with God, and be overwhelmed to overflowing with his grace.

> Always be joyful. Never stop praying. Be thankful in all circumstances, for this is God's will for you who belong to Christ Jesus.
>
> 1 THESSALONIANS 5:16–18

Lord Jesus, I don't know how, but give me the mind and heart to live these verses out today. Amen.

DIFFERENCE MAKER

Pick one of the three instructions and write it on your hand to remind yourself throughout the day what Jesus wants do within you.

SKY

Look at the sky. What do you see? How far can you see? What is up there? How does what you see change throughout the day? During the day, watch the clouds form and pass by in the atmosphere. If it is rainy, marvel at the science involved. If it is stormy, be humbled by the power of the winds and weather fronts. If it is sunny, feel the warmth of the sun on your skin. Enjoy the light it gives to reveal God's creation. At night, look at the stars. How many are there? Where are they all? Examine the detail of the moon. Think of the importance of its pull on the earth. Look at the sky. What do you learn about God and about what he created you to do?

> The heavens proclaim the glory of God.
> The skies display his craftsmanship.
> Day after day they continue to speak;
> night after night they make him known.
> They speak without a sound or word;
> their voice is never heard.
> Yet their message has gone throughout the earth,
> and their words to all the world.
>
> PSALM 19:1–4

Jesus, your love can be seen in the what you have made. Today, let me look up often and be amazed by you. Amen.

DIFFERENCE MAKER

Get outside and enjoy what God has made. Let the expanse of the sky cause you to wonder about how great he is and about your role on this earth.

STRUGGLE

Many people don't *struggle* with bitterness, they just let it waltz into their lives without a fight. Bitterness seems like a natural fit to hurting hearts. If they have been wronged, the company of resentment is often welcomed. If they have been disappointed, many people invite anger to take up residence in their lives. Once bitterness has taken root, however, it's not much of a stretch to invite retaliation to the party also. No one needs to get special training to become skilled in revenge. With resentment driving the heart, retaliation flows like lava. It wells up without much effort when bitterness kicks in its tectonic push. It's all too easy.

Many people, however, do struggle with forgiveness. To offer forgiveness seems almost like a heavenly pummel on top of bruises. It is a radical countercultural response to wrong. Extending reconciliation strains people when they have been wronged, because mercy demands that pride be put down and grace be picked up.

> Make allowance for each other's faults, and forgive anyone
> who offends you. Remember, the Lord forgave you, so you
> must forgive others.
>
> COLOSSIANS 3:13

Lord Jesus, I see your example of mercy and forgiveness and I am in awe.
Help me to live with the same heart. Amen.

DIFFERENCE MAKER

If you face the easy fall into resentment today, write this phrase on the first piece of paper you can find: *Jesus, help me to forgive.*

IF GOD WANTS

If God wanted to, of course, he could crash into our party and force us to listen. But he would rather get our attention through a gentle whisper. It's God's way of being gentle on our fragile hearts and ears. God's voice of wrath could tear the skin from our bones; his word could completely destroy us. Or God's voice of grace could create us. His breath could mend our tissue back together and his word could give us new life—if he wants.

But do *we* want it? Are we willing to listen to his gentle whisper? If yes, then God will call out gently. If no, then God might eventually need to clap his hands and thunder his voice in our direction.

"Go out and stand before me on the mountain," the LORD told him. And as Elijah stood there, the LORD passed by, and a mighty windstorm hit the mountain. It was such a terrible blast that the rocks were torn loose, but the LORD was not in the wind. After the wind there was an earthquake, but the LORD was not in the earthquake. And after the earthquake there was a fire, but the LORD was not in the fire. And after the fire there was the sound of a gentle whisper.

1 KINGS 19:11-13

Jesus, open my ears to hear you speak. Amen.

DIFFERENCE MAKER

Set aside uncrowded time today to listen for God's voice.

STUPID

Have you ever given a speech that you thought was incredible, only to have the teacher find some things wrong with it? You didn't realize that you had said um twelve times, but the teacher noticed. You thought your opening illustration about the space monkey and the alien was hilarious, but the teacher thought it would have been better if you could have tied it in to your main point somehow. You thought you showed enthusiasm, but your teacher thought you talked too fast.

Being corrected can feel really annoying if you're not looking for it. You might even be tempted to get angry with the one who corrects your mistakes. Maybe you're one of those people who always got a ribbon as a kid, even if you were in last place. Get over it. Learn from someone's discipline. And do even better next time as a result.

To learn, you must love discipline;
it is stupid to hate correction.

PROVERBS 12:1

Dear Jesus, let me find my confidence in you, and be willing to bear the weight of correction in my life. Amen.

DIFFERENCE MAKER

Find someone you trust and whose advice you would like to have in your life, and arrange a time for them to give you some constructive feedback on the plans you have for your life.

July

Jesus,

help me realize all that I could be,

and all that I could do,

with you shepherding my steps.

Amen.

-DOM

A suffix at the end of a lot of words is –dom, which refers to domain or rank. For example, a kingdom is the realm of the king, stardom is the realm of a popular person (a "star"), and boredom is hopefully not the realm you have just entered because of this silly grammatical study.

Freedom is the realm where a person can act or speak without prevention. When someone is free, they can do what they'd like and know that it is good. Freedom is not hedonism, where people choose to ignore the consequences and do whatever *feels* good (only to be forced to deal with their bad decisions later). Rather, freedom is so much better than a temporary suspension of morality. It is being able to walk where you need to go, say what you need to say, laugh when you need to laugh, and cry when you need to cry. Freedom is being able to wander with friends, dine with family, and enjoy what God has made. To enter the domain of freedom, people must follow the Spirit of the Lord. Life lived against the Spirit restricts people's ability to find true fulfillment.

> For the Lord is the Spirit, and wherever the Spirit of the Lord
> is, there is freedom.
>
> 2 CORINTHIANS 3:17

Lord Jesus, let me turn to you so that I can walk in freedom with you today.
Amen.

DIFFERENCE MAKER

Connect with a friend who is weighed down by his or her bad decisions. Invite them to turn to the Lord and walk in freedom today.

SET FREE

In *The Lord of the Rings*, when Gandalf is stuck and when he is truly in distress, he summons the eagles to come and help him. These aren't ordinary eagles, however. These are massive birds of prey with a forty-foot wingspan that are able to destroy orc armies and carry the heroes off to safety.

The Bible is full of times when God's people summon the Lord for rescue in the midst of distress. For whatever reason, they have found themselves in trouble. Sometimes it was stupid and sinful decisions that got them stuck right where they are, and at other times circumstances beyond their control overwhelm them. Repeatedly, as these individuals cry out to the Lord, they make this note: *And the Lord answered me and set me free.*

We don't always know the details of the distress, nor do we always know the details of the rescue either. The trouble and the escape certainly don't always look like the people expected. But we do know this: God rescues those who call out to him in their time of need.

In my distress I prayed to the Lord,
and the Lord answered me and set me free.

PSALM 118:5

Lord Jesus, I pray to you, and I ask you to please come to my aid when I find myself in trouble. Amen.

DIFFERENCE MAKER

If you get yourself stuck today, instead of trying to dig yourself out, start by praying to the Lord for rescue. Then, while placing yourself in his guidance, look for his path of rescue.

MESSIAH

Hundreds of years before Jesus was born, Isaiah gave a message to the people of Israel. Israel was suffering under the weight of bad decisions and oppressive nations. However, God had good news for them. He would send a Messiah, his Servant, who would restore people to freedom. This messianic Servant-King would focus his rule on healing, forgiveness, and rebuilding a nation that was released from the chains of oppression.

God's idea of a reigning king has always been radically countercultural to the human idea of a king who reigns. God's idea is that a king sacrificially walks in godliness, serves the people, frees them from any form of tyranny, and lifts them up to a status above himself. Ultimately, this was fulfilled in the reign of Jesus Christ, but it is also fulfilled in the way that we serve others through the good news of his kingdom.

> "The Spirit of the Sovereign LORD is upon me,
> for the LORD has anointed me
> to bring good news to the poor.
> He has sent me to comfort the brokenhearted
> and to proclaim that captives will be released
> and prisoners will be freed."
>
> ISAIAH 61:1

Lord Jesus, your concern is that I would share your good news with those who need to know you. Show me how and when to do this today. Amen.

DIFFERENCE MAKER

Ask yourself: Does my daily activity reflect God's good news kingdom mind-set?

FREEDOM

You may notice that the verse in today's entry looks exactly like yesterday's. That is because these words occur in two places in the Bible. The first was taken from Isaiah 61, when Isaiah introduces what the coming Messiah's ministry will be like. The second—today's verse—is taken from Luke 4, when Jesus read the very words from Isaiah 61 in his first sermon.

Jesus read these words in a synagogue gathering. He opened the scroll, read the messianic passage, sat down, and then said, "What you've just heard has been fulfilled this very day." Jesus was making a statement thereby proclaiming, "This is who I am and this is what I am going to do." As Christians, we follow Jesus, whose purpose was to share refreshingly good news and to proclaim unexpected release, renewal of sight, and the dignity of freedom.

"The Spirit of the Lord is upon me,
for he has anointed me to bring Good News to the poor.
He has sent me to proclaim that captives will be released,
that the blind will see,
that the oppressed will be set free."

LUKE 4:18

Jesus, because of your death on the cross, I am unshackled. Thank you for the good news of your freedom. Amen.

DIFFERENCE MAKER

Let off fireworks tonight in celebration of the freedom that comes from the sacrifice of life so that you can be truly free.

SHEPHERD

If you know that Jesus supports your cause, then you can be confident to tackle it full on. With Jesus standing behind you, ready to defend you and poised to refresh you, what have you got to lose? He has already laid down his life for you. He made it clear that he wasn't going to let anything snatch you away from his grip. He has absolutely given his whole self for you. So don't hold back anything from him or from the calling he has broadcast.

Jesus isn't urging you to go forward just because he wants you to follow his example (though he certainly does want you to do that). Jesus wants you to learn to be bold for him. There is no need to stand with trepidation; no need to let fear or timidity slow you down. There is no need to be a "Minnesota Nice" passive-aggressive believer. Jesus is absolutely good! And Jesus is your Shepherd—he is your Good Shepherd. And because he is the one who guides you and protects you, feeds you and grows you, challenges you and restores you, the calling he has given you is yours to pursue.

> "I am the good shepherd. The good shepherd sacrifices his
> life for the sheep."
>
> JOHN 10:11

Jesus, help me realize all that I could be and all that I could do with you shepherding my steps. Amen.

DIFFERENCE MAKER

Do something remarkably good for others today, something that you otherwise wouldn't have done, all because Jesus supports you with his life.

SHEEP

No offense, but you are a sheep. Just a dumb little lamb. Have you ever had a motivational devotional entry tell you that before? You are a wandering, stinky mess of an animal. A simple-minded, ego-headed, fragile hearted, bleating lamb.

The Lord, though, the Lord…he is your Shepherd. You are so significant that the Lord has chosen to shepherd your flock. Not some two-bit sheep, not some random hired hand, not a nomadic wanderer. The Lord alone shepherds you because he thinks you are worth his very life.

Just listen to what your Shepherd does for you. You don't need anyone or anything other than him. The Lord carries you, cleans you up, feeds you full, protects you, frees you, guides you, leads you, shears you, serves you, nudges you, pokes you, comes beside you, hears you, speaks with you, walks with you, calms you, excites you, instructs you, finds you, gathers you, waters you, mends you, quenches you, rests you, exalts you, lifts you, enjoys you, anoints you, tends to you, offers his life for you, and dwells with you—and he does this for all of your life. The Lord is your Shepherd. And he is so, so good.

> The LORD is my shepherd;
> I have all that I need.
>
> PSALM 23:1

Jesus, help me to live in the truth of this verse today. Amen.

DIFFERENCE MAKER

Avoid the temptation to fill your life with extra stuff today. Every time you are tempted to "need" something else, turn your attention to Jesus instead.

REST

Where is the most restful place you have ever been? A sandy beach, with the lapping waves and warm sun? A recliner chair with an ice-cold glass of lemonade after a busy day? If you were a sheep, your answer would be a green meadow, a gentle warm breeze, and a nearby source of fresh water. A good shepherd would navigate his sheep toward a place like this. The frantic environment of exhaust-spewing vehicles and noise-making appliances and retina-displaying screens and time-rushing schedules is not the proper ecosystem for sheep. Sheep fare better when their rhythm includes intervals of rest.

If a lamb wanders off to create a restful experience without the guidance of the shepherd, however, off-track bets are that the lamb will soon find itself in a precarious predicament. Rest is the one thing that was not created when God made the world. It was simply embedded in the Lord's shepherding rhythm.

> He lets me rest in green meadows;
> he leads me beside peaceful streams.
>
> PSALM 23:2

Lord Jesus, don't let me lead myself toward my own pursuits today. I want you to lead me toward those things that you desire for me. Let me rest in the knowledge that you are guiding me today. Amen.

DIFFERENCE MAKER

Set aside time in a comfortable place, with a comforting snack, and open up your Bible to Psalm 23 and let it sink into the rhythm of your soul.

GPS

In the old days, people used to unfold road maps over their steering wheels and on their dashboards. Then, in order to figure out where they were going, they would look up at the road, down at the map, up at street signs, down again at the map, up at visual markers, and down at the map again—eventually, hopefully safely, getting to where they needed to go.

Today, of course, things are quite different. Instead of a paper map, we have Siri. On your iPhone you can tell Siri to find the location you need to go and route you there. You merely follow her navigation (or his if you have changed its voice), including instructions to change lanes or to avoid construction. Many times you don't even know for sure that you are being led in the right direction, but you consent to follow Siri because you trust she/he knows where you are going.

Where do you need to go in your life? Siri can only get you so far. But Jesus can get you where you were created to be. Are you willing to let him tell you when to turn or when to take an exit? Do you trust yourself to his guidance, even if you don't always know all the steps to take? If you do, you will be strengthened by his Spirit to pursue your calling.

He renews my strength.
He guides me along right paths,
bringing honor to his name.

PSALM 23:3

Dear Jesus, I trust your steps of guidance for my life today. Help me listen to you.
Amen.

DIFFERENCE MAKER

The next time you use your navigation app, consider how it is a metaphor for how you should follow Jesus' direction for your life.

EVEN THOUGH

If you realize that Jesus is there for you, then you can be there for others who find themselves in need today. Once you recognize the comforting presence of your Savior next to you, it is the natural next step to reach out to someone else with the good news about the Good Shepherd.

Jesus has a deep desire to walk with anyone through even the most difficult of circumstances. He knows how raw real life can be. He knows there is not one person who doesn't walk through dark times. Jesus knows this because he came to walk with, to guide, and to shepherd his people. Once you realize his presence in the hardest of circumstances, you notice that his stride carries strength and his care provides protection. And when your fear dissipates, you want to let others know just how good the Good Shepherd happens to be.

Even when I walk
through the darkest valley,
I will not be afraid,
for you are close beside me.
Your rod and your staff
protect and comfort me.

PSALM 23:4

Jesus, thank you for being with me even though I go through difficult times. Empower me to reveal your presence to others too. Amen.

DIFFERENCE MAKER

Reach out to someone who is struggling today. Find a creative way to let them know that Jesus is ready to walk close beside them, and that so are you.

FEAST

Giordano deep-dish pizza. Lobster saturated in garlic butter. Turkey with thick gravy, potatoes on the side, and delicious stuffing. Slow-cooked barbeque pulled pork. Chipotle steak and queso burrito with corn, cheese, sour cream, and extra guacamole. The freshest Caesar salad you've ever had. Rich marble lava cake drizzled with strawberry cream. An unending chocolate fondue fountain with freshly cut fruit and those cool little wooden skewers. Iced tea and lemonade and cappuccinos. Serving after serving after serving placed in front of you. All of this doesn't even come close to the sort of attention that your Good Shepherd intends to lavish upon you.

You are worth it to Jesus. He wants you to be overwhelmed by his extravagant love today. Let his abundance disturb your comfort zone, shatter your walled-up insecurities, and cover your brokenness. All that has intended harm against you must cease, because your Savior has prepared a meal in your honor.

You prepare a feast for me
in the presence of my enemies.
You honor me by anointing my head with oil.
My cup overflows with blessings.

PSALM 23:5

Jesus, I don't know what to say, but thank you. Amen.

DIFFERENCE MAKER

Gather the people who are closest to you and share a vibrant feast together. Go overboard with your preparations and planning. Celebrate the life God has given you. And speak about this meal together as a metaphor for the communion Jesus offers all of you.

SURELY

In the old days, when a man fell in love, he courted the woman he wanted to marry—he "pursued" her. This didn't happen in some Neanderthal sort of way, nor in a creepy stalker sort of way. No, no, no, no, no. When a man fell in love, he tried to win the heart of the woman through gentleness, politeness, good intentions, and through proven stability and strength of character. He would have sent her flowers and written her notes (using his actual hand and a pen). He would have sacrificed his own well-being in order to lift up her life and treasure her.

This is the way Jesus pursues us. His goodness and unfailing love go everywhere we go. He tries to catch our attention with his kindness and his grace. He opens doors and prepares opportunities for us to get to know each other better. Because he follows after us in love, we learn to follow after him in love as well.

Surely your goodness and unfailing love will pursue me
all the days of my life,
and I will live in the house of the LORD forever.

PSALM 23:6

Lord Jesus, thank you for pursuing me, a wandering soul.
You have captured my heart. Amen.

DIFFERENCE MAKER

Everywhere you go today, imagine that Jesus is following you, trying to get your attention. Every now and then be sure to pause your activities to allow Jesus to share his life with you.

DOUBT

Is it okay to doubt God? That's a question many people often wonder about. We struggle as humans to completely trust anyone, including God. At times we're not sure God is really watching out for us, or we don't feel God cares about us. Or maybe we wonder why God allows tragedy to happen in our lives or even in the world at large. We are disappointed that God doesn't seem more real. Doubt is normal. But is it okay?

The Bible is filled with doubt. "Heroes" of faith appear to have serious trust issues. Gideon, for one, is a pessimist when it comes to God in his life. The Psalms echo with cries of bewilderment and despair. Martha was agonized that Jesus didn't arrive when she wanted him to. Peter and the disciples fail miserably on more than a few occasions. But is that okay?

Doubt can be a sign that we are trying to work out our faith in real life. For instance, we believe God is there, so we wonder why we don't feel him; we know God is good, so we struggle with all the bad in the world. When our doubt is lifted to God, it reveals our faith. And God honors the heart that trusts its deepest doubts to him.

The father instantly cried out, "I do believe, but help me overcome my unbelief!"

MARK 9:24

Lord Jesus, my faith is not always full, but whatever I have I lift to you. Amen.

DIFFERENCE MAKER

Entrust whatever doubt you have to the Lord in prayer today.

GRIEVE

Too often we are looking for the quick out. When we see someone grieve, we try to make them immediately feel better. Rare is the person who is willing to wait in pain with someone who is actively in pain. It is much too tempting to throw pleasantries and consolations of religion as if they were placebo drugs: "God has a plan for you," "Everything happens for a reason," "It will all be okay," and "Just trust God." Sometimes, one of the worst things we can do is encourage someone to stop grieving. After all, Jesus wept. He wept for Lazarus and his friends. Jesus wept for Jerusalem. He wept sweat from his pores in Gethsemane. Jesus grieved.

Love is the willingness to embrace pain. Yes, it is patient, kind, never failing, and it is not easily angered. Each of those attributes requires an intentional willingness to hurt for someone else. Endurance, perseverance, forgiveness, trust…each takes a purposeful step of entering into pain. Blessed are those who mourn. Love is not weakness; it is strength. We have a strong God who loves us, even in the midst of our pain.

> Then Jesus wept. The people who were standing nearby
> said, "See how much he loved him!"
>
> JOHN 11:35–36

Lord Jesus, give me the strength to love enough to grieve. Amen.

DIFFERENCE MAKER

Remember a friend who is hurting today. Do something for them to show that you are by their side in their time of grieving.

HASTY MISTAKES

Have you ever stopped at your local coffee shop for a vanilla skinny latte with extra whip cream, a bit weary eyed from too little sleep the night before, and in line just in front of you was someone you thought you knew? This person had the same hairstyle and the same coat and height as your friend Haley. From a quick glance, it was definitely her. So you said what you would normally say when you see your friend Haley—you said, "Hey, Haley!" But your friend didn't turn around. So then you did what any determined extroverted encourager would do in that situation—you took out your gloves and playfully smacked her in the back. You know, just to say hello. Well, this someone you thought was Haley turned around and looked at you with gaped astonishment. The only thing you could think of saying in the moment was, "Oops. You're not Haley." Real life reveals your deficiencies.

Enthusiasm without knowledge is no good;
haste makes mistakes.

PROVERBS 19:2

Jesus, thank you for loving me through my everyday mistakes. Help me roll with them today, slow myself down, and be more aware of what I'm doing. Amen.

DIFFERENCE MAKER

Take extra effort to take care of yourself today in order to limit your mistakes. Get good rest, eat healthy, don't rush your attitude, and breathe deeply.

WAKE UP

Have you ever wondered how Jesus woke up? Did he startle awake? Did he slowly yawn and stretch out his arms? Did he rub his eyes, grumble his voice, and gruff his shoulders? Do you think he smiled a sly smile, as if he knew something amazing was going to happen? Or do you think he wished he could hit his snooze button a few times?

One time Jesus woke up because he was awakened frantically by his disciples. They were in a boat, and the boat was in the middle of the sea, and the sea was in the middle of a storm. Jesus wasn't worried, however; he was obviously able to get comfortable enough to rest. Maybe he enjoyed the sensation of danger out there on the sea. The Creator of the Universe had the opportunity to ride in his own storm (which would be kind of like the creator of a roller coaster strapping himself in for the thrills). Jesus wasn't shocked by what was going on when he awoke. The chaos didn't overwhelm him. That day, just like any other day, was completely in his control.

> When Jesus woke up, he rebuked the wind and said to the waves, "Silence! Be still!" Suddenly the wind stopped, and there was a great calm. Then he asked them, "Why are you afraid? Do you still have no faith?"
>
> MARK 4:39–40

Jesus, give me even a small dose of your confidence for today. Amen.

DIFFERENCE MAKER

The next time you wake up, trust the circumstances of your day to Jesus.

NO LOBOTOMY

Here's some good news for you: Jesus doesn't want you to have a lobotomy. He's not asking for a turn-your-mind-off kind of commitment. He doesn't want numb faith. He wants you to thoughtfully give him your afraidness. If you find yourself in the middle of trouble, he doesn't want you to freak out. Rather, he wants you to think about who he is and where he is and what he is all about.

Even in the midst of the storm, Jesus is with you. He is not afraid, and neither should you be. He is in control, even if you feel like you're the only one trying to bail you out, or even if you feel alone in your struggle against the current. Jesus more often than not will reveal his posture of peace. That's right, in the middle of what is causing you your greatest panic, Jesus is holding himself together. He is amazing. In the end, he may either calm the storm or he may calm you, so in the middle of it you must remember to trust.

> "Don't let your hearts be troubled. Trust in God,
> and trust also in me."
>
> JOHN 14:1

Lord Jesus, you are the only person who could have genuinely made that statement. I trust myself to you in the middle of my circumstances today. Amen.

DIFFERENCE MAKER

When your stress level starts to rise, remember that Jesus is not panicking. So take a deep breath and walk confidently through it.

STAND IN HISTORY

At important moments of history, when rivers collided and torrents swelled, this world has needed people to take a stand for Jesus. If the opportunity was missed, if people failed to plant their feet, spectators were caught up in the rushing current and swept away. But when the opportunity was seized, when people stood up for what was right, the course of history was stabilized and Jesus brought healing to the scattered.

We are perhaps now at one of those moments. We need people bold enough to position their feet as a rock in the rapids, undeterred and unmoved. Then, with loving arms stretched out wide, we need those bold people to catch others before the pressure sweeps them away. For as soon as people are caught, they are enabled to catch their breath, steady their stance, and join in the rescue effort.

At one of these pivotal moments in history, Jesus asked Peter, "Who do you say I am?" Peter, against the current, stood boldly and unashamedly, and declared, "You are the Messiah, the Son of the living God."

> "Now I say to you that you are Peter (which means 'rock'), and upon this rock I will build my church, and all the powers of hell will not conquer it."
>
> MATTHEW 16:18

Jesus, give me the strength to boldly stand for you in this important moment of history. Amen.

DIFFERENCE MAKER

What would it practically look like to stand against the current and for Jesus today?

ETERNITY

If you knew you had the rest of eternity to pursue your goals in life, would it change the sort of goals you would pursue? Think about the long-term goals you have your life. If you had all the time in the universe, would those goals be big enough? If you had every day for thousands and thousands of years, what would usher its way to the top of your long-term priority list?

In the movie *Groundhog Day*, Bill Murray's character, a weatherman named Phil Connors, woke up on the same day over and over again. It has been estimated that Phil repeated the day 12,395 times. At first, Phil lived for himself, setting goals of manipulation and self-service. But then he discovered each time that these goals ultimately left him feeling empty. So, as eternity seemed to set in, he changed his priorities and began to deepen his character and strengthen his ability to help others. When we trust our lives to Jesus, we begin to live our days in light of eternity. And, as a result, our priorities and goals become grand endeavors that truly can change this world.

For you have been born again, but not to a life that will quickly end. Your new life will last forever because it comes from the eternal, living word of God.

1 PETER 1:23

Lord Jesus, make the goals I set in life reflect the eternal life you have given me. Amen.

DIFFERENCE MAKER

How would you answer the questions in the first paragraph of this devotion? Sit down with a friend today. Bring a pen along. Get out a napkin and begin dreaming big about what sorts of things Jesus might be calling you to do.

HOW YOU LIVE

People don't learn about Jesus just from going to church. In fact, most people learn most about Jesus through everyday, regular-life encounters with his followers. This means that if people regularly go to the grocery store, then they will repeatedly run into followers of Jesus who also naturally go to the grocery store. If people regularly sit down for meals, or spend hours at work, or hang out at community events, or watch a baseball game, it is very likely that followers of Jesus will be there too.

While good behavior at church is noteworthy, it could be argued that it is significantly more important how followers of Jesus live the other six days of the week in the regular routines of everyday life. It makes a difference what kind of words followers of Jesus use on Monday. It matters how they speak about others on Tuesday, how they stand in a checkout line on Wednesday, whether or not they are trustworthy at work on Thursday, how they spend their money on Friday, and if they are reliable as neighbors on Saturday. How we live seven days a week is important.

Be careful to live properly among your unbelieving neighbors. Then even if they accuse you of doing wrong, they will see your honorable behavior, and they will give honor to God when he judges the world.

1 PETER 2:12

Dear Jesus, change me every day of the week so that I can draw my neighbors to you. Amen.

DIFFERENCE MAKER

Next time you are not at church but still find that you are with people, consider how important it is to follow Jesus right in that moment.

LIVE DIFFERENTLY

Bashing the reputation of Christians can be a bit too popular in our culture today. They are an easy target. Christians are supposed to exhibit a different standard in society—not in terms of strict rules, but in terms of values and priorities and actions and lifestyle. They are supposed to be different. Almost everyone knows this. Because Jesus was so radically countercultural, so amazingly revolutionary in his bold love and humble authority, it is natural to expect that his followers are to be radical too. So when Christians pretend to be radical like Jesus, but turn out to be hypocritical messes, society rightly gets a bit critical.

The way to avoid the justifiable critique, however, is to actually live differently—not in a way that is removed from and judgmental of society, but in a way that is life breathing in every ordinary and dramatic circumstance of each day. Those who follow Jesus can dismiss public accusations simply by being consistently decent to neighbors, beneficial to their communities, and trustworthy in their words.

It is God's will that your honorable lives should silence those ignorant people who make foolish accusations against you.

1 PETER 2:15

Dear Jesus, let my talk and my walk be so saturated in you today that others will see you in me. Amen.

DIFFERENCE MAKER

Help a neighbor with something today without expecting anything in return.

BEAUTY WITHIN

Try filtering everything you do today through this earth-shattering concept: Who you are on the inside is much more important than who you make yourself to be on the outside.

The modern Western culture spends more money on outward beauty than half the world spends on food. This pursuit of unattainable beauty standards is worthless. Skin will wrinkle, muscle will weaken, and hair will gray. And while it is right and healthy to take care of your body, it is even more valuable to invest in those things that can mature and strengthen over time, such as wisdom and skills, character and reliability, loving relationships and faith in Jesus.

Peter, the brash disciple who lived everything outwardly, eventually grew inwardly mature enough to give some great insight. His words were directed to wives who, because of the culture's wrong standards, tried to impress their husbands in all the wrong ways. Peter's words could apply to most everyone in our society today.

> Don't be concerned about the outward beauty of fancy hairstyles, expensive jewelry, or beautiful clothes. You should clothe yourselves instead with the beauty that comes from within, the unfading beauty of a gentle and quiet spirit, which is so precious to God.
>
> 1 PETER 3:3–4

Dear Jesus, beginning in my heart, transform my life to reflect your beauty. Amen.

DIFFERENCE MAKER

Go a full day without looking in the mirror. Notice how the strong the temptation is to be self-conscious, and how conformed to the addiction of "looks" our society has become.

KEEP CALM AND...

"She gossiped about me! I have every right to spread rumors about her!"

"He cheated on me, so I should be able to get back at him!"

"What did that guy call me? Well, he's just a big $%##^^!"

Just because people do awful things to you doesn't mean you can do awful things in return. Keep calm and respond with gentleness. But in your response be shrewdly aware of the creative way that Jesus would like to work through you. Instead of repaying with retribution, try reimbursing someone's nasty deposit with a blessing. Surprise them in your dignity and graciousness. Don't let their stupidity destroy your dignity. Instead, as you recognize their idiocy, have pity and lift their distorted soul to the Lord. Take the posture of Jesus' blessing from the cross and leave any retribution to the Lord's good judgment.

> Don't repay evil for evil. Don't retaliate with insults when people insult you. Instead, pay them back with a blessing. That is what God has called you to do, and he will grant you his blessing.
>
> 1 PETER 3:9

Dear Jesus, this is a radical challenge to respond to evil in this world with the power of your goodness. Help me to live in the audacity of your authority today. Amen.

DIFFERENCE MAKER

When you feel anger and retribution welling up within you today, take a breath and pray for the person who has upset you.

ANSWER FOR HOPE

Is hope something you can actually hold? Is it tangible? Would you say that you can grasp enough hope that someone might notice that you have it? Or is hope something that you can't really hold, like a wish-upon-a-star-but-probably-isn't-likely sort of dream? The Bible says Jesus gives actual, relevant, and real hope when you intentionally become more and more defined by him in the everyday raw realities of life.

A real relationship with Jesus actually changes you. People notice that. If someone asked you about your hope, how would you answer? Would you shy away from the question, trying to avoid mentioning Jesus altogether? Would Jesus even come to your mind, or would your "hope" be based on your circumstances? In other words, is hope placed in Jesus or in your longing for things to work out for good (as in, "I have hope because of Jesus" versus "Boy, I really hope I have a good day")? What would you say if you asked these questions?

> Instead, you must worship Christ as Lord of your life. And if someone asks about your hope as a believer, always be ready to explain it.
>
> 1 PETER 3:15

Dear Jesus, increase your hope in me so that I may give it to those who ask me about it. Amen.

DIFFERENCE MAKER

If someone were to ask you, "Where do you get your hope?" what kind of answer would you like to hear yourself say?

GIVE UP BAD STUFF

Even though it might hurt, it is better to give up something harmful than to continue doing it. For instance, cigarettes cause premature aging, constriction of your blood vessels, trachea damage, cost an arm and a leg and a lung or two as well, and they lead to a little thing called cancer. It would be better to go through the misery of giving up smoking than to suffer for the addictive habit. The short-term frustration caused by doing the right thing can be intense, but, in a long-term view, the temporary suffering is well worth the pain.

Following Jesus might cause you some suffering in your life. It may even mean that people will treat you unfairly or speak against you at times. But as a result of your good decision to wholeheartedly follow Jesus, your life will thrive long term in Jesus Christ.

Remember, it is better to suffer for doing good, if that is
what God wants, than to suffer for doing wrong!

1 PETER 3:17

Dear Jesus, let me serve you no matter what it costs; let me stay true no matter what temptations arise. Let others see the hope you give in the everyday realities of life. Amen.

DIFFERENCE MAKER

What bad habit do you keep falling into? Resist that urge today. Instead, as tough as it may be, keep your conscience clear by following Jesus.

THE RIGHT STUFF

One of the greatest things about following Jesus is the difference he makes in your life. And one of the most difficult things about following Jesus is the difference he makes in your life. Jesus gives freedom and he urges restraint. Jesus gives fulfillment and he asks you to give up everything. Jesus gives you a high calling and he asks you to serve others.

This tugging in two opposite directions can be extreme at times, especially for those whose lives were dramatically transformed by Jesus. Some old friends or family might have difficulty understanding why you won't join them in some of your self-serving past activities. Your task, in the face of frustrated friends, is simply to listen to Jesus. He will help restore your spirit. Your calm focus and confident assurance in Jesus will keep you from flinching.

Of course, your former friends are surprised when you no longer plunge into the flood of wild and destructive things they do. So they slander you. But remember that they will have to face God, who stands ready to judge everyone, both the living and the dead.

1 PETER 4:4–5

Dear Jesus, I am tugged in multiple directions. Help me drown out the disruptive noise and stay true to you today. Amen.

DIFFERENCE MAKER

Take time to sit down with either an old friend or a new one and talk about how your life is different now because of Jesus Christ.

YOUR HOME

In his first letter, Peter offers great advice, challenging advice, and some downright oh-man-that-is-really-going-to-change-my-life advice. It was just the sort of advice that enabled the first followers of Jesus to transform the course of history. One piece of advice urged the early Christians to continually offer their homes to others. But, Peter said, don't open up your houses and beds and dinner tables begrudgingly. Don't do it as a "sacrifice" that burdens you. No, share all that you have with joy. Be happy about it. You get the chance to give what you have to someone else. How blessed you are to be able to bless someone else!

The example of early churches changed people. No one had ever seen such an unselfish, unencumbered community before. No one knew that humanity had such an incredible capacity to care for others. As this reality set in, neighborhoods, cities, and nations were turned upside down.

Cheerfully share your home with those who need a meal or
a place to stay.

1 PETER 4:9

Dear Jesus, let the generosity of your heart overflow in me. Amen.

DIFFERENCE MAKER

Do you know anyone who needs a clean bed or a warm meal, new clothes or house supplies, a used vehicle or payment of loans? Think of someone in need today, then share what you can spare.

YOUR GIFTS

If every year every person got every gift, this earth would become a miserably boring and overstuffed planet. Imagine all the Rock 'Em Sock 'Em Robots, Teddy Ruxpins, Bratz Dolls, and Xbox consoles piled up in every spoiled person's closet. If everybody got the same thing, then no one would get anything exceptional.

God blesses people abundantly with uniqueness—each person is gifted differently by God's design. He has the resources to give whatever he wants in whatever quantity and quality he desires. But he selects each gift precisely for each person.

The gifts God has given to you are intentional. He wants you to use your specific gifts so that you can bless others in extraordinary ways. You don't have everything, so you can't boast in arrogance, but you do have something that no one else has. Your mix of talent, passion, experience, context, and timing is unlike the gift mix given to anyone else. And, as a result, God has some very important work he wants you to do.

God has given each of you a gift from his great variety of spiritual gifts. Use them well to serve one another.

1 PETER 4:10

Dear Jesus, teach me to serve others through my unique gifting. Amen.

DIFFERENCE MAKER

Do something encouraging for others today according to the unique way God has wired you.

YOUR COMMUNITY

Stop. Look at your surroundings for a moment. What do you see? Describe the place where you are. Describe the street you are on, the activity level all around you, and the city where you reside. What kind of environment is it? What are the people there like? Think about all the nuances and noise and neighbors around you right now.

You know, where you are is where you represent Jesus. What a privilege that is. You. *You* get to represent Jesus. And you get to do this by caring for all that is around you. You have the opportunity to cherish God's creation, to treasure the rhythms and culture of families and communities, to uplift your city and celebrate its people. You have the incredible honor of praying for everyone around you. You can pray for blessing, for reconciliation, for restoration and prosperity and peace and joy and freedom and truth and whatever else your loving heart can think to pray. And, as you fill yourself with the practice of loving your neighbors, the Lord Jesus will honor you.

And work for the peace and prosperity of the city where I
sent you into exile. Pray to the LORD for it, for its welfare will
determine your welfare.

JEREMIAH 29:7

Dear Jesus, I praise you for the people and places of my community. I ask you to care for all of us today. Amen.

DIFFERENCE MAKER

Before you do anything else, stop and pray for God to deeply
bless your community.

THE NAME

God's name is too often tossed about like a dirty rag in a garage. If we slam our thumb in the door or if we get some frustrating news, we launch his name into the air like a ballistic missile fueled by our irritation. If someone cuts us off in traffic, we grab the Lord's name and throw it back in reaction. Or if we get a juicy morsel of gossip or some unexpected news, we erupt in a barrage of flippant repetitions of his name. And, sadly, we use various mutations of the name of Jesus—frequently laced with the vulgar power of profanity.

This needs to stop. We wouldn't want our own name discarded in the mud, cast carelessly about, and coupled with cursing. How can we dare do that with God's name then? Importantly, out of the Ten Commandments, God placed the honor of his name as number three. We must not misuse God's name, but rather seek to honor it in all that we do.

You must not misuse the name of the Lord your God.
The Lord will not let you go unpunished if you
misuse his name.
DEUTERONOMY 5:11

Lord Jesus, let me honor your name and, from this day forward,
never take it for granted. Amen.

DIFFERENCE MAKER

Put Deuteronomy 5:11 into action today. Check yourself and gently remind others. As much as you are able, in your presence today, make a difference in how Jesus is talked about.

RESTORATION

You know that day when you had hoped to rest, but instead had to catch up on all the work you neglected to do during the week? You know that test you had to cram for because you procrastinated on studying? By wasting time, you placed yourself in the stressful position of needing to stuff all of your needed work into the final moments of what should have been a rest-filled day. But instead of a day set aside for recuperation, you spoiled it into a day of preoccupation.

The idea of Sabbath, which is taken from the Bible, is that every seventh day people would pause their hectic lives in order to rest and remember what God has done in their lives. But it required that they do a couple things: First, they actually had to live and work for God during the week and, second, they actually had to rest with God on the seventh day. The goal was to set a rhythm in life that would help keep God's people healthy in every area of life. Sabbath was to be a day to *rest*ore all that was out of whack with the world—a day to rest in relationship with God and to remember all that God had done for them.

Observe the Sabbath day by keeping it holy, as
the LORD your God has commanded you.
DEUTERONOMY 5:12

*Jesus, teach me to live in rhythm with you so that I can find the restoration
I truly crave . Amen.*

DIFFERENCE MAKER

Within the next week, set aside an entire day to restore yourself with God
and with others.

MOM AND DAD

Let the following question stir deep feelings within you: What kind of relationship do you have with your mom or your dad? For some people, this is a question that erupts tears of reassurance because they have been loved by their parents and they have deep love and respect for their parents. However, others who hear this question want to hurl and harbor hurt and hatred. This can be such a visceral question because it evokes the deepest victories and vacuums of a person's identity.

God established parents as the key to transfer the hope and love of the Lord to a future generation. Parents who don't follow this call find themselves in a precarious position, not just with their kids but primarily with God. But God also established kids to set an example to their parents. As children grow to know the Lord, one dramatic way they are expected to display God's love is by showing respect and encouragement to their parents. This command isn't so much about whether the parents have raised their children well as much as it is about whether the children will follow God's instructions. This posture of honor for parents ultimately honors God, and, as a result, will have long-term benefits for the child.

> Honor your father and mother, as the LORD your God
> commanded you. Then you will live a long, full life in the
> land the LORD your God is giving you.
>
> DEUTERONOMY 5:16

Dear Jesus, let me learn how to love my parents with your love. Amen.

DIFFERENCE MAKER

Reach out to your mom or dad (or another significant mentor figure in your life) in a way that would meaningfully show them respect, gratitude, and love.

August

Jesus,
Let me dance your steps,
sing your songs,
and see your vision.
Amen.

LAUNDRY

Are your clothes getting stinky this summer? A little bit of BO? Are you the reason that "sweat" pants got their name? For the sake of everyone around you, please keep your laundry fresh. Each day try to wear what is clean, not what is old and crusty. Your socks should not be able to stand on their own. And change that pair of underwear.

In much the same way, the Bible encourages you to keep your attitude and actions fresh. Don't put on lazy heart clothes, with stained grudges, a nasty chip on your shoulder, and frayed emotions on your sleeves. Strip off any of your stinky old perspiring perspectives and instead put on a fresh outlook, washed in Jesus Christ. When you wake up in the morning, the first thing you should do is spray yourself with the eye-awakening fabric softener of Jesus. Then, piece by piece, put on the character and love of your Savior. Those around you will thank you.

> Since God chose you to be the holy people he loves, you
> must clothe yourselves with tenderhearted mercy, kindness,
> humility, gentleness, and patience.
>
> COLOSSIANS 3:12

Dear Jesus, if I could look half as good as you, everyone around me would be changed. Clothe me in who you are today. Amen.

DIFFERENCE MAKER

Want to make a difference in those around you? Do your laundry.
Take a shower. Brush your teeth. Put on fresh clothes.
And when someone asks you why you smell so good,
tell them it's because of Jesus—then see what happens.

TEXTING

Older generations can be confused by things like lol, rofl, or idc. If you add a ;) or >:(to the message, some older brains might not be able to handle the strain.

The early Christians probably would have loved texting. Just imagine all the networking they could have done. People like Paul, Peter, and John wanted to share with others what Jesus was doing in their lives. You can feel their sense of urgency in the New Testament letters. If they could do what you can do, they would have utilized texting and Twitter feeds and Instagram and a whole host of other social media platforms to get their message out to their friends.

Writing letters the old-fashioned way was the closest thing the early church had to texting. They had to use ink and paper (well, papyrus). But they did their best and were very prolific. When God put something passionate and important on their hearts, they couldn't wait to write to their friends about what Jesus was doing in their lives.

We proclaim to you what we ourselves have actually seen and heard so that you may have fellowship with us. And our fellowship is with the Father and with his Son, Jesus Christ. We are writing these things so that you may fully share our joy.

1 JOHN 1:3-4

Jesus, let me use the opportunities I have to share with my friends what you are doing in my life. Amen.

DIFFERENCE MAKER

Using whatever method of communication you want, share with some of your friends what Jesus is doing in your life.

KEEP YOUR WORD

Do you marinate your explanations with all kinds of filler words and excuses? A lot of people soak their answers in mazes of confusion and alibis because they are either too afraid to be honest, too afraid to hurt someone's feelings, or just too afraid to make up their mind. From politicians to puppets, confidence and clarity are rare traits of character these days.

Simply let your yes stand for itself and your no well defined. Gain your assurance of integrity from your walk with Jesus. Let your words stand firmly in him. Don't compromise your character by pandering to what seems politically correct or presently popular. Don't avoid honesty just to get out of an uncomfortable situation. Make your responses with clarity, your promises with conviction, and your comments with constructive truth and caring fairness. In the long run people will trust you and will seek your wisdom.

> "Just say a simple, 'Yes, I will,' or 'No, I won't.'
> Anything beyond this is from the evil one."
>
> MATTHEW 5:37

Lord Jesus, give me clarity to clearly articulate what you want me to say,
and then conviction to back it up. Amen.

DIFFERENCE MAKER

If someone asks you a direct question today, try answering succinctly and clearly. Give thought and honesty to your words. Don't meander around speaking the truth.

BE GENEROUS

There is a dreaded moment when your buddy asks you, "Can you help me move my things?" You would much rather be lazy—after all, it's a beautiful day for a nap. You've had a somewhat busy week and you were hoping to chill. And if you help, you're just going to get sweaty. And now that you think about it, your back feels a little bit stiff. Your knees suddenly begin to throb. And your pocketbook started crying because your friend probably isn't even going to pay you anything. This is a favor for a friend.

It is too easy to want to say no to someone who could use your help. But think about this for a moment—it usually isn't strangers asking you to come to their rescue; it's those who are close to you. If you truly cannot help, that's one thing, but if you can help and choose not to help, then what does that say about your friendship? Make a simple but remarkable difference in the lives of those around you. If they take the initiative to reach out to you, take the initiative to reach back to them.

> "Give to those who ask, and don't turn away
> from those who want to borrow."
> MATTHEW 5:42

Dear Jesus, help me get off my behind and help others today. Amen.

DIFFERENCE MAKER

As long as it is within your means, practice saying yes
to requests for help today.

BE ANONYMOUS

It's nice when people give to a church or a charity, or when they come to the aid of someone who is in need. But what if they brag about it? How does that make you feel about what they've done? What does that say about their motivation for giving in the first place? What does that reveal about their character?

Because God has allowed someone to have an abundance of possessions, that person should never boast about giving some of them away. Every good gift comes from God. Donations and offerings should be given in humility of heart and with a grace-filled gratitude. Someone who brags about their good deeds demeans those to whom their gifts were given. To puff up one's own grandeur at the expense of another person's dignity ultimately contributes to a continually oppressive cycle. Gifts should be given with a selfless burden to benefit the one who receives. The irony, of course, is that God will know and give honor to the anonymous giver.

> But when you give to someone in need, don't let your left
> hand know what your right hand is doing. Give your gifts in
> private, and your Father, who sees everything, will reward you.
>
> MATTHEW 6:3–4

*Jesus, let me trust you for my fulfillment and not seek glory
in my service to others. Amen.*

DIFFERENCE MAKER

Make a donation to a ministry without letting anyone else know. Ever.

PRAY LIKE THIS

When Jesus taught his disciples to pray, he gave them an example, almost like a template to follow. When you pray, Jesus modeled, start with your focus on God the Father. Remember who God is and don't take for granted that he holds the universe that holds you. Give honor and respect to his name, a name that is incomparable to all others.

Next, Jesus said, desire what God desires. Filter all of your own thoughts and requests through his will and kingdom. Consider what God wants to have happen in your life and in the world in which you live. Think about what God already is doing and get on board with that. Whatever God desires for his kingdom, desire that for your world, your community, your home, and your life. On earth as it is in heaven.

> "Pray like this:
> Our Father in heaven,
> may your name be kept holy.
> May your Kingdom come soon.
> May your will be done on earth,
> as it is in heaven."
>
> MATTHEW 6:9–10

Dear Jesus, in prayer, let my knee always be bowed to you
and my heart always be changed by you. Amen.

DIFFERENCE MAKER

Take time to pray. But this time, focus your prayer simply on God's greatness and God's great desire for the world. After a while, ask him how he wants you to respond.

PRAY GOD'S WAY

If we want something, we should simply ask for it. That's what Jesus told us to do. "How should we pray?" his disciples asked him one day. Jesus said that we are to start our focus on who God is ("Our Father...") and what God wants ("Your will be done"), and then ask away for what we need. When we remember how great God is and how great God's desire for this world is, then we are able to ask for those things that fit with his heart.

God provides for his people, so it is sensible to ask for what is needed today. Dependency on God is a beautiful characteristic. Independence and isolation from God, however, fending for ourselves, only creates a mess. God is gracious, so it is good to ask God to forgive us, even of our most terrible sin. As his heart saturates ours, we can't help but extend that same grace to others. And God is shepherding, so it is perfectly right to honestly put our fears and temptations at his feet and ask for his sheltering strength.

> "Give us today the food we need,
>   and forgive us our sins,
> as we have forgiven those who sin against us.
> And don't let us yield to temptation,
>   but rescue us from the evil one."
>
> MATTHEW 6:11–13

Dear Jesus, I place myself before you today. Feed me, forgive me, free me. Amen.

DIFFERENCE MAKER

Which aspect of the Lord's Prayer do you most need today?
Pick at least one of these and take time to pray through that request.

DO TO

Do you remember when you felt left out? Or laughed at? Or mistreated? How did this impact your perspective on life? On the other hand, do you remember when you felt invited and welcomed? Or encouraged? Or treated like royalty? How did this impact your perspective on life? The truth is that the way a person is treated can change his or her entire stance in life. If treated harshly, a person is understandably much more likely to develop a negative or despairing outlook. But if treated with dignity, a person is certainly more likely to flourish in their God-given purpose.

The way you treat someone says a lot about you. What erupts out of you reveals what is within you. If you harbor things like apathy or hatred in your soul, then you'll probably act uncaringly toward others. But if you have a love for God and a love for others embedded in your heart, then that is what will overflow in your daily practice, even when times get tough.

"Do to others whatever you would like them to do to you. This is the essence of all that is taught in the law and the prophets."

MATTHEW 7:12

Dear Jesus, fill my heart with your love so that my hands will act with your love. Amen.

DIFFERENCE MAKER

Out of God's love, do something profoundly kind today. For instance, when you get to the drive-through window to pay for your meal, pay for the person behind you as well.

WITH

One of the greatest words in the Bible is the word *with*. Again and again we learn in both the Old Testament and the New that God is *with* his people. Yahweh, the great I AM, is also Immanuel, who is God *with* us. He tells us over and over again throughout the Bible, "I am with you."

This concept of the Lord being so intimate and so near is especially important to the prophet Isaiah. The people of Israel, who at the time had become a scattered and scared nation, needed to know that God was not distant from them. In fact, God spoke, God heard, God loved, God moved, and God dwelt closely. "Everyone!" Isaiah shouted, "listen to what the Lord says! We are not alone! He is with us! So hold fast!" Knowing that God is near makes everything much more bearable.

> "Don't be afraid, for I am with you.
> Don't be discouraged, for I am your God.
> I will strengthen you and help you.
> I will hold you up with my victorious right hand."
>
> ISAIAH 41:10

Dear Jesus, I can be bold today because you are with me. No matter what circumstances I find myself in today, let me dance your steps, sing your songs, and see your vision. Amen.

DIFFERENCE MAKER

Think of a bold action, something that God has been wanting for you or for others but that you have been reluctant to tackle. Knowing that God is with you, take a step in the right direction today.

OVERFLOW

Could God ever be depleted of his resources? How many times can we keep asking for more? If we keep pulling up to God's station to fill up our tanks, will God eventually run out of energy? Will he finally say, "Enough! I can't take the pressure! Please ask somebody else"?

Come on. If God wanted to fill you, don't you think he could? The fact is that he does want to fill you, and he is totally able to do so. In fact, he's got more than you can ever bear. When he fills you up, it's not one of those leave-some-room-in-the-top-so-I-won't-spill sort of fills. No, God fills to overflowing. All of his unending hope, unlimited joy, and unrelenting peace is available in abundance for you. Perhaps the true question is this: Do you want him to fill you?

> I pray that God, the source of hope, will fill you completely
> with joy and peace because you trust in him. Then you will
> overflow with confident hope through the power
> of the Holy Spirit.
>
> ROMANS 15:13

Dear Jesus, I don't want to be empty, and I don't want to be filled with things that will leave me empty. Lord, I want you to fill me with your Spirit. Amen.

DIFFERENCE MAKER

It's summer (unless you are south of the equator!). Go outside and enjoy what God has made. Jesus, who fills the entire creation with his presence, is the same one who fills you with his vast love.

WORDS AND THOUGHTS

What if everything you ever said and everything you ever thought was pleasing to the Lord? Just think for a moment how radically different, for example, yesterday would have been. If every word that coursed through your brain and crossed over your lips was ordained by God's beauty, how would that have changed the direction of your conversations? How would that have impacted what you put your mind to?

Jesus is your rock, but he is also your redeemer. If you are like many people, in the traps of your words and thoughts, it is so easy to forget that he is there for you. Perhaps if your conversations and quiet times were to be saturated in God's patterns, in those things that please his heart, then today will bring a new level of recognition of the Lord's firm presence in your life.

> May the words of my mouth
> and the meditation of my heart
> be pleasing to you,
> O LORD, my rock and my redeemer.
>
> PSALM 19:14

*Dear Jesus, throughout this day, may my words and my thoughts
be pleasing to you. Amen.*

DIFFERENCE MAKER

This might feel really annoying at first, but choose one hour today where before you say a word you write the words down. Use this process as a filter for your mouth and your mind, so that everything you say and everything you think will become pleasing to the Lord.

SO MUCH

God wants to be with you so much that he would leave the comforts of heaven to walk with you on earth if he could. Oh wait. He can. And he did! There may not be a greater desire on his heart than to be with you. He wants to talk about news and sports and weather on your way to work. He wants to help you make a sit-down dinner and then throw soapsuds at you when you clean the dishes. He wants to throw a ball in the park and sing you a lullaby at night.

In the Bible, a guy named Zephaniah (Zephy to his mom, maybe), spoke about how God's joy hit its peak when he was with his people. Much like a parent enamored by their first grader in the Christmas concert, or a husband staring into the eyes of his bride on their wedding day, or a soldier who would give his life to save yours, the Lord loves you with an everlasting love.

> For the Lord your God is living among you.
> He is a mighty savior.
> He will take delight in you with gladness.
> With his love, he will calm all your fears.
> He will rejoice over you with joyful songs.
>
> ZEPHANIAH 3:17

Dear Jesus, thank you for delighting in me. Amen.

DIFFERENCE MAKER

Listen to praise music. Join others in singing. Go for a walk and enjoy what God has made. Whatever way you choose to worship, be sure to celebrate God's heart as he celebrates being with you.

SLOW WORK

The farmer knows how to work hard. Day in. Day through. Day out. Before the sun. During the sun. After the sun. Cold. Hot. Rain. Storm. Winter. Spring. Summer. Fall. It doesn't matter. The farmer works. Many people shy away from this kind of raw, real effort. They'd much rather just spontaneously drive through and buy food: "Ah, yes, I'll have a fast something now. Extra fast. Hold the slow. Oh, and I'll have an apple crisp too."

Throughout the Bible, our life of faith is compared to the slow, intentional process of planting, cultivating, and harvesting. A quick drive-through fix of faith, however, is how many of us tend to treat our walk with God: *Ah, yes, just fix this now, Jesus. Bless me fast. I don't really have time for this to take very long. Oh, and I'll have an apple crisp too.* God is invested in us over the long haul, not for the short term.

> So let's not get tired of doing what is good. At just the right
> time we will reap a harvest of blessing if we don't give up.
>
> GALATIANS 6:9

Dear Jesus, give me a depth of character committed to the long, slow work of faith. Amen.

DIFFERENCE MAKER

Today, as you may have done before, take time to prepare a meal. With each measurement and minute, consider what will result from your labor. Invite people to join you in the harvest of your work. And have a discussion about what it means to follow God day in and day out.

HAPPY

In his hit song "Happy," the pop poet Pharrell Williams sings, "Here come bad news talking this and that. Yeah, give me all you got, don't hold back, because I'm happy." How could he challenge hardship to not hold back? And how could he say he was happy even as bad news talked smack to his face? Is it possible for humanity to glimpse joy even in the midst of frustration and suffering?

Pharrell Williams, whether he intended to or not, touched on an old idea, one that the first followers of Jesus knew well. No matter what circumstances people find themselves in, whether dire or dry or dreaded, Jesus emboldens them to stand strongly with a remarkable joy. People who had been enfolded in the deepest darkness find in Jesus an infusion of light that lifts the heart. God truly does make us joyful despite our circumstances.

Always be full of joy in the Lord. I say it again—rejoice!

PHILIPPIANS 4:4

Dear Jesus, let your joy pierce the shroud around me. I need your light and life. Let my heart smile wider and wider and wider today. Amen.

DIFFERENCE MAKER

Smile. All day. Try it. Smile on your own. Smile with others. Exercise the muscles around the mouth all day long. And every time you do, remember that Jesus is dwelling in you, giving you strength and hope and lighthearted joy. Your cheeks will hurt tomorrow, but it will be worth it.

LET THEM SEE

When a person does what is good, they walk an interesting line. Sometimes the Bible says that good deeds should be done anonymously. After all, the world doesn't need anymore big egos. But at other times, the Bible says that good deeds should be put on display for others to see. This is not to be done in a boasting sort of way, but certainly in a publicly evident way, where attention is drawn to the good action.

What gives? Which is it? Good deeds, yes. But private or public? Well, it seems that sometimes good deeds can be contagious. If someone who respects you, who knows your heart, and who knows your motives, sees you serving others, what might they be likely to do as a result? And when you help people, that can spark something within them to respond in a similar way. Your unselfish actions encourage others to serve unselfishly as well.

Let everyone see that you are considerate in all you do.
Remember, the Lord is coming soon.

PHILIPPIANS 4:5

Dear Jesus, check my heart and kick me into gear. Let your good work in me spur me to serve others. Amen.

DIFFERENCE MAKER

Think of three people in your life and then find three simple ways you can surprise them with encouragement today.

FIX YOUR THOUGHTS

Are your thoughts broken? Do they work? Or do they sputter and smoke? Do they make that turning-the-key-but-the-engine-won't-start-because-the-battery-is-dead sort of grinding noise? Or do your thoughts make that muffler-busting blast that sends people to the ground for cover?

One of the benefits of knowing Jesus is that he is a great mechanic. He doesn't cut corners or swindle you into doing more than you actually need done. If your thoughts haven't been in for a tune-up for quite a while, or if they have gotten bent out of shape, Jesus is your guy. He is honest and tells you clearly what's wrong. Then—and this is the really good part—he can take your broken thoughts and fix them, and he can fix them on what is good.

> And now, dear brothers and sisters, one final thing. Fix your thoughts on what is true, and honorable, and right, and pure, and lovely, and admirable. Think about things that are excellent and worthy of praise.
>
> PHILIPPIANS 4:8

Dear Jesus, don't let my mind keep clogging and seizing up. Free me to focus on what I've been created to consider. Amen.

DIFFERENCE MAKER

Stretch your mind for a moment. What are those things that you should fix your mind upon? Write down at least five things you believe Jesus would like you to be thinking about today.

STRETCH ARMSTRONG

Stretch Armstrong was an elastic plastic wrestling toy whose arms could be pulled and stretched for several feet. And Stretch was supposed to be superstrong. But the sad thing was that Stretch couldn't really do anything. He couldn't actually lift any big object, or stop some bad guy. His stretchy strength was only imaginary. It wasn't real.

Is Jesus like Stretch Armstrong? Some people treat him in the same way. They think he's a great idea, and maybe if he were in a comic book fighting zombies that would make him even cooler. But he doesn't really do anything real, does he? He's a nice thought, yes, but is his strength actually real?

The apostle Paul was certainly convinced his strength was real. After Jesus knocked him to the ground with his mere words, blinded him with his very presence, and then healed him through another person's faith, Paul was forever convinced that Jesus had real power (Acts 9). Later, in a letter about the strength of Jesus, Paul wrote these very words:

> For I can do everything through Christ,
> who gives me strength.
> PHILIPPIANS 4:13

Dear Jesus, because you are truly strong, I can be strengthened to do what you want me to do. Amen.

DIFFERENCE MAKER

Put away your social media and roll up the sleeves of your soul for at least one hour today. Be prayerful and ask, *Jesus, what can I do in your power today?*

SUPPLY

What are you lacking today? Don't think about material things for a moment. What is it that you are missing inside your soul that you so desperately need? Don't think of something that just fills the void for a moment. No overstuffed and stocked-up warehouse could ultimately supply you with everything you actually need. Expand the search within yourself. Dig deeper. What do you lack, and that if you found it, your life wouldn't just be full, your life would be fulfilled?

The most famous psalm of David, Psalm 23, begins with these words: "The LORD is my shepherd, I have all that I need." Jesus famously told the woman at the well in John 4: "Those who drink the water I give will never be thirsty again. It becomes a fresh, bubbling spring within them, giving them eternal life." And having discovered that Jesus was true to his words no matter what circumstances he faced, the apostle Paul later wrote:

> And this same God who takes care of me will supply all your needs from his glorious riches, which have been given to us in Christ Jesus.
>
> PHILIPPIANS 4:19

Dear Jesus, whatever I face today, whether hardships or joys or busyness or rest, I invite you into my life because I really don't need anything else. Amen.

DIFFERENCE MAKER

Write the word *supply* on a piece of paper, then fold it up and put it in your pocket. For the rest of the day, think about what you truly need versus what you would like to have.

GIVE AWAY YOUR FAITH

Faith is not yours; rather, faith is yours to give away. God did not give you your faith so that you could keep it private, never to show it, or shut people out of it. Faith is not something that people have as an individual property right. Yes, faith is personal, but it is relationally personal, not isolationally personal. It is shared. It's not stolen or hidden; it is lived out and given away.

You have been entrusted with the good news of Jesus Christ. He has saved you and he has loved you, he is challenging you and he is calling you to make a difference in this world. He has given you faith in him so that you can give faith to others as well. Inspire people by the way you live out your faith today. Giving away your faith is one of the most important things you can do today.

> You didn't choose me. I chose you. I appointed you to go
> and produce lasting fruit, so that the Father will give you
> whatever you ask for, using my name.
>
> JOHN 15:16

Dear Jesus, thank you for giving me something so wonderful to give to others.
Don't let me keep it to myself today. Amen.

DIFFERENCE MAKER

Try sharing your faith with someone else today. Ask Jesus to open the opportunity. Trust him to lead you. And be ready to impact someone with the abundant life produced in you by Jesus.

GET CONNECTED

It's way too easy to be passive about relationships sometimes. It's nice to be noticed and to be loved. It's great when others ask you questions about yourself or celebrate things about you. But if you were to live every day wishing people would do these things for you, life would become a miserable monotony of isolating stress. It doesn't make healthy sense to spend your time getting anxious about others becoming your Facebook friend, or clicking Like on a post, or watching your Vine loops, or retweeting you.

What if you took the initiative to show love toward your friends? What if you were proactive about connecting with others rather than being passive? What if you took the step to ask your friends questions, to celebrate their unique qualities? Over and over again in the Bible, people are encouraged to become risk-takers for the benefit of others. Paul told the Romans, for instance, to use their unique gifts to sincerely connect and serve one another. Followers of Jesus are to set the pace in developing healthy, real relationships.

> Love each other with genuine affection, and take delight in honoring each other.
>
> ROMANS 12:10

Dear Jesus, motivate me to become someone who truly connects with others. Let me take the initiative to be a good friend. Amen.

DIFFERENCE MAKER

Look up ministry groups to get involved in this fall. Do some research and make some plans to get connected.

BE REAL

One of the most impressive things about the Bible is its raw honesty. Even the "heroes" of faith, like Moses, David, and Paul, are real people with real issues and real problems. In fact, their problems are absolutely astonishing at times. Each of these guys was a murderer, each of them had blatant public sins, and each of them had to make dramatic U-turns in life. They all needed Jesus to change them and heal them.

Perhaps you can relate to these guys? Each of them had a "past" that was filled with wrong decisions and regrets. But remarkably, even with all of their baggage, Moses, David, and Paul learned how to follow God. How can this be? God got ahold of Moses and helped him walk with a fire in his heart every night. God relentlessly worked to help David remember the pure-hearted faith of his youth. And God knocked Paul to the ground and used his once-blinded heart to change many people. In the process, each of them learned to be raw and real before God and others. As Paul told some dear Philippian friends of his, no fake celebrities here:

> We are in this struggle together. You have seen my struggle
> in the past, and you know that I am still in the midst of it.
>
> PHILIPPIANS 1:30

Dear Jesus, knock down the walls I have put up, and let me become a
vulnerably honest person. Amen.

DIFFERENCE MAKER

Examine your social media accounts. Do they represent a glamorized version of yourself, or do they reveal the true you?

IMPOVERISHED

This guy had it all together. He was wealthy. He had influence. He was good. He followed God's patterns. Surely he was handsome too. Hollywood producers would have tried to snag him to star in the next season of *The Bachelor*. He was as good a man as there is out there. But he felt like he was lacking something.

When the young man heard Jesus was in town, he went to ask him a question, which was a strange thing to do. Jesus, after all, was not wealthy. He wasn't a businessman. He didn't even own a pillow. And he probably wasn't that great looking. Their conversation went something like this:

"It looks like you've got life and faith all figured out," Jesus told the young man.

"Yes, I know it looks that way, but I'm still missing something. What is it?" the rich man asked.

"Well, you lack what you don't have," Jesus answered. "Nothing. You've got everything, but you're possessed by your possessions. To be truly rich, free your heart to follow me."

Jesus told him, "If you want to be perfect, go and sell all your possessions and give the money to the poor, and you will have treasure in heaven. Then come, follow me."

MATTHEW 19:21

Dear Jesus, let me fill my life with nothing unless it is you. Amen.

DIFFERENCE MAKER

Gather any extra stuff that you've accumulated over the years and drop it off at a local thrift store.

BEING AND SEEING

You are in a privileged role. You get to represent Jesus today. You! In your unique circumstances, with your unique character and gift mix, you can "be" Jesus to others through acts of service. Jesus said that when you follow him, you become part of his body, which is the church. In effect, with the Holy Spirit working through your actions, you become the hands and feet of the Savior.

And not only do you have this great responsibility to "be" Jesus to the world, but you also have the calling to see him in others. Jesus wants you to see where he is, what he is doing, and who he is with. He says over and over again that he is with those who desperately need him. So when you serve people, you are serving Jesus himself. In fact, Jesus identifies himself with the humble and he empowers you to be humble with him. Look for him today. Be with him. And take action with his love.

> "For I was hungry, and you fed me. I was thirsty, and you gave me a drink. I was a stranger, and you invited me into your home. I was naked, and you gave me clothing. I was sick, and you cared for me. I was in prison, and you visited me."
>
> MATTHEW 25:35–36

Dear Jesus, don't let me miss chances to love others today. Amen.

DIFFERENCE MAKER

Think of someone you know who has one of the needs Jesus mentions in Matthew 25:35–36. Figure out a way to serve that person today.

MIRROR

This is a mind-boggling thought: Jesus considers you better than himself. Now certainly you understand, and Jesus understands, that Jesus is greater than you—he will always be greater than you. After all, we know that he created everything that we can see, and even those things we can't see. He is the I AM. He is the Prince of Peace, Almighty God. He holds everything together by the word of his power. In him is life in abundance.

And yet, in his mind, in his sight, he considers you. In his vision, as he moves and acts in this world, is you. Given the choice between saving his own life or saving yours, he would save yours. In fact, that's exactly what he has already done. So how could you, or anyone, keep returning to selfishness? How could anyone still try to impress others as if they think they need to their approval? You already are being lifted up in the loving gaze of the Savior.

> Don't be selfish; don't try to impress others. Be humble,
> thinking of others as better than yourselves. Don't look out
> only for your own interests, but take an interest in others, too.
>
> PHILIPPIANS 2:3–4

Dear Jesus, forgive me for filling so much of my life with myself. Help me to put others first today. Amen.

DIFFERENCE MAKER

For fifteen minutes, walk around using only a handheld mirror for sight. While doing it, think about how difficult it becomes to navigate through life when you're only looking at yourself.

CITIZENSHIP

In which country does a follower of Jesus most belong? The United States? Canada? Britain? Perhaps Brazil or Argentina? Maybe even China, because there are millions of Christians there. Or how about India? The Philippines? Israel? Egypt? Russia or Ukraine? Perhaps Italy or France or Mexico? Singapore? Hong Kong? Japan? Where should followers of Jesus call home?

How about heaven? What if we were actually strangers in the land, making our home here for a lifetime as landed immigrants? What if we were to invest our time and heart and energy into our local communities and schools and neighborhoods because Jesus wanted us to be his ambassadors representing our true home with him? And what if we began to long for our true home? What if we kept out heart connected to our Savior-King while we carried out the instructions of our current assignment? I think this world would be much different.

But we are citizens of heaven, where the Lord Jesus Christ lives. And we are eagerly waiting for him to return as our Savior.

PHILIPPIANS 3:20

Dear Jesus, don't let me forget that you have adopted me into your kingdom. Remind me to live as a part of your family wherever I happen to be. Amen.

DIFFERENCE MAKER

Write at least two of your local government representatives, thanking them for their service and letting them know that you are praying they will be blessed and they will follow God's character and patterns in their decisions.

ALWAYS PRAY

Some people don't think it makes much of a difference to pray. It would be better, they assume, to actually get something done rather than pray. Prayer, after all, doesn't make much sense in an achievement-based society because it can be difficult to see the immediate outcome of time invested in prayer. It would make more sense, to some people, to be get hands dirty in real "work."

But, lest we're mistaken, prayer *is* hard labor. Prayer gets knees dirty in passionate commitment to God and others. It also gets hearts dirty through love, worries, desires, fears, and joys—through trusting life to God. And prayer also gets movements started. Through prayer God strengthens commitments and raises awareness; he also invites people to join his passion and action already at work in the world.

No one could ever question the action-based mind-set of the apostle Paul. And yet he prayed perhaps more than he did anything else because he wanted so much to participate with what God and his friends were doing in the world. We are to always pray, giving thanks to God—it is worth the time

We always pray for you, and we give thanks to God, the
Father of our Lord Jesus Christ.

COLOSSIANS 1:3

Dear Jesus, right now I pray for my friends and family, both near and far. Thank you for their investment in my life. Please draw them closer to you and bless them today. Amen.

DIFFERENCE MAKER

Use social media to your advantage today. Scroll through your contacts and stop to pray with thankfulness for people as God gets ahold of your heart.

DON'T STOP PRAYING

There isn't anything magical about prayer. You can't say any special formula that will twist God's arm or trick him into doing what you want him to do. God will never say, "Oh, you got me there. You said the secret password." Prayer is much more simple than that. It's about matching what is on your heart with what's on God's heart. No tricks. Just a relationship.

One of the things that is always on God's heart is his care for people. He's already thinking about others, so he loves it when you lift people up to him in prayer. When you pray for others, you match the very rhythm of God. The apostle Paul was amazing at this. He begins many of his letters with this sort of heartbeat:

> So we have not stopped praying for you since we first heard about you. We ask God to give you complete knowledge of his will and to give you spiritual wisdom and understanding.
>
> COLOSSIANS 1:9

Dear Jesus, I pause everything else right now and ask you to bring to my mind those you would like me to be praying for. Amen.

DIFFERENCE MAKER

In a continued posture of prayer, listen for God's lead as he brings names of people in your life to your mind. Take several minutes to pray for those people right now.

DREAM

On August 28, 1963, over 250,000 people gathered around the reflecting pool by the steps of the Lincoln Memorial. A young preacher named Martin Luther King Jr. stood up and gave what has been considered the greatest speech of the twentieth century.

At one point, with most of his prepared speech completed, Martin Luther King Jr. was beginning to wrap it up. Near him on the stage was an internationally famous gospel singer named Mahalia Jackson. As he was about to finish, she yelled over to him, "Tell them about the dream, Martin! Tell them about the dream!"

Martin, without hesitating, pushed his notes to the side of the podium, stared out to the river of people before him, and with words from Isaiah and prayers from his heart, he began to paint a picture that changed the nation: "I have a dream that one day…"

> Then the glory of the LORD will be revealed,
> and all people will see it together.
> The LORD has spoken!
>
> ISAIAH 40:5

Dear Jesus, may your justice roll through our land, bringing a righteousness that changes my heart toward you. Amen.

DIFFERENCE MAKER

Get online today and watch Martin Luther King's "I Have a Dream" speech. Don't skip a word of it. Let it soak in. (And, if possible, plan a trip to Washington, DC to stand on the very place where this speech was delivered.)

TELL OTHERS

In the first chapter of Colossians, the apostle Paul gives a heartfelt greeting to his friends in Colossae (a town in what is now southwest Turkey), writing about how much he prays for them. He also gives thanks for them because they are a part of the spread of the good news about Jesus "all over the world." And that's a great thing, Paul writes, because Jesus has rescued people from sin. The world needs to know that even though we were once enemies of God, Jesus, the "visible image of the invisible God," "in all of his fullness," made peace through his death on the cross. It's a lot to pack in the first chapter of a small letter! But his point is simple: Because the Colossians were a part of a growing movement that was sharing Jesus with others, many people were developing a life-saving relationship with Jesus.

> So we tell others about Christ, warning everyone and teaching everyone with all the wisdom God has given us. We want to present them to God, perfect in their relationship to Christ.
>
> COLOSSIANS 1:28

Dear Jesus, motivate me to be a part of the vast movement of people, spanning history and geography, who have told the world about you. Thank you for those who shared your life with me. Help me to do the same with others. Amen.

DIFFERENCE MAKER

Tell someone about Jesus today.

TREMBLE?

What are you afraid of? Why do you hesitate? What stops you from doing what you are called by God to do? Is the obstacle confusion, apathy, or perhaps a lack of conviction? Maybe you are tired, or hungry, or upset at someone? Or perhaps you are struggling with a nagging sin? Do you feel alone in pursuing God's call? Are you worried about how people might respond to you?

What are you afraid of? The Lord is flawlessly focused. God is passionate. He restores your verve for life. He fills your soul. The Lord heals your hurt and forgives your sin. He gives you strength to overcome your weaknesses. He offers companionship and invites you to join others in his mission. The Lord reassures you that he will respond to you with joy and blessing, even if others don't. So what are you afraid of? In the Lord's power, live for Jesus today.

> The LORD is my light and my salvation—
> so why should I be afraid?
> The LORD is my fortress, protecting me from danger,
> so why should I tremble?

PSALM 27:1

Dear Jesus, I choose to stand for you today. Amen.

DIFFERENCE MAKER

What are you facing today that causes you concern? What could you do differently knowing that the presence of Jesus is with you?

EYES

You can usually tell when people are afraid or lying or unconfident because their eyes dart all around when speaking to them. It's as if they think they're being followed, or that they're feeling too insecure or too intimidated to look someone in the eyes. Such a lack of focused vision causes people to make mistakes, either intentionally or unintentionally, out of chaos or anxiety.

But those who perseveringly follow Jesus keep steady eyes. A steady gaze on Jesus allows people to notice and absorb his already focused gaze upon them. Their concentration on their Savior teaches them to walk securely in situations that seem impossible to eye rovers. This is the way of Jesus. Eyes secure. Sight enabled. Vision clear. Steps assured.

Look straight ahead,
and fix your eyes on what lies before you.
Mark out a straight path for your feet;
stay on the safe path.
Don't get sidetracked;
keep your feet from following evil.

PROVERBS 4:25–27

Dear Jesus, halt my wandering eyes today. Enable me to steady my gaze on you and in the direction you want me to go. Amen.

DIFFERENCE MAKER

What do you need to do to take the next intentional step in your life to focus on Jesus? Write it down and post it where your eyes will see it throughout the day.

September

Jesus,

I refuse to get lost in the fleeting

experiences of this world.

Amen.

GET TOGETHER

Finding a small group of people to study the Bible with is one of the most important habits you can develop during your lifetime. By meeting with people regularly to focus on Jesus, you'll be encouraged to grow deeper in your faith and make healthy decisions in your life. You'll find people who will support you, care for you, laugh with you, and pray for you. Such a group can become one of those deep gatherings where every word is cherished and treasured, where the surface serves not as a barrier but as an invitation to know what's underneath.

As you head into this fall, be sure to intentionally find such a group. It is too easy to fall into hectic schedules or slip into mundane routines of life that usurp an active relationship with God. Don't let that happen to you. Gather others around you to keep you present in relationship with Jesus Christ.

For where two or three gather together as my followers,
I am there among them.
MATTHEW 18:20

Jesus, thank you for promising to be present with me if I am present with others who follow you too. Let me be an encouragement to a small group of people this fall. Amen.

DIFFERENCE MAKER

Be proactive. Contact local ministries or churches, ask friends who are already plugged in somewhere, or gather some people you trust and ask them to start a small group with you.

GET CONNECTED

The book of Romans is a soaring theological argument. For fifteen chapters, the apostle Paul explains humanity's history with God. He summarizes profound truths with memorable phrases and simple language. He writes things like "we all fall short of God's glorious standard," "for the wages of sin is death, but the free gift of God is eternal life through Christ Jesus our Lord," "nothing can separate us from God's love," and "don't copy the customs of this world, but let God transform you."

With all of this amazing clarity, many people overlook the last chapter. After all, instead of eloquent rhetoric, there is just a bunch of people Paul writes to and about. Dozens by name and hundreds, perhaps thousands, of people by reference. Some were famous (like the apostles), while others were obscure (like Junia, or Nereus and his sister, or Rufus' dear mom). Romans 16 should not be overlooked, however, because in this real-life network of people is the real-life theological truth of Romans. What Paul talks about actually works in the everyday fabric of people's lives. Jesus unites people in a growing network that changes everything in this world.

Greet each other with a sacred kiss. All the churches of
Christ send you their greetings.

ROMANS 16:16

Jesus, give me the jump start I need to network with others who are living for Jesus. Amen.

DIFFERENCE MAKER

Contact a local ministry group so that you get plugged in this fall.

NICKNAME

His real name was Joseph, but the leaders of the early church gave him the nickname Barnabas, which means "Son of Encouragement" (Acts 4:36). This guy, Joseph…*er*, I mean Barnabas, was a Jewish man from the tribe of Levi, and had come to Israel from the island of Cyprus. The book of Acts describes how he had owned a field, had sold it, and had given all of the money to the leaders of the church so it could be distributed to those in need.

Barnabas repeatedly came alongside people who needed support and lavished them with encouragement. Just read the book of Acts and you'll see what I'm referring to. He believed in Paul when no one else did. He raised money for the poor, he advocated for the outcast, and he stood by John Mark. Anybody who knew him could say, "Oh, Joseph? Yeah, he totally gives me courage!" If people who know you gave you a nickname that reflected the way you live, what would that nickname be?

> Barnabas was a good man, full of the Holy Spirit and strong
> in faith. And many people were brought to the Lord.
>
> ACTS 11:24

Dear Jesus, let the way I live today represent what you have gifted me to do.
Amen.

DIFFERENCE MAKER

Be proactive about equipping people today. Focus on identifying and affirming their God-given qualities.

KICKOFF

People all around the country are preparing for several months of frenzied worship on Sundays. They're going to fill their coolers, grill their burgers, turn on their TV sets, plop down on couches, froth and scream as their favorite football teams kick off inflated pigskins in packed-out stadiums.

Other people all around the country (some who are also deeply embedded in the category above!) are preparing to launch several months of activities and events designed to bring people closer to God. They're going to fill their kitchens, pray for needs, get their hands dirty, lean on each other, welcome new guests, study the Bible, sing and serve and enjoy the proactive fellowship that comes from people who have been changed by Jesus. This is an answer to the prayer of Jesus that he prayed just before he was arrested and crucified. He wanted his followers to get involved, to get connected, and to change the world through their fellowship.

I am in them and you are in me. May they experience such perfect unity that the world will know that you sent me and that you love them as much as you love me.

JOHN 17:23

Jesus, kick me in gear to get involved in a ministry group this fall. Help me to follow through with connecting deeply with others who follow you. Amen.

DIFFERENCE MAKER

Take another step today toward a deeper commitment to a local ministry group.

SPEAK UP

"What? Did you say something?"

Justice is the process of restoring people to their created relationship with God. Justice fights against whatever it is that unjustly shackles. It gives dignity to those who are being crushed, and it fights for life for those whose lives are being cut off. It lifts up downtrodden souls, forgives the debts of those who have fallen short, and advocates for those who are trapped in unbreakable cycles. Justice gives more hope to those who hope less. It gives voice to shut mouths. It speaks up and lifts up and rises up on behalf of those who are caught in the despair and oppression of this broken world.

But if you act in justice, it will cost you something. In fact, it must cost you something. Justice impoverishes your resources and it disturbs your comfort. Justice takes your effort, your compassion, and your determination. It doesn't take your revenge, your pity, or your charity. Justice takes you. In other words, justice isn't fair—it is love.

> Yes, speak up for the poor and helpless,
> and see that they get justice.
>
> PROVERBS 31:9

Jesus, let me love. Not for my own sake, but for the sake of others. Amen.

DIFFERENCE MAKER

Whom do you know that needs an advocate today?
Creatively think of a way you could speak up on their behalf.

PRUNE

A prune is a fruit. Or, it was a fruit. Actually, it is (or was?) a plum—a plum which is preserved by being dried and becoming all dark and wrinkly. But to prune is also an act of cutting off parts of a plant that are dead, that aren't producing fruit, or even healthy aspects that the gardener believes will be better for the life of the plant in the long run. A gardener decides to remove a branch or bud so that the plant can flourish in times to come. Pruning something like a grapevine requires specialized attention so that it can become more abundantly fruitful.

Jesus promises that those who want to follow God will go through the pruning process too. God wants his people to become fully what he intends. You can try to be a prune and fight against getting pruned or you can let Jesus prune away in your life so that you can produce more prunes. Or something like that. Jesus said it so much better when he was talking to his disciples.

> "I am the true grapevine, and my Father is the gardener. He cuts off every branch of mine that doesn't produce fruit, and he prunes the branches that do bear fruit so they will produce even more."
>
> JOHN 15:1–2

Jesus, remove those things from my life that keep me from becoming all you created me to be, and from doing all you created me to do. Amen.

DIFFERENCE MAKER

Buy a bonsai tree, learn how to care for it and prune it, and keep it in your room all fall and winter as a reminder of the difference God makes in your life.

REMAIN

Imagine that your relationship with Jesus is fastened together with duct tape—you hold his hand and you both strap that magical silvery gluey adhesive around your wrists. As long as you are fastened to Jesus, whatever you do begins to produce abundance in your life. Your ugly habits begin to disappear because you are securely connected to Jesus who sanctifies you, and your beautiful habits begin to flourish because you are being grafted into Jesus who nourishes you.

Imagine, however, what would happen if you decided to loosen the tape just enough to slip out of relationship with Jesus—just for a moment here and another moment there. Not for good, of course. At least, not at first. It's just that those ugly old habits are so alluring at times. *Just a minute, Jesus. I'll be back soon.*

Remain in me, and I will remain in you. For a branch cannot produce fruit if it is severed from the vine, and you cannot be fruitful unless you remain in me.

JOHN 15:4

Jesus, don't let me slip away. Tighten our relationship today. Amen.

DIFFERENCE MAKER

Wrap a piece of duct tape around your wrist or finger (not too tightly!). Wear it as a reminder today to be in close relationship with Jesus.

FRUIT

Fruit maker—that's what you are. You are a producer of fruit. Fresh fruit; the kind of fruit that people love and pick up at the grocery store, examine, and bring home; the kind of fruit that people crave, like a beautiful strawberry or a delicious orange. You are a producer of the kind of fruit, you know, where one a day keeps the doctor away; the kind of fruit that restores a quenched soul, like a watermelon on a warm summer day. You produce the kind of fruit that, when planted, seeds a harvest of fruit into others.

The way you produce fruit, of course, is through abiding in Jesus. He delights in giving you everything you need to make a refreshing impact on others. So reach deeply toward Jesus today. Rely upon him for your nourishment, your resources, your rest, your stretching, and your productivity. Trust him today with your interactions, schedules, and dreams, and he will yield magnificent results through you.

When you produce much fruit, you are my true disciples.
This brings great glory to my Father.
JOHN 15:8

Jesus, I am yours. Produce in me the abundant fruit of a deep relationship in you. Amen.

DIFFERENCE MAKER

Buy some fruit from the store and offer it to friends today. Use this simple offering as a reminder to stay close to Jesus and to let him produce life change in you and through you.

JESUS HAD YOU IN MIND

Jesus had you in mind. Right before he was arrested and crucified, Jesus had a strategic time of prayer. He and his disciples had finished their Last Supper and walked to the garden of Gethsemane. Jesus spent his time in the garden praying. He prayed for his disciples, who were about to get scared and scattered. And he also prayed for you.

In his prayer, Jesus looked forward to the day when you would be tested as his follower. Would you run and fall, like the disciples would later that night? Would you be restored and empowered to spread his good news, just as the disciples soon would? Jesus prayed in the garden for you—he had you in mind. He prayed that you would stand close to him so that the world would be changed through you.

> "I am praying not only for these disciples but also for all who will ever believe in me through their message. I pray that they will all be one, just as you and I are one—as you are in me, Father, and I am in you. And may they be in us so that the world will believe you sent me."
>
> JOHN 17:20–21

Jesus, thank you for praying for me. May your prayer be true today. Amen.

DIFFERENCE MAKER

Be intimate with Jesus through a dedicated time of prayer and reading the Bible, and then share his message with someone today.

SO MUCH MORE

We haven't begun to understand all that Jesus has done or all that he will yet do. The Bible only begins to reveal the great works he performed, the great love he shared, and the great hope he restored. Healings and miracles, signs and wonders. He fed, he healed, and he walked on water. Oh, and he created everything. Jesus is a pretty big deal.

So much more—that's what Jesus did. So much more. He did more than could be written about. He did more than his followers would ever be able to explain or share. So much more. That's what Jesus will do for you and for me. So much more. Our greatest desires for change in this world are but a scratch of what Jesus has envisioned. John, his closest follower, who wrote down so much that we know about Jesus, said it so simply toward the end of his book.

The disciples saw Jesus do many other miraculous signs in addition to the ones recorded in this book.

JOHN 20:30

Jesus, there is so much more to you than I know. Let my eyes be full of wonder.
Let me see more of your miraculous works in action today. Amen.

DIFFERENCE MAKER

Pray and look. Pray for the miraculous work of Jesus in the lives of others. Remember all that he has already done and look expectantly for what he will do today.

9/11

It is the beauty of that day that adds shock. The eternally brilliant blue sky was broken by the sudden strike of horror. How can a day so beautifully clear be clouded with such darkness? The mechanics of death, moving across the highest reaches of the sky, drew hell to earth.

God's presence stands in stark contrast to the visceral hate-filled nature of evil. God runs to the disarray, concerned for his earth, fighting through the smoke, embracing the hurting, carrying the fallen, paying honor and restoring dignity to those stripped of life; he is weeping with those in fear, mourning with those in loss, emboldening people with courage, and thus making our hearts alive in the valley of the shadow of death.

> O LORD, I give my life to you.
> I trust in you, my God!
> Do not let me be disgraced,
> or let my enemies rejoice in my defeat.
> No one who trusts in you will ever be disgraced,
> but disgrace comes to those who try to deceive others.
>
> PSALM 25:1–3

Jesus, I remember those lost in the debris caused by evil. I remember those who responded with your courage and love, offering their own lives for the sake of others. I hate evil, Lord. May your brilliance overcome it. Amen.

DIFFERENCE MAKER

Ask some people where they were on this day in 2001. Listen to their stories. And then pray together for Jesus to restore peace to this world.

TRUST, DO, AND THEN...

Trust in the Lord. This was the Lord's number one message to his people. He repeated it over and over again. Trust in the Lord, lean not on your own understanding, rely upon your God. Let him restore you, empower you, and sustain you.

Do good. This was the Lord's second message to his people. Trusting in the Lord led to an overflow of care for others. Doing good in life is a command, but it is actually more of a response too. When people trust God, they are so dramatically changed by his love that they learn to live in God's patterns.

Then, as people trust the Lord and do good, the Lord gives blessing. Communities and nations that learn to do these things become safe and productively fruitful places. Trust in the Lord, do good, and then watch God bless all that is around you.

Trust in the LORD and do good.
Then you will live safely in the land and prosper.
PSALM 37:3

Jesus, help me to do these two things today. Help me trust you with whatever is ahead, with whatever is pressing on my mind and heart. And help me to put others first in all that I do. Amen.

DIFFERENCE MAKER

Practice serving people all day long through acts of politeness and kindness. Trust that the Lord will bless you and others as you serve.

TRAINING

Usain Bolt is the fastest person on the planet. He holds world sprinting records and gold medals. But he didn't become that way overnight. He grew into it. He disciplined himself and the gift he was given. In fact, he has dedicated his entire life to a dramatic training regimen. His workouts are plyometric, meaning he engages in rapid exercises that maximize power in explosive succession. Sounds tiring? Or exhilarating? Both?

Following Jesus asks for a similar type of dedication. Part of the reason for *Make a Difference* is that we need a daily push to practice our faith. We are called to run through this world, spreading the good news and sharing its blessings. We need the determination of Rocky Balboa, mingled with the coaching of Knute Rockne, and the unflinching focus of Jesse Owens. Even as competitors try to defeat us or even take us out, we grow strong in the life of Jesus.

All athletes are disciplined in their training. They do it to win
a prize that will fade away, but we do it for an eternal prize.

1 CORINTHIANS 9:25

Jesus, discipline my routines and my focus so that I can exercise my faith today.
Amen.

DIFFERENCE MAKER

What aspect of your faith feels ill prepared? Whom could you ask to coach you and strengthen you daily in this area of your life?

ENDURE

Every day you will have opportunity to flail and fall and flop. There will always be chances for you to be sidetracked or sideswiped or blindsided. You can give in yourself or be lured into the snare. Every day. And you are not alone.

You also have the opportunity to stand every day. There will always be chances for you to remain strong in the face of fear, or to resist the trap of temptation. In the throws of an alluring struggle you have the authority to choose freedom. You do not have to relent. You can endure. And you are not alone.

God wants to walk with you and empower you to do what is right. He does not expect it will be easy for you, but he does expect you, just as he expects everyone else, to follow him through every struggle, every day. You can endure with his help and his empowerment.

The temptations in your life are no different from what others experience. And God is faithful. He will not allow the temptation to be more than you can stand. When you are tempted, he will show you a way out so that you can endure.

1 CORINTHIANS 10:13

Jesus, fight by my side today. Show me the way through each trap. Amen.

DIFFERENCE MAKER

You know yourself. What traps are waiting for you today? Identify them by name. Don't let them catch you off guard. How might God be leading you to avoid them or overcome them?

CONSTRUCTIVE

Have you seen those talent shows where the contestant argues with the judges? Even though the person may have just sung completely off key or stumbled through their dance, still they stand there and refuse to accept any avenue for critique.

When someone tells you that you're wrong, and it's clear they're right, how do you handle it? If a teacher corrects your error, do you make excuses? If a friend points out one of your annoying traits, do you point out two of theirs right back? If an expert shows you a better way, or an older person gives you instructions, or a coach tells you to work harder, are you patient and thankful and willing?

Accepting feedback is evidence of godly character. Resisting feedback and reacting negatively to feedback, however, evidences a lack of understanding and maturity. We need to be people who accept feedback in whatever form it comes so we can live looking more and more like Christ.

If you listen to constructive criticism,
you will be at home among the wise.
If you reject discipline, you only harm yourself;
but if you listen to correction, you grow in understanding.

PROVERBS 15:31–32

Dear Jesus, search me and point out those things in me that need correction or realignment with your will. Amen.

DIFFERENCE MAKER

Take some deep breaths and ask a trusted friend to offer you constructive feedback on a recent project, on an assignment, or perhaps on your leadership skills.

WORK

You've heard the stories, right? Some lucky guy strikes it rich in the state lottery, only to squander it all away carelessly. All of his money didn't stand a chance against all of his spending. What once seemed like an endless supply of resources one day leaked away to nothing.

It's great to have dreams and have passions. It's wonderful to want to travel and play. It's even okay to pray for an unexpected windfall. But, ordinarily, to truly obtain the sort of stable life that puts food on the plate and clothes on the back takes healthy planning and hard work. Food doesn't magically appear on the plate and savings don't miraculously appear in the account. Ask any aging pop-culture child superstar or any one-hit musical wonder. The combination of fantastical consumption mixed with a lazy attitude depletes the reservoirs of life.

> A hard worker has plenty of food,
> but a person who chases fantasies ends up in poverty.
> PROVERBS 28:19

Jesus, kick my butt into gear. Let me become known as a hard worker and a person of character. Amen.

DIFFERENCE MAKER

No procrastination on any projects today. Finish your to-do list before allowing yourself to play.

ALIGN

Do know what happens when the tires on your car get out of alignment? They start to wear unevenly, balding on one side. Then picture a man who went bald on the left side of his scalp but still had full treads on the right side—and then he tried to do that comb-over thing. Not a fabulous look. Okay, mixed metaphors here. Maybe they are not helpful. Back to the tires. When the tires of your car lose their hair on the left side, the car wants to veer you out of your lane even if you try to steer straight.

This wonderful mash-up of metaphors is just like your life with Jesus. If you let yourself get out of alignment with him, two things happen: first, you begin to work harder to keep yourself from veering off the road, and second, even though you try to hold it together, people eventually begin to notice the inconsistency in your life. It's called hypocrisy. And trust me, it's not a fabulous look on anyone.

> So we are lying if we say we have fellowship with God but go
> on living in spiritual darkness; we are not practicing the truth.
>
> 1 JOHN 1:6

Jesus, let me be true to you. Align me with your Spirit. Amen.

DIFFERENCE MAKER

Where is your lifestyle out of alignment with your faith? Take one deliberate step to practice integrity in your life today.

DE-JUICE

Did you ever see *Willy Wonka and the Chocolate Factory*? Remember the kid who turns into a blueberry? Her name was Violet Beauregard. Violet was addicted to chewing gum. Oh, dear.

When Mr. Wonka reveals a new type of gum in his inventing room, Violet can't contain herself. The gum serves as a full meal, complete with different courses of meat and dessert. Mr. Wonka instructs that the gum isn't ready for humans yet, but Violet snatches the gum and plops it in her mouth. Once she begins to taste the blueberry pie, her skin turns indigo and she begins to swell into an enormous blueberry. To save her, Violet needs to be de-juiced.

Well, in a way, Jesus offers to de-juice us. We've snatched what never belonged to us, we are paying the horrendous price of that sin, and we need to be rescued before we explode.

> But if we confess our sins to him, he is faithful and just to forgive us our sins and to cleanse us from all wickedness.
>
> 1 JOHN 1:9

Jesus, I've become swollen with pride and arrogance and harmful habits. Forgive me and restore me to what you created me to be. Amen.

DIFFERENCE MAKER

Whatever sin you have been holding onto, let it go today. Confess your sin to Jesus and accept his forgiveness in its place.

NO COVER

When you were a kid and did something wrong, it is likely that at some point you ran to your room and buried yourself under the covers. Your deprived and depraved thinking process was that if you couldn't see out, perhaps your parents couldn't see in. You were covered. Or so you thought.

There is an old adage: "Everyone eventually gets caught." Sin, in whatever form, eventually undermines your life. It sneaks up and snatches control of you. It can slowly erode your willpower to do what is right, and, if you try to hide, it can twist your perception of truth. No amount of covering actually conceals your sin.

The irony of covering up wrongs, of course, is that the crime committer always knows—and God always knows too. It is never a secret to everyone. The best way to deal with sin is to expose it. Be honest with God, yourself, and others. Fess up. Change your heart. And let God uncover you in a shower of mercy.

People who conceal their sins will not prosper,
but if they confess and turn from them, they will receive mercy.

PROVERBS 28:13

Jesus, no more hiding. I am right here. And I admit you can see me. Amen.

DIFFERENCE MAKER

Confession is not easy. But if there is any concealed sin in your life, turn it over to God right now and take steps to gain freedom from it today.

THE WORLD OFFERS...

Take a look at all your stuff. Then take a look at your schedule. Then take a look at your goals and then take a look at your wish list. What have you added to your heart that complicates your simple walk with God or with others? What have you tied yourself to? What anchors have you purchased?

Today might be the day when you choose to let go, quit stressing, quit filling, and quit consuming. The options will still be there. The tractor beam of the next great item or opportunity will still pull on you and try to suck you into its vortex. The question is whether you will let yourself be induced into those things rather than motivating yourself to pursue Jesus. Don't let the fragmented shards of society trick you. They are but a broken image of what is good. Gaining more fragments gives you less room to thirst for God.

Do not love this world nor the things it offers you,
for when you love the world, you do not have the love
of the Father in you.

1 JOHN 2:15

Jesus, give me discernment to choose what is good from your perspective.
Help me to stop pursuing all the offerings of the world, and instead
to pursue you alone. Amen.

DIFFERENCE MAKER

Ask someone to sit down with you and help you prioritize your
commitments, contents, and calling.

...TOO MANY CHOICES

You've consumed too much and now you're are hovering over the bowl to belch, burp, and barf. You say, "But there was so much to take in! So many desirable things!" *Belch*. "There were just so many options!" *Burp*. "How could I say no to things that make me feel so good?" *Barf*.

Um, have you seen yourself lately? You don't look like you actually feel so good. You had a craving for pleasure, but you tried to fill it the wrong way. No wonder you turned green with envy and putrid with excess. Gluttony has gotten you nothing but sick. Your stuffed-up life hasn't fulfilled you. You look more like a dog that returns to its vomit even though it can't gratify its true needs (Proverbs 26:11). And, sadly, in the broken crevices of our world, there is a seemingly endless cafeteria of vomit.

> For the world offers only a craving for physical pleasure, a craving for everything we see, and pride in our achievements and possessions. These are not from the Father, but are from this world.
>
> 1 JOHN 2:16

Jesus, I need you. Why do I keep pursuing other things? I need only you today. Amen.

DIFFERENCE MAKER

Whatever empty thing to which you would normally return to today, resist it. Instead, do something more proactive to bring lasting life to your soul.

GOD OFFERS...

What a day this is. It was made just for you. God created this day as a taste of what you could have forever. He offers you another chance to spend your day living in step with him. He is already knocking on the door of your heart, asking to be vibrantly linked with you in all of your journeys today. Since the day you were born he has had in his mind this day, and every day for the rest of eternity, to spend with you.

Of course, sin would love to derail that everlasting experience. It has tried. Sometimes it even seems like it is withering everything. But you won't let it win out, right? Why would you? Of course you won't. No way. You'll follow hard after Jesus. You'll seek his will for you today. You'll pursue what he has created you to embrace: life forever with him.

> And this world is fading away, along with everything
> that people crave. But anyone who does what pleases God
> will live forever.
>
> 1 JOHN 2:17

Jesus, I refuse to get lost in the fleeting experiences of this world. Instead, I choose to be found in everything that is marked by your good, pleasing, and perfect will. Amen.

DIFFERENCE MAKER

Think through your plans and desires for today. Filter out what won't matter in the long run and pursue what will matter.

YOU AND THE HOLY SPIRIT

There is a lot of talk in our culture today about people leaving churches. This isn't true everywhere in the world, but it does seem to be a common theme in our society. You probably know many people who once were a part of a church but who just don't seem to be interested anymore.

The apostle John, as an older man, wrote to followers of Jesus in the first century about the same concerns. He discussed how many people had been leaving churches because they were unwilling to commit to the truth of Jesus. But he counseled those who stayed: "You must remain faithful to what you've been taught." But John wasn't worried because he knew God wasn't worried. God would continue to spread his message and grow his movement around the world. John could see this and he wanted people to know it too. Jesus, after all, had sent his Spirit to encourage, embolden, and employ his people in his mission.

> But you are not like that, for the Holy One has given you his
> Spirit, and all of you know the truth.
>
> 1 JOHN 2:20

Jesus, fill me with your Spirit so that I may stay true to you. Amen.

DIFFERENCE MAKER

Reconnect with some people you know who were once connected to church with you, but who have, for whatever reason, walked away.

DISCERNMENT

Have you noticed how some older and wiser people don't waste their words? It's as if they have learned to measure what they say in order to have maximum impact with their message.

When the apostle John chose to write a letter to the early Christians, he didn't want to waste words either. As an older person, he wanted his "children" to live freely in the eternal truth of Jesus and not get caught up in the trends of culture that ebb and flow throughout history. He wasn't going to throw away words and ink and papyrus on people who weren't going to listen. He knew that these early followers of Jesus would be strengthened by his message.

How do you receive advice and encouragement from older people in your life? Are there some experienced people in your life who have wisdom to share with you? How are you going to make time to listen to them today?

So I am writing to you not because you don't know the truth
but because you know the difference between truth and lies.

1 JOHN 2:21

Lord Jesus, thank you for the wisdom and guidance of those who have led the way for me in faith. Amen.

DIFFERENCE MAKER

Connect with an older person who know you has some wisdom to pass on to you. Consider asking him or her to become a mentor to you in life and in faith.

VIGILANT

Are you vigilant? Like a dog sniffing the air and scanning the horizon, are you on the lookout? Some people keep falling into the same traps over and over again. They repeatedly walk into the same pitfalls and perils, each time just as surprised as the last. *How did this happen?* or *Why do I keep doing this?* become common mantras. For some reason they just haven't learned to notice the signals, to scout the land, and ready the defenses.

Are you like that? Do you get caught unaware, even though you knew trouble was brewing, or you knew the temptation was coming, or you knew someone would try to undermine your purity, your message, your good work, or your success? You're shrewder than that, right? This world needs you to be. Don't give in to apathy only to be jolted upright by failure. Don't give in to a reactionary life, surprised by the perils that find their way to you. Be ready. Be strong. Be close to Jesus.

> I am writing these things to warn you about those who
> want to lead you astray.
>
> 1 JOHN 2:26

Dear Jesus, help me to outwit any trouble ahead today. Let me be sensitive to your guidance and strength. Amen.

DIFFERENCE MAKER

Scan the day ahead. What potential obstacles might you face? Develop a plan to remain resolute in the things God would have you do today.

BE STRONG AND COURAGEOUS

"Remember that time when Jesus healed the demoniac? I was so scared by that guy. And that time when he told the authorities they were hypocrites? They wanted to kill us, which might have been even scarier," one disciple said.

"Which time was that? He did that almost every day," some of them replied.

Another disciple said, "I was even more afraid when he fed the thousands of people with virtually nothing. Every time I passed the basket it trembled under the weight of all the food. Then there was that storm. He just stood up and told it to shut up. I was thinking, 'Who is this guy?'"

"Hey guys, how about when I walked on water? Ha! I bet you wet your tunics," Peter teased.

"We did! We soaked them. But so did you, Peter, when you got scared and sank."

"Yes, that's true. But he saved me, didn't he? I guess I've learned to fear him much more than anything else in this world."

> This is my command—be strong and courageous! Do not be afraid or discouraged. For the LORD your God is with you wherever you go.
>
> JOSHUA 1:9

Jesus, you are more powerful and more present and more amazing than anything or anyone. Let me walk courageously today. Amen.

DIFFERENCE MAKER

Name an action God has put on your heart that you know will be a blessing to others. Knowing that Jesus is with you, pursue it today.

NO LONGER I

We know, in the hindsight of the resurrection, that the crucifixion of Jesus is beautiful terror…or terrible beauty. It wasn't just the beatings—as wretched as they were. Nor the insults—as hideous as they were. And it wasn't even the nails—as horribly awful as they were. It was also the asphyxiation. The very breath that Jesus gave to us at the creation of the world, stolen from him. He couldn't keep leveraging his legs to push himself up enough to catch air in his lungs. And still he mustered enough strength, swallowed more pride than all of humanity combined, and spoke out those resoundingly refreshing words, "Father, forgive them."

My old self has been crucified with Christ. It is no longer I who live, but Christ lives in me. So I live in this earthly body by trusting in the Son of God, who loved me and gave himself for me.

GALATIANS 2:20

Jesus, just as you gave your life for me, I give my life for you. As I am stretched out and lifted up, may people be drawn to you, and may they find forgiveness and peace, salvation and hope. I trust you to lovingly lead others to life through me today. Amen.

DIFFERENCE MAKER

Speak to some people today about the hope of the cross. As you risk your pride and comfort, invite them into deeper relationship with God through the loving work of Jesus.

THE PLANS

What a special day this is. A day uniquely set aside for you to follow the Lord. A day when your steps can be placed on his path. A day when you won't need to fear what will be. This day, and all the days to come, are in God's hands. He knows what will happen and he knows what won't happen.

You are incredibly precious to the Lord. He sees his own reflection in your eyes. He hears his own rhythm in your heart. He made you to be with him for the rest of eternity. He has done and will do everything necessary to be with you. While you may not comprehend all that he does, embrace the good that the Lord has for you. Cherish the challenge to trust yourself completely to him today.

> "For I know the plans I have for you," says the LORD.
> "They are plans for good and not for disaster,
> to give you a future and a hope."
>
> JEREMIAH 29:11

Lord Jesus, thank you. I trust myself to your plans today. Amen.

DIFFERENCE MAKER

This verse was written to the scattered people of Israel during their exile under King Nebuchadnezzar. In their circumstance, they struggled to see how the Lord was planning good for them. Where do you struggle to see God's good plan in your own life? How can you reconcile this with the Lord's promise?

ACCIDENTAL WORDS

It happens in slow motion. You can sense your lips separating, feel your muscles forming, and hear the sounds emerge from your vocal cords, and still you can't stop the words from screeching out of your mouth, through the red light, and into the intersection. The accident caused by your words ruins relationships, opportunities, cooperation, and even hope. The debris of your words can shatter people and can be a mess that others need to clean up.

One of the best impacts you could have on this world is to learn when to speak and what to say when you actually do speak. Those who speak with right words and right timing speak life. But those who speak with harmful words and harmful timing speak only ruin.

Jesus was a master with his words. He is even called the Word by the apostle John. Jesus spoke everything into existence, and he speaks truth even now into your heart and mine. He responded wisely in tricky circumstances, gently in heated moments, and truthfully in the face of sin. He knew just what to say and how to say it so that people would be able to discover God.

Those who control their tongue will have a long life;
opening your mouth can ruin everything.

PROVERBS 13:3

Jesus, give me your words and prompt me when to use them. Don't let my mouth get in the way. Amen.

DIFFERENCE MAKER

Challenge yourself to not speak unless necessary today. Practice going through the day only saying those things you believe Jesus would want you to say.

HOTHEAD

Hothead. Jesus was never called this, but Peter was. Certainly. He was ready to retaliate, to take a swipe at someone if necessary. But Jesus told everyone to put away their swords. Chill out, Peter. Calm down, Andrew. James, that's enough. Take it easy now.

Jesus had passion. Buckets of it. But somehow he was able to harness this passion into effective action rather than ineffective anger. Even as the rulers plotted against him, as the mobs rejected him, as the disciples slept while he wept, Jesus never lost his cool.

His holiness was at his fingertips. His wrath at his disposal. His creative and destructive capability within the sound of his summons. But he kept them sheathed. He would only use it when needed against those who would dare try to stop his eternal plan. He would only let it simmer when people were oppressed from finding him. His anger was only and ever righteous. And it was under his control.

> People with understanding control their anger;
> a hot temper shows great foolishness.
>
> PROVERBS 14:29

Lord Jesus, make me like you. My temper has done more to destroy relationships than to create them. Forgive me and help me wisely control my anger today. Amen.

DIFFERENCE MAKER

Try taking ten long, slow, deep breaths anytime you get fired up today. As you breathe, pray for God's control in your life.

October

Jesus,

Every good thing comes from you.

Produce good things in me so that I can be an

encouragement to others.

Amen.

AUTUMN HOPE

October 1 is another one of those wrong-side-of-history days for the Chicago Cubs. In game three of the 1932 World Series, the Yankees had come to Wrigley Field. Babe Ruth was being ridiculed by some Cubs players, so he famously (or infamously?) pointed to the bleachers, took his stance, waited for the pitch from Chicago's Charlie Root, swung, and hit the ball to deep center. Home run. The Cubs, who hadn't won a World Series since 1908, had lost once again. For Cubs fans, though, there is always a chance. Once more the autumn games will come, and once more the Cubs will win. Eventually. Right?

The Psalms tell us to look ahead to the future, to what God will do. Don't get lost in the calamities that have happened, because God will restore all things. He proves it each year by the seasons. Just as the leaves change colors, just as the weather brings rich moisture, so he will bring blessing to his people. And maybe, just maybe, the Cubs will win a World Series again.

Rejoice, you people of Jerusalem!
Rejoice in the LORD your God!
For the rain he sends demonstrates his faithfulness.
Once more the autumn rains will come,
as well as the rains of spring.

JOEL 2:23

Jesus, let me trust your promises to your people. Amen.

DIFFERENCE MAKER

Root, root, root for the Cubbies. Or gather some friends and make plans in a few weeks to rake leaves for people who could use some hope.

HOW TO BE A FOOL

Here is a time-tested way to guarantee foolishness: Don't ever learn anything. Just refuse to do it. If someone corrects you, reject their input. If a teacher marks an answer as wrong, just get mad and blame him. If a police officer tells you to use your blinker, just go ahead and swear up a blinkin' storm and tell her you're no longer going to pay taxes. If a friend offers you some constructive feedback, tell him to shove it.

In John 21, when Jesus corrected Peter, it wasn't a comfortable scenario by any means. But Peter had begun to learn. His foolhardy tendencies were (mostly) behind him. He was ready to discipline his life according to the patterns of Jesus. In other words, he was ready to be a learner of Jesus, for a disciple is a learner (they are the same word in the New Testament).

> People who accept discipline are on the pathway to life,
> but those who ignore correction will go astray.
>
> PROVERBS 10:17

Dear Jesus, let me learn you today. Let me absorb your training in my life.
Let me not be closed to instruction, but be an approachable, teachable person.
Amen.

DIFFERENCE MAKER

Pick an area of your life where you need more discipline. Ask someone to hold you accountable, to correct you when you are wrong, and to help you learn.

SEASONS

The leaves beginning to change color, and summer is gone. The warm days are behind us. Winter is just around the bend. Colder weather is ahead. Fall is the transition.

The Autumn Blaze Maple tree grows to be about fifty feet tall and forty feet wide. It is a beautiful fast-growing, leafy green tree in the summer, providing deep shade. It is strongly resistant to pollution and its robust health helps purify air all around it. It also flourishes in various environments. But in the fall its leaves turn a vibrant orange-red that transforms the landscape.

Many of us try to live our lives without seasons. We'd like to have predictability and safety all year long. But change in us, especially when generated by Jesus, produces brilliant opportunities to change the world in which we live.

> For everything there is a season,
> a time for every activity under heaven.
> A time to be born and a time to die.
> A time to plant and a time to harvest.
>
> ECCLESIASTES 3:1–2

Lord Jesus, change me through the seasons of my life so that I might bless others. Amen.

DIFFERENCE MAKER

Gather some friends and spend a day together at a corn maze or a pumpkin farm. Enjoy this month. And let Jesus' work in you give vibrancy to others.

THE GOOD FIGHT

Were you ever told not to fight as a child? Did you know that whoever told you that was wrong? You are supposed to fight at times. You aren't supposed to just let yourself fall apart, and you aren't supposed to just let the world crumble around you. You are supposed to stand up for what is right and repel what harms the people of this planet. You are supposed to join in the struggle, the resistance movement, the revolution that refuses to allow evil to have its way. You are supposed to pick up the weapons of Jesus' powerful grace and mercy and wield his enduring love. You may, at first, find that others are afraid to stand with you or afraid to understand why you take risks to represent Jesus. But hold tight to this calling and don't hesitate to call others to unite with you.

But you, Timothy, are a man of God; so run from all these evil things. Pursue righteousness and a godly life, along with faith, love, perseverance, and gentleness. Fight the good fight for the true faith. Hold tightly to the eternal life to which God has called you, which you have declared so well before many witnesses.

1 TIMOTHY 6:11–12

Jesus, in this world's struggle against good, you fought with an unyielding love. Thank you for inviting me to join you. Amen.

DIFFERENCE MAKER

Find other followers of Jesus and start a weekly prayer meeting for the revival of your community.

MORTALS

So there is water on Mars, eh? It's cool that we found that out. But this is no surprise to God. It's ironic how we can be so proud to discover things that God already knows. It's not truly a discovery, except to us.

It's no different than Columbus "discovering" by accident a "new" land. "North America" and "South America" were already there in 1492. They didn't suddenly appear when Christopher Columbus accidently ran into them. There were already trees and rivers and mountains and animals, and, wait for it, families who made the land their home with farms and livestock and livelihood.

In some ways our "discoveries" reveal more about our limitations than our achievements. The more we find the more we realize the feebleness of our advancement. This is ironic, because it is precisely our desire to steal knowledge that led us to disavow the Creator in the first place. We failed to acknowledge God; will we continue to miss knowing him as well?

When I look at the night sky and see the work of your fingers—
the moon and the stars you set in place—
what are mere mortals that you should think about them,
human beings that you should care for them?

PSALM 8:3-4

Dear Jesus, I fall to my knees as I consider the works of your hands. Amen.

DIFFERENCE MAKER

Go to NASA's website and explore the universe with a posture of humble awe toward our Creator.

FACE TO FACE

It wasn't easy for the early church to connect. Not only were they missing out on Facebook, but they also had little issues of communication to deal with, like, say, an authoritarian Roman Empire threatening to arrest and execute them.

One guy who knew this reality very well was one of Jesus' closest disciples, a man named John. For decades, John himself was displaced as a result of the persecution and scattering of Christians. Yet, even in transition, John was determined to carry on friendships with those he had shared so much of his life with.

In his third letter, he wrote specifically to a friend named Gaius, a name both familiar and strategic in the New Testament. Gaius was a key figure in the spread of the good news about Jesus. And John, somehow now separated from him and distressed by conflict, missed the encouragement of his friend and was determined to see him soon. He wanted to be face to face with him once again.

> I have much more to say to you, but I don't want to write it
> with pen and ink. For I hope to see you soon, and then we
> will talk face to face.

3 JOHN 13–14

Dear Jesus, thank you for the encouraging friends you have placed in my life. Amen.

DIFFERENCE MAKER

Sit down face-to-face with a friend today, then share the peace of Jesus as you remember old times and old stories together.

SAVIOR

In the middle of the Bible is an important question. At least it's a critical question to those who understand what it means to be in trouble. "I look up to the mountains," the psalmist writes, "where does my help come from?" (Psalm 121:1).

The concept of "salvation" can be difficult to understand for someone who has never felt in need of rescue. People who have lived fairly comfortably postpone discomfort and, as a result, can struggle to comprehend the desperation caused by trouble. It's one reason Jesus said that it's harder for the rich to get into heaven than for a camel to fit through the eye of a needle (Matthew 19:24).

Eventually, though, everyone's constipated comfort gives way to the need to be rescued. Something inevitably breaks through the coziness: sin, evil, sickness, death, or separation from God. Something eventually urges everyone to cry out for Jesus. Those who choose to look up and ask for his help will be saved and shout with joy.

And they were shouting with a great roar, "Salvation comes from our God who sits on the throne and from the Lamb!"

REVELATION 7:10

Jesus, you are my Savior. Amen.

DIFFERENCE MAKER

If you have never stopped to accept salvation from Jesus, recognize your need and look to him now and ask for it. Then encourage someone else today to look to Jesus for salvation too.

SANCTIFIER

Fruit is best when it is ripe and washed, but fruit that is forced is bitter. Fruit that is infected is sickening and fruit that goes wasted is rotten. I'm sure glad that Jesus produces ripe, clean fruit in you. As you root deeply into him, he prepares his characteristics to emerge from you and have tremendous impact, both in your life and in the lives of those around you. In this way, Jesus changes you and he changes everything every day through you.

Jesus is hard at work in your life. He doesn't just check in with you when you are afraid and call out to him. He checks in with you constantly. He is connected to you. You have infiltrated his heart and he is flowing through you. Allow him to separate you from sin and dedicate you to a new life in him. Allow him to conform you to his Spirit, to be made like him in the way you think and in what you imagine is possible.

And I will give you a new heart, and I will put a new spirit in you. I will take out your stony, stubborn heart and give you a tender, responsive heart. And I will put my Spirit in you so that you will follow my decrees and be careful to obey my regulations.

EZEKIEL 36:26-27

Jesus, as you are producing your good within me and through me, let me be a blessing to others. Amen.

DIFFERENCE MAKER

In trials and temptations, choose not to rely upon yourself. Instead, draw near to God and give the test to him.

HEALER

Jesus came to heal. Our self-dependent culture can overlook that fact sometimes. Jesus came to heal. In just one chapter in Matthew, for instance, he heals a man with leprosy, he heals the paralyzed servant of a centurion, he heals Peter's mother-in-law of her fever (which must have won her son-in-law some brownie points!), he heals many demon-possessed people with a simple command, and he healed many others who were sick. Oh, and, by the way, he calmed a storm.

That's an impressive chapter indeed. And these sorts of miracles weren't out of the ordinary for Jesus. Matthew wanted us to know that this is what Jesus does. "This fulfilled the word of the Lord through the prophet Isaiah," Matthew wrote, "who said, 'He took our sicknesses and removed our diseases'" (Matthew 8:17).

> Then Jesus said to the Roman officer, "Go back home.
> Because you believed, it has happened." And the young
> servant was healed that same hour.
>
> MATTHEW 8:13

Jesus, I trust you to restore people to relationship with God. I ask that you would
bring healing to my life and use me to bring your healing to others too. Amen.

DIFFERENCE MAKER

Pray to the Lord for healing, either for yourself or for someone you love.
Don't be afraid to ask the Lord for what is honestly on your heart. And don't
be afraid to gather others to pray with you.

THE COMING KING

J. R. R. Tolkien's third volume in The Lord of the Rings series is called *The Return of the King*. In the story, the prophesied rescuer, Aragorn, returns to the land of Gondor, fights victoriously against evil forces, and is joyously crowned king. As a result, the land is restored, creatures return home, and refreshing peace reigns over the land.

Tolkien's story had Jesus in mind. The prophecies spoke about Jesus' coming to launch his rescue mission, but they also promised he would return to fight an apocalyptic battle to destroy evil and complete his restorative work.

Jesus is called the Alpha and the Omega—the beginning and the end (Revelation 1:8). What he started he will finish. He has promised to return to gather us—all of us—to him once again (John 14:1–3). Having once carried our sin, he has promised to return to save us absolutely and finally from it (Hebrews 9:28). He wants us to watch for him (Matthew 24:44) because he has promised to fight for those who look for him (John 6:39–40).

> Look! He comes with the clouds of heaven.
> And everyone will see him—
> even those who pierced him.
> And all the nations of the world
> will mourn for him.
> Yes! Amen!
>
> REVELATION 1:7

Jesus, when you return, let me not be caught looking for something other than you. Amen.

DIFFERENCE MAKER

Look for Jesus today. Look for glimpses of his coming and anticipate the stirring of his Spirit. Be aware of his work. Don't miss him.

GENEROUS WAYS

Jesus changes lives. It's actually what he's good at doing. And those who are changed by Jesus change lives too. From one person to the next, there is a passing on of Jesus' generosity, life overflowing with life because Jesus has given himself in abundance. Here are just some of the generous ways someone who has been changed by Jesus can live today:

- Leave a 25 percent tip at a restaurant.
- Give a larger than normal offering to a church or nonprofit organization.
- Listen to a friend longer and less distractedly.
- Give assistance to someone who is overwhelmed with a project.
- Tutor a younger person in a subject you can handle pretty well.
- Buy a second meal and give it to someone who is hungry.
- Visit someone who is going through a rough time.
- Spend time encouraging patients in a children's hospital.
- Be the first one to set up and to clean up.
- Look someone in the eyes during a conversation.
- Smile. A lot. Naturally. Let the muscles form and let it happen.
- Volunteer your time on a mission trip, either locally and internationally.
- Mentor teenagers in a local youth group.

The generous will prosper;
those who refresh others will themselves be refreshed.

PROVERBS 11:25

Jesus, you are changing me. Help me to live that way today, letting you work through me to change others. Amen.

DIFFERENCE MAKER

Choose at least one of the generous ways listed above to put into practice.

PLANT IT FORWARD

Those who do good things encourage others to do good things too. It really is a simple formula. One person doing something good leads to another person doing something good, and so on. Before long, good deeds pile upon themselves into an expanding difference-making movement.

Good deed x good deed x good deed = world change.

This really is the regular love-your-neighbor calling of everyone on this planet. A true follower of God is someone who follows the LAW (love, action, walk) of God. It is not about a list of commands, not about a rulebook to be followed, and not about a set of bylaws to implement. Following God involves personally living out God's heart of love, God's patterns of action, and God's walk on this earth alongside others. When people live according to God's good heart and God's good acts, the world is transformed by God one small footstep at a time.

The seeds of good deeds become a tree of life;
a wise person wins friends.

PROVERBS 11:30

Jesus, every good thing comes from you. Produce good things in me so that I can be an encouragement to others. Amen.

DIFFERENCE MAKER

Spend the day doing good things for people. Everywhere you go, intentionally and spontaneously sow kindness into the lives of others so that they can flourish.

CAN YOU SEE?

Stop and hear this. The Lord cares deeply for those who have lost the most basic of human abilities. It surprises many people to hear that the Old Testament was ahead of its time in terms of promoting access and respect for those who were physically disadvantaged. The Lord elevates those with physical disabilities to a high status in society, and he calls others to serve them with honor.

Stop and see this. The Lord himself came to the aid of those with physical limitations. If someone who is deaf is mocked, the Lord takes it personally—very personally. If someone who is blind is ridiculed, God says we are messing with him directly. Jesus himself says that the way we treat people who are in disadvantaged situations is how we treat him (Matthew 25:31–46). He will not stand by idly as we mock, neglect, or create difficulties for those who are less fortunate physically.

> Do not insult the deaf or cause the blind to stumble.
> You must fear your God; I am the LORD.
>
> LEVITICUS 19:14

Lord Jesus, you came to heal eyes and ears. Help me to honor you by honoring those you deeply care about. Amen.

DIFFERENCE MAKER

Sign up for an introductory course that teaches sign language or braille so that you can better empathize with someone who is deaf or blind.

PLAYING FAVORITES?

Can you see beyond labels? Can you see people for who they truly are? Are you willing to make decisions based on the truth of their heart and their actions? Or will you bend to peer pressure and make decisions based on the winds of culture?

At times the court of opinion favors the wealthy, because there is benefit to the judge and politicians, or to the community, or to the news outlets, or to _____ to have leniency on those with the power of influence. At other times, the court of opinion favors the impoverished, because there is benefit to the judge and politicians, or to the community, or to the news outlets, or to _____ to have leniency on those with the power of critical mass. Jesus doesn't care about whom the court of opinion favors. Jesus judges people according to what they have done and according to how they respond to him.

Do not twist justice in legal matters by favoring the poor or being partial to the rich and powerful. Always judge people fairly.

LEVITICUS 19:15

Lord Jesus, thank you for dying on the cross for each person, no matter their status in society. Amen.

DIFFERENCE MAKER

Make a plan to attend a public session at the local courthouse. With a prayerful attitude, survey the aspects that seem fair and those that seem biased.

RESPECT AGE

God loves old people. Do you?

He loves their long stories and deeply grained smiles. He loves their rascally outlook and feisty concern for the world. He loves their wrinkles and wisdom and wit. He loves people who have aged like good wine, without whining, of course. He loves those young-hearted warriors who have lived through generations, through wars, through terrors, through economies, through leaders, and they still stay simple and focused on what is right and true.

God seems to believe that someone who has lived a long life has earned the right to be respected. The years haven't always been easy on them. For every ring of the tree they have borne the weight of joys and sorrows, jubilation and loss. Their memories are both sweet and bitter. And the Lord knows every fiber of their being and he loves them with every fiber of his being.

Stand up in the presence of the elderly, and show respect
for the aged. Fear your God. I am the LORD.

LEVITICUS 19:32

*Dear Jesus, how can I expect to be respected if I fail to respect those who have come before me. Help me to honor you by honoring those older than me.
Amen.*

DIFFERENCE MAKER

Do something that shows respect for an older person, such as sending a thank-you note, extending an invitation to lunch, offering to do yard work, going fishing, or simply sitting down for a long conversation.

LEGACY

When Israel's leader Joshua died, a remarkable comment was made. It was said that during his lifetime that the people of Israel "served the Lord." The way that Joshua lived his life encouraged people long after he died to continue following hard after God. He left a remarkably good legacy for the generations to come.

If you could look ahead many years into the future, what kind of legacy would you like to have left on this earth? One way of thinking about this is to consider what kind of words you would like spoken about you at your funeral, or what phrase you'd like written on your epitaph (the message that is etched onto your tombstone). This isn't a morbid thought about death. Rather, it is a proactive thought about your life.

How will you have lived? What stories do you want told? Do you want others to follow in your footsteps? What difference do you want to have made in this world? Living in the light of our legacy should cause us to live for eternity rather than the fleeting pleasures of this world.

> The people of Israel served the Lord throughout the lifetime of Joshua and of the elders who outlived him—those who had personally experienced all that the Lord had done for Israel.
>
> JOSHUA 24:31

Jesus, let my choices today leave a positive impact on others for years to come. Amen.

DIFFERENCE MAKER

Write an epitaph for yourself that you would be proud to have etched on your tombstone.

MIDNIGHT

Paul and Silas healed a slave girl. They healed her! And her masters got upset because they made a lot of money off of her affliction. And because she was now healed, they had lost their ability to profit from her. So the masters grabbed Paul and Silas and incited the authorities against them in the city's marketplace. Because they had disrupted the unjust economic system, a mob formed against them. Paul and Silas were severely beaten and then thrown into prison, where they were chained by their feet to the walls. Then Paul and Silas sang praises to God.

Around midnight Paul and Silas were praying and singing hymns to God, and the other prisoners were listening.

ACTS 16:25

Dear Jesus, I'm not sure that would have been my response in this situation. How were they able to bring themselves to sing praise after being treated so harshly? How were they able to continue praising you publicly? The jailer heard them, the other prisoners heard them, and you heard them. Lord, give me the heart to praise you today. Amen.

DIFFERENCE MAKER

At midnight tonight, gather some people together, read through Acts 16:16–36, and have someone lead in singing praises to the Lord.

CAUSING TROUBLE

Paul and Silas kept traveling and sharing about Jesus. From town to town. The more they shared, the more they seemed to disrupt the economies and political structures of the regions. When they came to a city called Thessalonica, several people, including a lot of prominent women, gave their lives to Jesus. This upset the local marketplace, which relied upon the corrupt worship system in the local temples. So a mob started a riot. They were so angry they attacked the home of a man named Jason, where Paul and Silas had been staying. They dragged Jason to the city council, along with some other Christians, and threatened them with treason against the government. How would you respond in this situation? Would you stand tall in faith and love them, even in the midst of their threats?

Not finding them there, they dragged out Jason and some of the other believers instead and took them before the city council. "Paul and Silas have caused trouble all over the world," they shouted, "and now they are here disturbing our city, too."

ACTS 17:6

Dear Jesus, I understand that there will be people who reject the good news because it disrupts their habits and desires. This might mean they'll reject me too. Give me courage to stand tall in faith and love, even in the midst of threats. Your gospel turns the world upside down. Use me to make a difference in this world for you. Amen.

DIFFERENCE MAKER

Pray for those who follow Jesus to be loving and bold within their communities.

THEOLOGICAL EYES

Through what lens do you see your culture? Do you notice that the good news of Jesus is embedded in the popular stories of your society? Look with theological eyes for a moment. That great story about human survival is so riveting because God created us to live life eternally. That great song about the heartache of a broken relationship is so true because God created us to live in communion with him and with others.

At one point in his life, the apostle Paul walked around the city of Athens. He could have seen everything wrong with the false system of worship there, but instead, as he observed that culture, he found connection points to share Jesus. We must learn to view our world through the theological eyes of the Lord.

So Paul, standing before the council, addressed them as follows: "Men of Athens, I notice that you are very religious in every way, for as I was walking along I saw your many shrines. And one of your altars had this inscription on it: 'To an Unknown God.' This God, whom you worship without knowing, is the one I'm telling you about."

ACTS 17:22–23

Lord Jesus, thank you for making your message evident throughout the world. Give me eyes to see where your story breaks into the story of others. Amen.

DIFFERENCE MAKER

The next time you watch a popular movie or listen to a popular song, try to find the theological connection points or the gospel story embedded within.

AN EXAMPLE

Mother Teresa didn't call attention to herself. She was just determined to work hard for Jesus on behalf of the poor. As she continued steadily in her humble tasks of caring for those with afflictions, her hard work won her an incredible following. Her example of helping those in need in Calcutta inspired others to launch life-changing efforts to help those in need around the world.

One reason why Christianity spread so rapidly was because the first followers of Jesus led by example in caring for the poor. They worked tirelessly on behalf of widows and orphans. They started movements to support those suffering from famine and they constantly addressed the needs of the afflicted. Through these efforts the world could tell that there was something remarkably genuine and refreshing about those who followed Jesus.

And I have been a constant example of how you can help those in need by working hard. You should remember the words of the Lord Jesus: "It is more blessed to give than to receive."

ACTS 20:35

Jesus, you are the ultimate example of how to help those in need. Help me to follow your lead. Amen.

DIFFERENCE MAKER

Be an example of how to help those in need. Work hard to organize food and clothing drives, after-school youth drop-in programs, or a trip to a local rescue mission or food provider. Set the example so that others will join in.

KNELT DOWN AND PRAYED

Praying with others, especially praying out loud, can be an intimidating experience for many of us. As a result, many of us leave the praying up to someone else, or we just avoid prayer times completely. We might be afraid to say the wrong thing, or say something that sounds stupid, or simply be afraid to say anything at all.

Prayer is indeed a solemn activity, but it is also supposed to be a relational activity as well. Prayer is simply talking with God. And when several people pray together, it is really a group conversation.

When the apostle Paul was preparing for his final big endeavor in life, he shared with some close friends what he thought his plans were going to be. Afterward, through tears and friendship, they got down on their knees and prayed for one another. They didn't worry about what they sounded like or who was better, they simply had a conversation with God together.

When he had finished speaking,
he knelt and prayed with them.

ACTS 20:36

Lord Jesus, give me the courage to pray with people. Amen.

DIFFERENCE MAKER

At certain points today, as you feel led by the Holy Spirit, ask people if you could pray for them and the situations they are facing. If it helps, use the ABCs of praying with others—keep it audible, brief, and Christ centered.

NACHO LIBRE

Many of us struggle with God's calling on our life. We are tempted to think that if God wants something from us, then he'll make the path clear for us. But when we hit fog and gravel, we can grow uncertain about the path God has. Nacho Libre, the Luchadore, found himself wondering about the same thing. (Yes, this is from a movie, and it is a bit cheesy, but be patient with me here.)

At one point, after losing another match in the ring, Nacho grew quite concerned about his calling to wrestle. So first he prayed: "Precious Father, why have you given me this desire to wrestle and then made me such a stinky warrior?" Secondly, he didn't let go of the yearning. No matter what testing he faced, he wouldn't let go of his holy angst to do something for God. This determination, along with the support of his closest friends, refined Nacho's heart. He came to comprehend that God wanted him to serve his calling rather than be served by his calling.

> Therefore I, a prisoner for serving the Lord, beg you to lead a
> life worthy of your calling, for you have been called by God.
>
> EPHESIANS 4:1

Jesus, let me never give up my pursuit of how you want to use me in this world.
Amen.

DIFFERENCE MAKER

Pray. Then serve your calling from God. What can you do today to pursue
his will in your life?

BETTER THAN A SNOOZE BUTTON

When that alarm goes off, say at 6:15 in the morning, do you hit the snooze button with a bad attitude? Do you ask God to help get your mind in the right frame for the next nine minutes? When the alarm goes off again at 6:24, do you feel any more refreshed than when it went off nine minutes earlier? Did those minutes rid you of your grumpiness? Or do those problems in the world, including your own flaws and festering worries, continue to mock you and make you want to go back to bed?

When that alarm goes off, you may not feel like you are ready for what's ahead, but God believes you can do good work today. All he asks is that you give him your attention. He gave you his Word to help you prepare for your day. Nine minutes in the Bible can be much more effective than hitting the snooze button and getting nine more minutes of sleep.

All Scripture is inspired by God and is useful to teach us what is true and to make us realize what is wrong in our lives. It corrects us when we are wrong and teaches us to do what is right. God uses it to prepare and equip his people to do every good work.

2 TIMOTHY 3:16–17

Jesus, use me to help others by changing me through your Word. Amen.

DIFFERENCE MAKER

Instead of hitting the snooze button tomorrow morning, use those extra nine minutes to read 2 Timothy.

FUTURE GENERATIONS

Psalm 22 is a messianic lament that is intermingled with hope. Even though the writer, David, is going through terror, his song offers a prayer of blessing for future generations. He envisions a time when his generation's unselfish faith and sacrifice will produce abundance among the generations who are yet to come.

The unborn take a place of importance in David's vision. They are, perhaps, the most important generation to be considered in the foundation being established. David foresees that those alive today should consider the practice of faith of those yet to be born. One generation is to equip the faith of the next, who in turn equips the faith of the next, who in turn equips the faith of the next, and so on, for generations to come. David believed that how people respond to their circumstances today impacts how generations not yet born will respond in the future.

> Our children will also serve him.
> Future generations will hear about the wonders of the Lord.
> His righteous acts will be told to those not yet born.
> They will hear about everything he has done.
>
> PSALM 22:30–31

Jesus, right before you gave your life on the cross, you had the same attitude when you prayed in the garden for future generations. Amen.

DIFFERENCE MAKER

When you face your next frustrations, consider how your reactions could impact the faith of future generations.

MIGHTY MOWER
OF THE YARD

Our world is full of monstrous men who fear nothing other than peace. And to be honest, on the world scene, most of us worry about that. But what if we were to truly trust the words of the Bible? How would our engagement with the world change? Would our actions be driven by faith and hope and love rather than fear? Would we be empowered that in the end God would not allow evil to triumph?

There is nothing in the Bible to interpret as soft or mindless. There is no avoidance of conflict. In fact, conflict and strife are inherent in the raw reality of the words of the Bible. There is, after all, historically and cosmically, a fight launched by principalities who would wreak destruction against the everlasting hand of God. In God's power, we are called to stand against the world's adversaries without buckling our knees.

After all, why should we be afraid? Whose arm of might and justice will prevail? We choose to join sides with the Mighty Mower of the Yard, the Almighty Trimmer of the Flowers.

> Don't worry about the wicked
> or envy those who do wrong.
> For like grass, they soon fade away.
> Like spring flowers, they soon wither.
>
> PSALM 37:1–2

Jesus, give me the courage to trust you today. Amen.

DIFFERENCE MAKER

Take some time to attend to the news today without fear. Instead, pray and give courage to your community through the confidence of God.

TAKE DELIGHT

Take delight in the Lord. Let God be your definer. Let your will be saturated by his. Let what you want be shaped wholly by what God wants. For as you delight in the Lord, the desire of your heart becomes what he wants for your life. When you learn to align your will with his, your desires merge with what God wants to give you. Your hearts delights in what God desires, and God delights in giving you what your heart desires.

Does that mean if you live perfectly in his will that you won't suffer loss or pain today? No, this verse doesn't say that. It doesn't say that if you are good, you will get a big house and live a trouble-free life and be healthy and wealthy. No one should read that into this verse. But if you follow after the Lord, if you do his will and delight in him, then you will receive the desire of your heart: God himself.

> Take delight in the LORD,
> and he will give you your heart's desires.
>
> PSALM 37:4

Dear Jesus, teach me to want what you want. Amen.

DIFFERENCE MAKER

Stop right now to ask God what he desires for you. And then ask him to make that your desire too.

COMMIT TRUST

Today may not make much sense; in fact, it may be a struggle. We may feel blind to the way God is working and wonder what in the world is going on. Partially because it's so important, and partially because our struggles are so real, the Bible reinforces the instruction to trust in God. As difficult as it may be to maintain that focus, it is what we must do. Our daily actions are to be subjected to the eternal scope of the Lord, not to our short-sighted understandings.

God sees our daily toil. He is aware that division and deviousness in this world detracts from our ability to live fully. He is aware that the sin and destruction of others hinders our own pursuits. God is fully cognizant that things don't always work out the way we want them to work out. So we trust everything we do to him because he is going to use our work to make a difference in the world in which we live.

> Commit everything you do to the Lord.
> Trust him, and he will help you.
> He will make your innocence radiate like the dawn,
> and the justice of your cause will shine like the noonday sun.

PSALM 37:5–6

Jesus, every action of mine today is yours to use. Amen.

DIFFERENCE MAKER

Use this question as a filter today: What difference would it make to commit this action to the Lord?

WAIT

Is there anything more difficult than waiting quietly? Probably. But by the way many of us act when we are supposed to be calm and watch time pass by, you would think we we were having a root canal done on our funny bone! (Not really sure what that means, but it sounds really uncomfortable!)

The phrase "good things come to those who wait" is not in the Bible. But it seems like it should be. It is a proverb, probably, that has been used by Heinz ketchup. You can't rush a good thing. Don't count your chickens before they hatch. What did you expect, it's McDonald's? The early bird gets the worm and then gets eaten by the eagle.

We want God's salvation now, our worries to go away now, evil people to be gone now, our families to be blissful now, our health to be perfect now, and money to fall into our lap now. Perhaps we need to chill out right now, in this instant. We cannot afford to wait any longer. But it is good to wait on the Lord.

> The Lord is good to those who depend on him,
>   to those who search for him.
> So it is good to wait quietly
>   for salvation from the Lord.
> LAMENTATIONS 3:25–26

Lord Jesus, I struggle to be willing to wait for you to act. Help me to trust you.
Amen.

DIFFERENCE MAKER

Practice waiting today without taking out your phone. Fill the void instead with an active pursuit of God.

TRAIN WRECK

A train wreck disrupts the rhythm of creation at the end of Psalm 104. The psalm is an awe-inspiring ride through the skillful wonder of the earth and sky and oceans. The waters are stretched out like a garment and bursting through the ravines, the mountains erupting, the seas teeming with life, the whales playing games, the lions depending on God, the birds nestled in the trees along the streams, the night active with life, and the day provided for the gathering of food.

And then the train wreck. It's as if the gentle song of creation suddenly hits a dissonant crash. The psalmist is jarred from considering God's wondrous work when the shocking vision of the work of humanity enters into his mind. The writer's mind is suddenly flooded and defiled by the thought. The murders, the wars, the adultery, the profanity, the abuse, the destruction, the lying, the betrayal, the envy, the arrogance—all of this insurrection in stark contrast to the beautiful dance of the planet. The point of the psalm is to refuse to step into the fall of creation, but to instead be reconciled to a waltz with God on the dance floor that he has made.

> May all my thoughts be pleasing to him,
>   for I rejoice in the LORD.
> Let all sinners vanish from the face of the earth;
>   let the wicked disappear forever.
> Let all that I am praise the LORD.
>   Praise the LORD!

PSALM 104:34–35

Jesus, let my steps be in rhythm with yours today. Amen.

DIFFERENCE MAKER

Dance in wonder of what God has made. Hike or drive or just sit marveling at the wonder of creation. And pray for humanity to be restored to God.

PRODUCES GOOD

You can be confident that God will use you to make a difference in this world because he is at work right now making a difference in you. Every time he chisels a sin out of your life, every time he prunes away a fear, every time he molds your faith into shape, the Lord is preparing you. He asks a lot from you because he knows he can empower you. God trusts himself to generate good work through you. God accepts the fact that he is pretty masterful at producing the right results in your life. He is removing anything false in you so that his truth will be brilliantly evident through all you say and do.

For once you were full of darkness, but now you have light
from the Lord. So live as people of light! For this light within
you produces only what is good and right and true.

EPHESIANS 5:8–9

Jesus, I am yours. Make me as you intend. Amen.

DIFFERENCE MAKER

Buy some Play-Doh and make things out of it all day long. Carry it around and use it as a stress reliever if necessary. And as you shape the dough, consider how the Lord is shaping you into the person he wants you to be so that you can do what he wants you to do.

WHAT TO DO TONIGHT

Some followers of Jesus think we should avoid Halloween because of its flirtation with evil and the busy occult behaviors taking place every October 31. It would be incredibly foolish, these people would say, to open ourselves up to such demonic activity. Other followers of Jesus think we should participate in Halloween because it is the one night of the year when our neighbors are all outside interacting with one another. It would be ironically wrong, these people say, to be the only dark house on the street on Halloween night.

Wherever we fall in the great Halloween debate, our concern should be twofold. First, we should seek to love the Lord in everything we do, and second, we should seek to be a loving light for our neighbors in a darkened world.

So be careful how you live. Don't live like fools, but like those who are wise. Make the most of every opportunity in these evil days. Don't act thoughtlessly, but understand what the Lord wants you to do.
EPHESIANS 5:15–17

Dear Jesus, give me creativity and discernment as to how to be a loving witness to my friends and neighbors today. Amen.

DIFFERENCE MAKER

Whatever you do tonight, make the most of your opportunity to keep Jesus and your neighbors as the focus of your heart.

November

Jesus,

Help me to use the gifts
you have given me for your glory.

Amen.

SHARING TRUTHS

Why is it that many of us who have long ago left the realm of childhood can learn more from children's messages than all of the hymns and sermons of "big church"? Perhaps this is because children's messages capture the simplistic beauty of Jesus while also drawing us into a more profound life, and adults have an inherent need to share their faith rather than sit on it. Something spectacular happens to people when they see young people come alive with vibrancy of faith and hope and love through Jesus.

Faith should not be reserved to the realm of adulthood. Faith is not ours; rather, it is ours to give. Someone at some point introduced us to a life-changing relationship with God, and now it is our turn to creatively and passionately pass that faith on.

O my people, listen to my instructions.
Open your ears to what I am saying,
for I will speak to you in a parable.
I will teach you hidden lessons from our past—
stories we have heard and known,
stories our ancestors handed down to us.
We will not hide these truths from our children;
we will tell the next generation
about the glorious deeds of the LORD,
about his power and his mighty wonders.

PSALM 78:1–4

Jesus, if I ever become an old tightwad who is reluctant to share my faith,
loosen me up—a lot! Amen.

DIFFERENCE MAKER

Connect with your local church children's ministry director and ask how you can support them (either with time or resources or encouragement).

GENERATIONAL VISION

Broaden your scope today. As you go about your own business, consider the impact that your actions have, not just immediately but for the long term. Consider not just the impact your actions have on you, or on your immediate family or friends, but on those who will come after you.

The scope of vision in the Bible is incredibly forward thinking. When we make our lives only about the here and now, when we make church or faith about the current benefit, we squander the immensity of impact visualized within Scripture. Our faith was meant to impact generations. Those who came before us passed faith down through the generations, and eventually that faith in Jesus was entrusted to us. Now it is our turn to equip those who follow us with faith, so that they not only embrace faith but are enabled to empower the generations after them to follow Jesus too.

> For he issued his laws to Jacob;
> he gave his instructions to Israel.
> He commanded our ancestors
> to teach them to their children,
> so the next generation might know them—
> even the children not yet born—
> and they in turn will teach their own children.
>
> PSALM 78:5–6

Dear Jesus, let my vision of faith never be navel-gazing. Amen.

DIFFERENCE MAKER

Ask yourself this question: Am I helping to equip people in the next generation in such a way that they will be able to pass faith on to the generations that follow them?

SERIOUSLY, DO I HAVE TO?

"That guy absolutely drives me crazy. Why do I need to be patient with him? Why can't I be caring just toward the people I like? Why do I have to show love to people who suck the life out of me?" Because that's what Jesus would have done. In fact, it's what he did. There were days when he was tired, exhausted, exasperated, fed up, weary, lonely, upset, and he still kept serving. He didn't give up being humble and gentle and patient and forgiving, because of his intense love for people.

Jesus isn't calling you to absolutely step into destruction. When he needed restoration, he would step away for lengths of time to find refreshing with God the Father. He often withdrew to solitary places to rest, pray, and be revitalized. Distinguish yourself as a follower of Jesus in the way that you care for others and rely on Jesus to refresh you as you give of yourself.

> Always be humble and gentle. Be patient with each other,
> making allowance for each other's faults because of your love.
>
> EPHESIANS 4:2

*Lord Jesus, in your love you are humble, gentle, patient, and forgiving of me.
Don't let me forget that as I grow weary of others. Amen.*

DIFFERENCE MAKER

Think of somebody you struggle to withstand, and take even the smallest of steps toward extending them a loving attitude today.

ONE...

People in this world seem to understand that followers of Jesus, if they are true, are a united community rather than divided. There is something terribly wrong when Christians tear each other down, rip each other apart, fight publicly, react vehemently, or judge harshly. Jesus states what people all around the globe affirm: "Your love for one another will prove to the world that you are my disciples" (John 13:35).

Jesus draws people to himself, which means those who gather around him are naturally supposed to draw together. Imagine a scene where people gather around Jesus, but in frustration and jealously, in anger and a heated sense of righteousness, they start spewing venomous vocabulary and pummeling each other. We know there is such a thing as heresy of doctrine, but there is also such a thing as heresy of behavior. The church is called the body of Christ for a reason—it should never be dismembered.

> Make every effort to keep yourselves united in the Spirit,
> binding yourselves together with peace. For there is one
> body and one Spirit, just as you have been called to one
> glorious hope for the future.
>
> EPHESIANS 4:3–4

Lord Jesus, enable me to tirelessly build up others who follow you. Let me be an encouragement to your people so that the world will know you are love. Amen.

DIFFERENCE MAKER

Check yourself. If you have spoken or acted inappropriately against another follower of Jesus, take a step toward forgiveness and reconciliation today.

SEND ME

Awe-inducing angels called seraphim (meaning "fiery") gathered around the Lord, who was sitting on a throne. The angels sang, "Holy, holy, holy is the Lord Almighty. The whole earth is filled with his glory!" Their resounding praise shook the foundations of the temple and filled the sanctuary with smoke.

As Isaiah had this vision, he became certain that his destruction was sealed. How could any human stand in the presence of Almighty God? He was overwhelmed. But one of the seraphim flew over to Isaiah and touched his lips with a burning coal, telling him, "Your guilt has been removed. Your sins are forgiven." Then the Lord wanted to know who would share the message.

> Then I heard the Lord asking, "Whom should I send as a
> messenger to this people? Who will go for us?" I said,
> "Here I am. Send me."
>
> ISAIAH 6:8

Lord Jesus, let me have the heart of Isaiah. Overwhelm me with your presence
and clean my lips so that I can share your words with others. Amen.

DIFFERENCE MAKER

Spend some time with the Lord, asking him to prepare you and to send you to share the good news of Jesus with those you will see today.

YET

Of the entirety of his creation, God's greatest joy is reserved for his chosen people. For regardless of how much God possesses, and regardless of how broken people become, his most esteemed treasure is humanity.

To Nicodemus, Jesus said, "For this is how God loved the world: He gave his one and only Son, so that everyone who believes in him will not perish but have eternal life" (John 3:16). In other words, people were in a state of perishing, yet because of his deep love for his people God chose to initiate the process by which his people could be reclaimed.

In the whole of the Bible, it is clear that God is holy, yet he has chosen to offer forgiveness to people (Romans 3:23–24). The Psalms resound with wonder as they recognize that creation is so marvelous, yet God gives humankind his utmost affection (Psalm 8:5). Isaiah reveals that humanity has gone astray, yet the Suffering Servant of God will carry humanity's weakness, sorrow, and punishment (Isaiah 53:4–6). The *yet* of God is a wonderful gift indeed.

> Look, the highest heavens and the earth and everything in it all belong to the LORD your God. Yet the LORD chose your ancestors as the objects of his love. And he chose you, their descendants, above all other nations, as is evident today.
>
> DEUTERONOMY 10:14–15

Jesus, I am a sinner and yet you love me. Thank you! Amen.

DIFFERENCE MAKER

Take a few moments and allow yourself to be overcome by the yet of God. Give thanks for his amazing love that is found in Christ Jesus.

(IN)FORMATION

Information gives us control. We access information, we search for it, and that information gives us power. Because we live in an information-driven world, we tend to open the Bible for information, like some archaic magical Google. We look for information about God, about life, about faith, about a decision, about parenting, about work, about _____.

The Bible wasn't written to fill our heads with information, however. It's true that within its pages the Bible contains some interesting and helpful material. But even more than solid information, the Word of God is focused on our formation as God's people. The Bible exists so that we can be shaped and transformed and empowered by God.

> Have you never heard?
> Have you never understood?
> The LORD is the everlasting God,
> the Creator of all the earth.
> He never grows weak or weary.
> No one can measure the depths of his understanding.
> He gives power to the weak and strength to the powerless.
> Even youths will become weak and tired,
> and young men will fall in exhaustion.
> But those who trust in the LORD will find new strength.
> They will soar high on wings like eagles.
> They will run and not grow weary.
> They will walk and not faint.

ISAIAH 40:28–31

Jesus, change me through your Word. Amen.

DIFFERENCE MAKER

Read prayerfully through these verses from Isaiah a few times. As you do so, ask God how he would like to form you today.

PRAY FOR YOUR LEADERS

This is the time of year when politicians seek your vote. As you sift your way through the myriad of sound bites for streams of truth, you are considering electing leaders who will make a significant impact in the lives of millions of people. That's a big deal. So your vote makes a tremendous difference. Elections have consequences.

It is essential, no matter how you feel about a leader, to pray before voting for him or her. Pray for the nation and pray for its leaders. The push to pray for healthy and safe governance has always been a prevailing perspective for followers of Jesus.

> I urge you, first of all, to pray for all people. Ask God to help them; intercede on their behalf, and give thanks for them. Pray this way for kings and all who are in authority so that we can live peaceful and quiet lives marked by godliness and dignity. This is good and pleases God our Savior, who wants everyone to be saved and to understand the truth.
>
> 1 TIMOTHY 2:1–4

Jesus, encourage me to use the energy that I put into complaining about elected leaders toward praying for my leaders. Amen.

DIFFERENCE MAKER

If this is a voting year, be sure to vote. Be sure to support and pray for candidates who will champion your ability to peacefully follow God's patterns.

LIVING ROOM

Your soul is a living room. It is not a storage closet or a garage. It's not a garbage bin or an attic. Your soul is where you invite God to make himself at home.

Imagine if Jesus walked in and sat down among all the clutter, in the midst of stains, crumbs, filth, dust, and the garbage you'd been putting into your soul. And before you could protest, Jesus gets the vacuum out, the carpet cleaner, the dust rag, and the window cleaner, and he repairs the rip in the couch and throws away the trash and puts his Word out on the coffee table. And then he sits down on the sofa and puts his feet up with a smile. *Ah.*

That's when you ask your guest, "Um, can I do anything for you, God? What have you been up to lately?" And that's when Jesus tells you all about his life, what he does for fun, his relationships around the world. And Jesus asks you about your life, and you share a laugh together, you invite others to come in genuinely, you revel in songs of joy, and you play vintage Super Nintendo because it was the best video game console ever. Your soul is the living room where Jesus wants to take up residence.

> Jesus replied, "All who love me will do what I say. My Father will love them, and we will come and make our home with each of them."
>
> JOHN 14:23

Jesus, please come in and make your home in my soul. Amen.

DIFFERENCE MAKER

Clean up your physical residence today. As you do, think about Jesus making himself at home in you.

WALK OF DISCOVERY

Jesus wants to walk with us and talk with us so that we can discover who he is. There is no greater way to change everything in our lives than to spend time in personal conversation with him.

On the Sunday of the resurrection, two of Jesus' followers were walking about seven miles outside of Jerusalem. He suddenly caught up to them, but he kept them from realizing who he was at first. "You seem to be having a deep conversation," he said to them.

"You must be the only person who hasn't heard what happened the last few days!" they replied. And they went on to describe to Jesus how they thought he was the Messiah but the rulers had executed him. Then they shared how his body was no longer in the tomb, and how angels declared that Jesus was alive.

Jesus responded in disbelief at their confusion. "This shouldn't surprise you!" he said. "Wasn't it clearly predicted that the Messiah would have to suffer all these things before he entered his glory?"

Then Jesus took them through the writings of Moses and all the prophets, explaining from all the Scriptures the things concerning himself.

LUKE 24:27

Lord Jesus, would you give me just a taste of that conversation? Walk with me intimately today, unveiling my eyes to see you and my ears to hear you. Amen.

DIFFERENCE MAKER

Get together with some other followers of Jesus and investigate what Jesus might have said on this walk.

LOOK AT WHAT GOD LOOKS AT

We love looking at good-looking people. We elevate the glamorous, we celebrate the stylish, we exalt the pretty face, and we spend a lot of time and energy and money on cosmetics. As Billy Crystal's old character, Frenando, used to say, "Yooouuuu look marvelous! And it's better to look good than to feel good, you know what I'm saying to you, darling?"

The world has bought into this ideology for a long time. Three thousand years ago, Israel was searching for a king. The Lord told the prophet Samuel to anoint a king from the family of Jesse, a shepherd from Bethlehem. As Jesse's oldest son, Eliab, was presented to Samuel, the prophet was convinced he had the "looks" of the next king. But the Lord gave Samuel a bit of a rebuke. For God sees things differently than we are initially inclined to see. The Lord is concerned about something other than good looks—he cares about our hearts.

> But the LORD said to Samuel, "Don't judge by his appearance or height, for I have rejected him. The LORD doesn't see things the way you see them. People judge by outward appearance, but the LORD looks at the heart."
>
> 1 SAMUEL 16:7

Lord Jesus, help me care more about my relationship with you and my heart for others than a shallow approach to life. Amen.

DIFFERENCE MAKER

Don't take a selfie for the entire next week. Instead, take pictures that highlight others doing good things (would that be called an "otherie"?).

YOU CAN DO MORE THAN YOU THINK

It was remarkable for David, a teenager, to slay Goliath. It wasn't just how he did it, with a slingshot and a rock, but also *that* he did it. The fate of an entire nation was in his arm. But this wasn't the first time David had done the remarkable. He had already killed lions and bears that had tried to attack his sheep. He had already been anointed as the next king, and he had the guts to stand up to the current one face-to-face.

David, as a young man, also managed the family business. When he was instructed by his dad to bring supplies to his brothers at the battle lines, David had the authority to put another employee in charge while he was away. Perhaps our society doesn't champion young people enough? Perhaps we don't challenge ourselves enough either? We can do more than we think we can do, especially if God is with us.

So David left the sheep with another shepherd and set out early the next morning with the gifts, as Jesse had directed him. He arrived at the camp just as the Israelite army was leaving for the battlefield with shouts and battle cries.

1 SAMUEL 17:20

Jesus, challenge me to step up my level of responsibility and action. Don't let me listen to the lies that young people are not ready to do great things. Amen.

DIFFERENCE MAKER

Tackle a higher-level responsibility today that you had not yet felt encouraged to do.

STEALING COMPLIMENTS

It is a sad reality of our culture that those who consistently do the best work often don't get the recognition they deserve. It's like a fun little game called "stealing compliments." You should try it sometime. If someone says, "Oh my, that is a beautiful sunset!" you simply say, "Thank you!" If someone says, "I love the paint color in this restaurant," then you say, "Thanks for noticing." And if someone says, "The Bugatti is the coolest sports car ever," you say, "Thank you. I'm glad you think so."

This is a ridiculous game, of course, because someone else is responsible for the work behind each of those items. Someone else designed that car, painted that restaurant, and someone else created that sky. But it is also ridiculous that our culture takes for granted, or even steals praise from, the effective influence of a person of creative integrity and productive talent. It's as if the fruits of their work are stolen from them. Many of our best and brightest people could use more resources, more acknowledgement, and more encouragement than they are given.

Do not withhold good from those who deserve it
when it's in your power to help them.

PROVERBS 3:27

Jesus, I have often been blind to those around me who deserve my praise. Help me to recognize their work, to invest in their future, and to enthuse their hearts. Amen.

DIFFERENCE MAKER

Celebrate someone who has done good work without much fanfare (like a teacher or a grandparent or a volunteer). Think of a way to honor their trustworthy contributions and to champion their future success.

USE YOUR GIFT

When a basketball player releases a jump shot from the three-point line, giving the ball a perfect arc on the release, and thousands of fans watch the ball swish straight through the hoop, nothing but net, it's one of those moments when everything seems to slow down, harmony and precision combine to form in wonder, and life just seems to make sense. But unless we are mistaken, those moments only come from a player's dedicated commitment to improving their skill over a period of years. Investment. Hard work. Study. And joy.

In his grace, God has given us different gifts for doing certain things well. So if God has given you the ability to prophesy, speak out with as much faith as God has given you. If your gift is serving others, serve them well. If you are a teacher, teach well. If your gift is to encourage others, be encouraging. If it is giving, give generously. If God has given you leadership ability, take the responsibility seriously. And if you have a gift for showing kindness to others, do it gladly.

ROMANS 12:6–8

Jesus, thank you for investing in me. I pray that you will motivate me to invest in improving my skills so that I can use them to make a positive difference in others. Amen.

DIFFERENCE MAKER

What skill set has God gifted you with to use for the benefit of others? What do you need to do, both today and also in the long term, to become even better at it?

YOU NEVER KNOW HOW

Four young men had been displaced by war. They were removed from their homes and relocated to the enemy's capital. They were forced to give up their families, to change their diets, to change their names, and to lose much of their heritage. But they never waivered in what mattered most to them, which was their faithful commitment to the Lord.

Not one of us knows exactly how God will end up using us to impact the world. But he will use us. These four men had every reason (in the world's standards) to let down their guard and let go of their pursuit of God. Instead, they dedicated themselves to a life of integrity and character and excellence in the ways that God called them to live.

When the moment came to use their gifts to impact the world around them, they were ready. The enemy king took notice of the outstanding character and skills of these young men. And before long, God used them to change an empire.

> God gave these four young men an unusual aptitude for
> understanding every aspect of literature and wisdom.
> And God gave Daniel the special ability to interpret the
> meanings of visions and dreams.
> DANIEL 1:17

Jesus, no matter how you choose to do so, prepare me to serve you today.
Amen.

DIFFERENCE MAKER

If you were to lose everything else, what would be the one thing that would keep you pursuing the Lord?

EXCEL

Jesus sees your unique role. You are a part of his body, working to bring good change to this world. You have a unique, significant, and strategic role to play in God's mission on this earth. He loves seeing you use the gifts he has given you to make a difference around you for his glory.

The Lord has always gifted people differently so that each person can love him completely and serve others fully according to their unique abilities. When each person draws upon the excellence of the Lord to use their distinctive gifts to serve one another, then the world is built anew.

> The LORD has filled Bezalel with the Spirit of God, giving him great wisdom, ability, and expertise in all kinds of crafts. He is a master craftsman, expert in working with gold, silver, and bronze. He is skilled in engraving and mounting gemstones and in carving wood. He is a master at every craft. And the LORD has given both him and Oholiab son of Ahisamach, of the tribe of Dan, the ability to teach their skills to others. The LORD has given them special skills as engravers, designers, embroiderers in blue, purple, and scarlet thread on fine linen cloth, and weavers. They excel as craftsmen and as designers.
>
> EXODUS 35:31–35

Jesus, help me to use the gifts you have given me for your glory. Amen.

DIFFERENCE MAKER

Grab three friends. Together, identify and affirm three unique things that each one of you loves to do really well. Then dream up a mission project you could do together using your gifts.

FIRST

Humility is one of those personal characteristics that is nearly impossible to admit you have. Right? Once you admit it, do you still have it? This is the intentionally tricky logic of Jesus. He is shrewd. He knows that we humans love to be recognized for being great, which really makes us not so great. So he ensnares his followers with a little teaser about humility. "So," he said, "you'd like to be recognized for being great, eh?" (Yes, Jesus can speak Canadian English.) "Well, then just make sure you treat everyone else as if they are greater than you."

The disciples, learning the secret formula to God's great sauce, must have been excited at first. "Aha! Now we'll be greatest in the kingdom of heaven!" Little did they know that by continuing to serve others, by continuing to make themselves "last," the disciples would be transformed. In the persistence of their good service, they would be changed more and more into the likeness of Jesus.

He sat down, called the twelve disciples over to him, and said, "Whoever wants to be first must take last place and be the servant of everyone else."

MARK 9:35

Jesus, thanks for tricking me into being transformed by you. Amen.

DIFFERENCE MAKER

Serve people today. Open doors. Wash dishes. Clean up messes. Vacuum. Carry things. Sit down and listen. Make eye contact. Don't interrupt. Let others go first in line. Speak up in defense of someone. Give extra help when needed. Serve people today.

GIVE

No one goes to heaven because he or she puts money in the offering plate at church. Giving to church was never about being a "rule" or a price of membership; rather, giving to the assembly of God's people has always been about the attitude of the heart. The Bible talks about tithing, where a person gives back to the Lord a tenth of what the Lord has blessed them with. The Bible also talks about laying down one's whole life for God and for others as a result of all that Jesus has done on our behalf.

At Israel's major annual festivals, the people of God were encouraged to remember the ways that God had blessed them throughout the year. As a sign of gratitude for all of God's blessing, people were to offer a "gift" to the Lord. The gift was to be personal and related to the blessings the Lord had given them. To appear before God without a heart of thanksgiving showed a lack of forethought and respect. We give because he first has given to us.

All must give as they are able, according to the blessings
given to them by the LORD your God.

DEUTERONOMY 16:17

Lord Jesus, help me to pause long enough today to recognize all you have done for me this year. Amen.

DIFFERENCE MAKER

Out of the response of your heart for all Jesus has done, give 10 percent of this month's income to your local church.

GREET WELL

Whassup! How we greet each other says a lot about how we think about each other. The way that the writers of the New Testament greet people reveals an incredible attitude of blessing. Focusing on how to greet well is a good way to enter these winter months when some people tend to retreat and hibernate. Greeting people well prioritizes our hearts, gets us out of our shells, and prayerfully encourages others.

Paul begins all of his letters with some form of this greeting: "May God our Father and the Lord Jesus Christ give you grace and peace." Peter launches his letters with these words: "May God give you more and more grace and peace." John starts his third letter with a remarkable greeting to his friend Gaius: "To Gaius, my dear friend, whom I love in the truth." And Jude begins his letter this way:

> This letter is from Jude, a slave of Jesus Christ and a brother of James. I am writing to all who have been called by God the Father, who loves you and keeps you safe in the care of Jesus Christ. May God give you more and more mercy, peace, and love.
>
> JUDE 1–2

Jesus, remind me to intentionally greet others with a blessing. Amen.

DIFFERENCE MAKER

Say something more profound than hello today. Put thought into a simple prayer of blessing when you greet people.

FOR EVERYTHING

Give—Ah, come on! That one hurts. Whatever I have, I need to give it?

Thanks—Oh, okay. So I just need to give the gratitude I have. Okay, I can do that. Give thanks. Cool. I've got some things I could give thanks for, I guess.

For everything—Huh? What was that? You don't mean *every thing*, do you? Like, the opposite of nothing? That's what I'm supposed to give thanks for? You mean the most anti-no-thing there is? Everything. Really?

To God the Father—Well, okay. I've got no problem with giving God thanks, but I'm still stuck on *everything*. Could we compromise on this a bit? Meet halfway perhaps?

In the name of our Lord Jesus Christ—Oh, um…so I have to mean it too? I can't just say thanks, like, according to the way I feel in the moment? I shouldn't just say thanks for the things I like? You mean I should put myself in the perspective of Jesus? Ah man, I thought you might say that.

And give thanks for everything to God the Father in the
name of our Lord Jesus Christ.

EPHESIANS 5:20

Jesus, help me be saturated in who you are today so that I can learn to be truly thankful. Amen.

DIFFERENCE MAKER

Contact a local homeless shelter and make a plan to serve a meal during
the Thanksgiving week.

FOR HE IS GOOD

There is so much bad in this world. We are sick and tired of how sick and tired this world is. And yet we keep asking for it. We are glued to our news sources looking for more and more bad news. If there is a disaster, the ratings go up and news providers and advertisers make more money. Even the coverage of bad news is bad.

God is so different—he is so good. Why don't we gravitate toward the Lord instead of getting sucked into another terrible vortex day after day? Why does "bad" entice us more than "good"? What's wrong with us that we keep giving "bad" undue attention while ignoring all the good things that are going on around us? Why do we let the one bad tree withdraw our attention from God in the garden? We sensationalize what is bad, when what is good is right before us. This Thanksgiving, don't give in to bad. Give thanks to the Lord, for he is good.

Give thanks to the Lord, for he is good!
His faithful love endures forever.

PSALM 107:1

Jesus, let my eyes attend to you and you alone. You are so good! Thank you! Amen.

DIFFERENCE MAKER

Write the words of this verse on a sticky note and paste it to something you will see throughout your day.

FOR WHAT HE HAS DONE

Stop. In the margins of this page, or on a napkin, or a blank piece of paper, brainstorm all of the things God has done for you. Just start listing whatever comes to your mind. Think of things both large and small, grand and intricate, massive in scale and microscopic to the eye, beautiful and strange, wonderful and surprising, overwhelmingly powerful and perplexingly gentle. Think of things he has promised and things he has fulfilled. Think of things he has said. Think of songs he has written and dances he has led. Think of meals he has prepared and sacrifices he has made. Think of the authority he has used and the hope he has shown. How could you begin to give thanks for all of these wonderful blessings? How could you begin to tell the world about what God has done?

> Give thanks to the Lord and proclaim his greatness.
> Let the whole world know what he has done.
>
> 1 CHRONICLES 16:8

Dear Jesus, you are so great and have done so much to reach this world, to rescue and redeem this world. Thank you! You've changed me forever. Teach me how you'd like me to tell people about you so that they will be changed too. Amen.

DIFFERENCE MAKER

Using the list you have made and the creative talent you've been given, create a work of art, a poem, or a song that proclaims the greatness of God.

FOR HIS MIGHTY POWER

Anarchy isn't all it's cracked up to be. Or is it? Whatever anarchy is, it is certainly a mess that cannot control itself. Controlled anarchy would be the opposite of anarchy, after all. Anarchy is a void of power and the absence of control. The flames of it spread through terror and false agreements, fear and disasters. What people initially think of as "freedom from authority" quickly devolves into a civil war between power mongers.

Isaiah was concerned about this very thing 2,700 years ago. And yet, he had a vision. He saw the Servant of the Lord, the Messiah, rising out of the destruction of a nation, with the Spirit of the Lord resting on him, defending the poor and the exploited, ruling against the wicked and destroying them with the commissioning of his breath, and overwhelming them with fairness and truth (Isaiah 11–12). Isaiah's fear of the disintegration of society was overcome by the coming King. Aren't you glad someone is actually in control?

> In that wonderful day you will sing:
> "Thank the LORD! Praise his name!
> Tell the nations what he has done.
> Let them know how mighty he is!"
>
> ISAIAH 12:4

Jesus, you are the hope of the nations.
Commission me to tell the world about you. Amen.

DIFFERENCE MAKER

Take some time to pray for the spots of chaos in our world. Pray for people to discover the peace of Jesus in the midst of turmoil.

WORDS FROM THANKSGIVING

If you take the letters of *thanksgiving* and scramble them up, you can create some great vocabulary omelets. Words like giving and thanks are obvious, but think of all the others: think, hang, tang, gnat, king, gang, sing, singing, hanging, skiing, than, thin, snag, thing, nag, kin, stinking, thanking, thinking, hank, gain, gin, sang, it, at, is, as, gist, gas, its, ant, tan, shin, gash, kit, hat, saint, skit, angst, taking, van, skin, hint, sting, hint, asking, tasking, ah, sin, in, an, gig, inn, gag, tag, tank, stag, staging, aging, gist, ski.

The Bible speaks often about other words that derive from a heart of thanksgiving. An attitude of gratitude causes people to erupt in thankful expressions. For instance, in 1 Chronicles 16:8–36, David overflows with thanksgiving, which creates in him a litany of other words too: sing, praise, tell, miracle, generations, glory, acts, wonderful, name, known, nations, good, joy, rejoice, remember, seek, face, Lord, strength, dwelling, declare, ascribe, resound, splendor, holiness, tremble, heavens, salvation, everlasting, people, say, amen.

> Give thanks to the Lord, for he is good!
> His faithful love endures forever.
>
> 1 CHRONICLES 16:34

Jesus, giving thanks to you produces wonderful things in me.
Keep creating a thankful heart within me. Amen.

DIFFERENCE MAKER

This may seem like the cheesiest devotional entry you have ever read before. But imagine doing this with people over the Thanksgiving holidays. What other words overflow from a heart of thanksgiving?

WITH ALL OF MY HEART

What does "all" of your heart look like? When the Bible encourages you to praise the Lord with "all" of your heart, what does it have in mind…*er*, I mean heart—what does it mean? Can you praise God with just three out of four chambers? What if you put all of your ventricles into it but let your atria rest? How about the arteries? The inferior vena cava and pulmonic valve too?

Put your hand over your heart for a moment. Do you feel it pumping? Your heart, your whole heart, right now, is pumping deoxygenated blood from the body in the right atria and the right ventricle, and your heart is pumping oxygenated blood from the lungs through the left atria and the left ventricle. The blood that comes into the heart must be pumped out, otherwise the heart would seize up in an attack.

When you receive life from the Lord, you must pump out praise. When someone helps you see what Jesus has done for you, you can't contain that joy and wonder, and you must push it on. The truth of God that fills your heart must come out or you will seize up.

I will praise you, LORD, with all my heart;
I will tell of all the marvelous things you have done.

PSALM 9:1

Lord Jesus, keep my heart beating for you! Amen.

DIFFERENCE MAKER

Take time to write a heartfelt thank-you note to someone who has made a difference in your life by telling you about Jesus. Include Psalm 9:1 in the note to show your gratefulness for the way God used them to impact you.

WITH THE RIGHT WORDS

Consider all the effort we spend on profanity. Much of the most popular music, media, and Internet outlets are riddled with it. Our culture has become saturated in obscenity, which, of course, makes it seem less obscene with each passing day. This is a difficult path to walk for those who want to follow Jesus. The prevailing winds of culture that blow against us on the path shape so much of what we think and speak on a daily basis, often without us stopping to realize it.

Paul, a man who was certainly not afraid to use provocative language when necessary (for the right reasons), encouraged people to substitute words of thanksgiving for words of vulgarity. What if, he thought, instead of spending our energy on poisonous words, we spoke gratefulness? How would we be changed? And how would our example have a slow, steady impact on those around us?

Obscene stories, foolish talk, and coarse jokes—these are
not for you. Instead, let there be thankfulness to God.
EPHESIANS 5:4

*Jesus, make me aware today of the words I say. I pray that my heart would
overflow with thankfulness today. Amen.*

DIFFERENCE MAKER

To retrain your mind and mouth, try to say thank you at least a hundred different times throughout the next twenty-four hours. (Keep track with simple tally marks.)

WITH GLADNESS

Do you know that church isn't supposed to be boring? Did you know that? Some people have been engrained to think that church is always supposed to be solemn and respectful and ordered and hallowed (which sounds especially seriously religious if you pronounce it Old English-style: "Hal-low-ed"). But this just isn't a full picture of church.

Can you see Jesus being satisfied to fall asleep as a speaker drones on and on? Can you imagine Jesus looking blank faced as choruses are repeated and a pew bench cramps his lower back? Can you picture Jesus trying to draw something on the bulletin with that little tiny golf pencil found next to the old red hymnal?

Or do see Jesus engaging in discussion about the Bible? Do you imagine him smiling as people make discoveries about the greatness of God? Do you picture him preparing a meal over a fire and giving thanks for the food and for time with his friends? He loved being with the gathering of his followers! When he entered Jerusalem, as people rallied to him, he declared, "Even the stones will burst into cheers!"

Shout with joy to the LORD, all the earth!
Worship the LORD with gladness.
Come before him, singing with joy.

PSALM 100:1–2

Jesus, let my heart come alive with joy before you today. Amen.

DIFFERENCE MAKER

Pick up some musical instruments or get a karaoke machine. Then gather some friends, put on smiles and laughter, and spend some time loudly singing praise songs.

WE ARE HIS

If a congressional special committee were to examine every aspect of your day—all your e-mails and Internet traffic, how you spend your money, what you say, what you think about—would it be clear that the Lord is your God? Would your actions from an hour ago, or an hour from now, be in line with someone who follows after Jesus?

The irony here is that whether we act like it or not, the Lord already is God. What we think about him or the way that we treat him has nothing to do with whether or not he is God. Our opinion doesn't change who the Lord is at his very core. What is changeable, what is subject to our opinion and actions, is whether or not we will acknowledge that the Lord is our God, that we are his people, and that he is our Shepherd.

Go ahead and let that special committee examine you. As they find all the warts and all the flaws, publicly confess this one thing: "Yes, I am a sinner. But the Lord is God, and I choose to belong to him."

Acknowledge that the LORD is God!
He made us, and we are his.
We are his people, the sheep of his pasture.
PSALM 100:3

Jesus, I really am just a dumb sheep sometimes. Thank you for being my Shepherd. Guide me today in my every step I take. Amen.

DIFFERENCE MAKER

Think ahead one hour from now. What could you do that would evidence that the Lord is your God?

WITH THANKSGIVING

We are coming to the end of November. As you look back at the last eleven months, how would you describe God's work in your life and in the lives of those around you? Are you able to see his faithfulness, even in the difficulties? Are you able to recognize his hands through the ebbs and flows of daily routines? Do you notice those moments where he tried to get your attention? Did you feel him tugging at your heart to respond to others, to care, to love, to do the right thing in the hard moments? Can you feel him drawing you gently into his presence right now? The Lord loves you. From generation to generation, from season to season, from month to month, and even on this very day, he is faithful to give you his unfailing love.

Enter his gates with thanksgiving;
go into his courts with praise.
Give thanks to him and praise his name.
For the LORD is good.
His unfailing love continues forever,
and his faithfulness continues to each generation.

PSALM 100:4–5

Lord Jesus, I come to you with praise and thanksgiving today. Thank you for loving me. Amen.

DIFFERENCE MAKER

Go to the homes of friends and neighbors collecting cans of food for a local food pantry. When someone gives you a can, hand them a thank-you note with Psalm 100:4–5 written on it.

NEW MERCIES

His mercies are new every morning. Repeat that phrase. His mercies are new every morning. It doesn't matter what yesterday was like—his mercies are new every morning. It doesn't matter how you feel about how how you did, for his mercies are new every morning. Even if you feel like you blew it, his mercies are new every morning. Whether you feel like you'll never get another chance or whether you'll never recover, his mercies are new every morning.

The truth is this: Jesus loves to redeem and he loves to restore. And he loves a fresh new day because he gets to lift you up again and walk with you. His mercies are new every morning. So don't try to take a twisted advantage of God's mercy, where you sin a little bit while anticipating that he'll forgive you again tomorrow. Instead, take full advantage of his mercy! Live in it! Let it refresh you and change you into a new person who lives in his faithfulness each and every day.

> The faithful love of the LORD never ends!
> His mercies never cease.
> Great is his faithfulness;
> his mercies begin afresh each morning.
> LAMENTATIONS 3:22–23

Jesus, thank you. Thank you that I can wake up tomorrow and embrace your mercy deeper and fuller than today. Overwhelm me. Amen.

DIFFERENCE MAKER

Be merciful to others today, just as God has offered you mercy.

December

Jesus,

You came to earth because you were willing to

be real with me.

Now I pray that I will be real with you.

Amen.

HIDE

Some people hide things so they won't be found, while others hide things so that they'll be discovered. Which type of hider are you? It is important to bury God's Word deeply in your heart so that it can be discovered there. Don't wallow in the shallow end of your heart because life is meant to be lived deeply. Seed the Word of the Lord into you heart. This way, when a relationship calls for deep commitment, you'll find sacrificial love there. When a challenging moment probes the depths of your character, you'll find integrity. When people need a stable leader, you'll find a treasure of endurance. And when justice demands an advocate, you'll find God's voice speaking out from within you.

> I have hidden your word in my heart,
> that I might not sin against you.
>
> PSALM 119:11

Jesus, find your way to the deepest parts of my life so that when called upon, I will reflect your heart and respond in action just like you. Amen.

DIFFERENCE MAKER

To help you embed truth in your heart, write this verse out on ten small sticky notes. Then hide the notes in places where you might need the reminder in the coming week.

SEEING

It is often said that leaders who make the most significant difference in our world are people who have "vision." They see what is and they envision what could be. They don't waste the focus of their sight on despair, they don't allow their sight to be distracted by sin or selfishness, and they don't develop blurriness or nearsightedness from binge-watching the wrong things.

Leaders who make a significant difference in our world have keen insight into the immediate landscape and also crisp foresight on the horizon. They choose to see the God-created potential in humanity and they help others to see it too. A. W. Tozer (why do all the cool writers get initials for first names?) once wrote, "Faith is the gaze of a soul upon a saving God." In other words, looking and believing are the same thing. What we choose to see reveals what we believe should be the focus of our lives.

Turn my eyes from worthless things,
and give me life through your word.

PSALM 119:37

Jesus, let me see you and you alone. Repair my sight and fix my eyes upon you.
Amen.

DIFFERENCE MAKER

As you use your eyes today, imagine that Jesus is seeing what you see. How would that change the way you look at people? How would that change what you look at?

PRIORITIES

Would you rather be incredibly wealthy or have instructions from God? Think about that for a moment. Would you rather receive millions upon millions of dollars deposited right into your bank account for you to use in whatever manner you deem fit, or would you like to have God give you instructions on how to live?

Which of those options would be more valuable to you? Which would last longer? Which would change your life more? And which would be better for the people around you? You probably know the right Sunday school answer, but is that the right answer practically for your life?

The writer of the longest chapter in the Bible played the Would You Rather game and felt passionately about his answer. In prayer, he turned to the Lord and made his turn-the-world-upside-down decision.

Your instructions are more valuable to me
than millions in gold and silver.

PSALM 119:72

Jesus, where are my priorities today? Would I rather follow you or follow my own desires? Please walk with me and shape my thinking. Amen.

DIFFERENCE MAKER

Prayerfully filter your goals in life against this verse. Where do your priorities match up and where do they clash? What could you do today to reinforce your connection to God's purpose for your life?

PERFECTIONISM MERSCHMECTIONISM

No wonder perfectionists are always dissatisfied! Perfect is never good enough. Even if everything were completed to its most excellent potential, it still would fall short. The problem is that perfection sets a bar—a very high bar—that has a limit. Once it is reached, if it ever truly is, it leaves a person feeling incomplete because it is limited. The enjoyment of perfectionism is limited, the scope of perfectionism is limited, and the lasting effect of perfectionism is also limited.

But God's patterns have no limit. They are boundless. Perfectionists are always dissatisfied because they are chasing the wrong pursuit! God's commands blow right past the limited gratification of perfectionism and open the door to abundant, overflowing life—life that is more fulfilling than any limited human goal could ever dream to be.

Even perfection has its limits,
but your commands have no limit.

PSALM 119:96

Jesus, don't let me stress ever again about being perfect. Let me strive to hear your voice and pursue your commands for my life. Amen.

DIFFERENCE MAKER

Make a to-do list. Draw a line across the middle of the paper, then on the bottom side list everything important you think you really need to accomplish, and on the top side write Pursue Jesus. As you work to complete the important bottom items, seek your satisfaction in the one item on the top.

LIGHT FOR MY FEET

LEGOs are the most spectacular toy ever invented. You can create anything your ingenious mind allows—vehicles, spaceships, buildings, abstract works of art, and on and on and on. But there is also a dark side to LEGOs. Inevitably in the voracious generative process a few pieces get scattered and go missing. Somehow, those pieces find their way to the middle of your bedroom floor in the middle of the night. Angry from being neglected, they plot out their revenge and lie in wait for your nightly ritual to the bathroom, at which point they will position themselves under your footstep so that excruciating pain will scream up to your brain. All it would have taken to avoid the agony of a misplaced step was a simple light for your feet.

Your word is a lamp to guide my feet
and a light for my path.
PSALM 119:105

Jesus, let my eyes see where you are leading and let my childlike feet find their traction in your footprints. May your Word guide the direction of my life today. Amen.

DIFFERENCE MAKER

In the dark hours of the morning or evening, go for a walk in a well-lit, safe place (or use a flashlight in your room!). Use the light to guide your steps while you pray about where God wants your life to go.

PURPOSE AND INFRASTRUCTURE

Every building, every society, every product, every family, and every person has some sort of purpose and some sort of infrastructure that supports it or them. Whether those things or those people have success is directly relational to whether the infrastructure serves the purpose. If a building was meant to be fifty stories high and house hundreds of high-tech office spaces, it would be a farce if the infrastructure were made out of wood and a few dial-up modems.

It has been said that the "chief end" of humanity is to glorify God. But humans have often created a dilapidated infrastructure around themselves that has hindered their pursuit of their purpose. The good news is that through Jesus, God has given humanity the foundation and the resources it we need to love the Lord and to love our neighbor as ourselves.

Let me live so I can praise you,
and may your regulations help me.
I have wandered away like a lost sheep;
come and find me,
for I have not forgotten your commands.
PSALM 119:175–176

Jesus, forgive me for those times I have used the wrong materials to build my life. May I always follow your blueprint so that I can bring glory to you. Amen.

DIFFERENCE MAKER

What long-lasting materials do you need to invest your life into today? Choose at least one of the following to build yourself up: God's Word, serving others without calling attention to yourself, time spent in prayer, or mentoring a younger person in their walk with God.

DAY OF INFAMY

The attack on Pearl Harbor startled the nation. Three hundred and fifty-three Japanese planes crippled the United States Pacific Fleet and nearly 200 aircraft. Worse than that, however, over 2,400 people were killed that day. The next day, the United States declared war on Japan—a war that would involve the death of hundreds of thousands of soldiers and civilians over the next few years.

The horror of war reminds us that life and peace on this earth are fragile. Fear strikes unexpectedly and wreaks long-lasting devastation. Yet the Lord is stronger than the worst war. He will restore this world from its rubble, he will honor those who offer their lives for the good of others, and he will reestablish our steps as we follow him.

Even though the fig trees have no blossoms,
and there are no grapes on the vines;
even though the olive crop fails,
and the fields lie empty and barren;
even though the flocks die in the fields,
and the cattle barns are empty,
yet I will rejoice in the LORD!
I will be joyful in the God of my salvation!
The Sovereign LORD is my strength!
He makes me as surefooted as a deer,
able to tread upon the heights.

HABAKKUK 3:17–19

Jesus, this world needs you! I place my hope in your salvation today. Amen.

DIFFERENCE MAKER

Look through the news of turmoil around the world and pause on each geographic location mentioned and pray for the people in those regions.

RECORD

Jesus makes you free. Did you know that? He loves you so much that he does not keep a record of your sins. Every time you mess up, he is not going to bring out *The Book of Sin* with your name on the cover, open up to page 1,378, and say, "Aha! See! I knew you were no good! You're always failing!" That's just not the way of Jesus. He won't do that.

In fact, when you mess up he might actually pull out another book that we call the Bible. He might open to a myriad of different passages like 1 John 1:9, which says, "But if we confess our sins to him, he is faithful and just to forgive us our sins and to cleanse us from all wickedness," or Isaiah 43:25 where God says he "will blot out your sins and will never think of them again." Jesus might even quote from the "love" chapter of the Bible, 1 Corinthians 13, which says that love "keeps no record of wrongs." This is the way of Jesus, and it makes you free.

> LORD, if you kept a record of our sins,
> who, O Lord, could ever survive?
> But you offer forgiveness,
> that we might learn to fear you.
>
> PSALM 130:3–4

Jesus, a record of my wrongs is not a record I'd like anyone to keep. Thank you for keeping forgiveness in your heart for me. Amen.

DIFFERENCE MAKER

As the Christmas season approaches, string up new lights, bake some gingerbread cookies, listen to carols, and share the good news of Jesus with others.

THE ADVENT OF IMMANUEL

The birth of Jesus Christ is such a powerful event that Isaiah explains it as if it is just around the corner. Good as gold. Seven hundred years before Jesus is born, Isaiah already knows it is about to happen. The child is as good as born. His birth is bigger than past, present, and future itself. It's as if his birth was planned outside of time to impact all of time. His birth is the all-time greatest birth.

Isaiah is seeing it happen. He understands it is a birth yet to come, for back in Isaiah 7:14 he declares it as a future event. This child will be born among us, he will be with us, Isaiah declares. We will know him as "God with us."

> All right then, the Lord himself will give you the sign. Look! The virgin will conceive a child! She will give birth to a son and will call him Immanuel (which means "God is with us").
>
> ISAIAH 7:14

Lord Jesus, your plan is greater than time itself. Thank you for having us on your mind through all of time. Amen.

DIFFERENCE MAKER

If possible, volunteer to babysit for someone you know who has a baby. Consider how Jesus was once a child just like this.

CHILD

Back in Isaiah's day, the nation of Assyria inflicted intense physical distress and spiritual misery upon Israel. But not to worry, because Isaiah proclaimed that a child would be born. A child. "Hey don't worry, everyone—a baby is coming." Well, this wasn't just your normal, cute little bubble-blowing baby. The power and majesty of this child would be utterly astonishing. Isaiah was not afraid to emphasize this.

Child is the prominent word in Isaiah's prophecy. For upon this child would hinge everything. If you were to take the child out, the entire prophecy falls apart. If this child is not born and does not step into darkness, the entire world collapses. If this child does not make an impact, the world's very soul crumbles. Without this child being born, darkness still reigns, oppression still weighs people down, despair and struggle and restriction still overwhelm. And they always would, if it was not for the amazing capacity of this child to change everything.

> For a child is born to us,
> a son is given to us.
> The government will rest on his shoulders.
> And he will be called:
> Wonderful Counselor, Mighty God,
> Everlasting Father, Prince of Peace.
>
> ISAIAH 9:6

Jesus, how did you come in such fragility and still know you would change the world? I am in awe of you. Amen.

DIFFERENCE MAKER

Give someone a thoughtful, encouraging, early Christmas gift today.

JESUS IN CHARGE

In Isaiah 9:6, the prophet wasn't joking. The Christ child would not be just another boy. His responsibility would be the heaviest burden any person could carry: "The government will be on his shoulders."

Isaiah foresaw that Jesus wouldn't simply rule a local community or write a constitution or enforce laws. This child would rule everything—all of creation. The scope of the responsibility of administration and management and care and livelihood of the entire planet would be upon him. The weight of the world—the consequences of justice and redemption—would rest upon his shoulders. His kingdom would extend beyond borders and jurisdictions (John 18:36). He would have complete authority (Matthew 28:18) and would hold everything together (Colossians 1:15–20), both in heaven and on earth (John 13:3).

The reason Christmas brings so much joy is because a child is born, a child whose shoulders are greater than all nations, greater than all powers, greater than all darkness, and greater than all sin both now and forever. And this child was to be born as a baby and be laid in a manger.

> And I will give you the keys of the Kingdom of Heaven.
> Whatever you forbid on earth will be forbidden in heaven, and
> whatever you permit on earth will be permitted in heaven.
>
> MATTHEW 16:19

Jesus, thank you for carrying me on your shoulders. I trust you to govern my life.
Amen.

DIFFERENCE MAKER

Speaking of government, take time today to write an encouraging Christmas note to one of your city or state leaders, congress members, or senators. Include Isaiah 9:6 in your message.

WONDERFUL COUNSELOR

In Isaiah 9:6 are four sets of word pairs that are used to describe the child who would be born to us. The first is "Wonderful Counselor." By itself in English, this is pretty cool. Imagine putting this title on his birth certificate: "Yes, that's what I said. His name is Wonderful Counselor." But this title is even more impressive in Hebrew, the language Isaiah used. It is a title of awe. The Hebrew is *pele yoetz*.

Pele means "wonder." In the Old Testament this word usually refers to God and his miraculous works. He is astonishing and marvelous and indescribable. *Pele* hints at the deity of this child who is to be born. It is a word that could even stand alone, and Isaiah 9:6 could be translated, "He will be called Wonder."

And not only will he be called Wonder, but he will also be called Counselor. The Hebrew word *yoetz* means "counselor," "adviser," or "advocate." This child will sit on the throne of the world with wisdom and with judgment. He is a counselor who needs no other consultants or analysts around him. This child does not need a cabinet to help him make decisions. He himself is the Counselor to whom everyone else will turn. The child born among us is called Wonderful Counselor.

> The LORD says, "I will guide you along
> the best pathway for your life.
> I will advise you and watch over you."
>
> PSALM 32:8

Jesus, if you find I am not in awe of you, shake me up a bit today. Amen.

DIFFERENCE MAKER

Entrust your concerns, worries, and troubles to Jesus today.

HERO GOD

The second word pair that is used in Isaiah 9:6 to describe the child that will be born to us is "Mighty God." Is that really what Isaiah 9:6 says? How could a child actually be called "Mighty God"—especially in the monotheistic Hebrew worldview? But Isaiah says *El-Gibbor*, which is "Mighty God."

El is the Hebrew word for God. Isaiah never uses it in reference to anyone other than the one true God of Israel. For Isaiah to use this title upon a child is absolutely astonishing. The reason people in the future will rejoice, the reason darkness will be destroyed, the reason light is coming into the world, is because somehow a child who is God himself will overturn all the consequences of sin and despair and distress and misery.

And this God is mighty. *Gibbor* literally means "hero." This child is the hero God. God is going to be the hero of the story. Are you walking in darkness? Don't fear, because God will give you light! Are you oppressed? Hang in there, for God is coming to the rescue. Is your soul imprisoned? God will free you! Are your struggling? God will revive you! He is the hero God who comes to save the world.

He heals the brokenhearted
and bandages their wounds.
He counts the stars
and calls them all by name.
How great is our Lord! His power is absolute!
His understanding is beyond comprehension!

PSALM 147:3–5

Jesus, if I am not blown away by who you are yet, get my attention today. Amen.

DIFFERENCE MAKER

If Jesus is the hero God, what does that mean for you as his follower?
Do something heroic for someone else today.

FOREVER FATHER

The third word pair that is used in Isaiah 9:6 to describe the child who will be born to us is that he is the "Everlasting Father." The Messiah, this child who was to be born, this son upon whom the weight of the entire world would be carried, will be known as "Father." The Hebrew for this title is *Abbi-'ad. Abba* means Father, while *'ad* refers to endlessness. That means this child will be a father to his people forever and ever.

When God's children return to God the Father, Isaiah says, they will return to this child. He will stand guard over them, supply their needs, and cascade them with tenderness and protection and love. He will shepherd them, guide them, and lay his life down for them. All of this is not for a brief period of human life; rather, this child will be their Father forever (Isaiah 63:16), a Father who will never abandon his children (Matthew 28:21).

> "I give them eternal life, and they will never perish. No one
> can snatch them away from me, for my Father has given
> them to me, and he is more powerful than anyone else.
> No one can snatch them from the Father's hand.
> The Father and I are one."
>
> JOHN 10:28–30

Lord Jesus, during this Christmas season, help me to not see just a sweet baby in the manger. Help me to see Jesus as the Everlasting Father who is with me forever. Amen.

DIFFERENCE MAKER

How would your regular routines today be different if you were to remember that Jesus will be leading you forever?

PEACE PRINCE

The fourth and last word pair used in Isaiah 9:6 to describe the child who will be born to us is the "Prince of Peace." Prince of Peace. *Sur-Shalom*. Physical distress and spiritual misery will be conquered through the power and authority of this Christmas child. He will establish peace, a peace that is very much more than a temporary ceasefire. His power and rule will launch a new heaven and a new earth. All suffering and frustration and angst and weapons of darkness will be obliterated.

Shalom is the wholeness and fulfillment that only God has. *Shalom* is the purity and the perfection and the knowledge and summary of everything that is right. And it will come from a child, a child who is the ruler of peace. This peace will come from child who has in his hand the power to dispense peace. It will come from a child who will inherit *shalom* from God the Father because he is God's Son, the heir to the throne of all creation. This child is going to be one who rules with the power of eternity, a child who is born among us and for us, a child who is too wondrous to describe with just one name. He will be the child who holds titles unimaginable, a child who saves the world, and a child who inaugurates the *shalom* of God.

> Therefore, since we have been made right in God's sight by faith, we have peace with God because of what Jesus Christ our Lord has done for us.
>
> ROMANS 5:1

Jesus, let your peace fill my anxious soul today. Amen.

DIFFERENCE MAKER

Because Jesus is the Prince of Peace, pray about this: If you are separated from someone because of something you have done, take the necessary steps to make peace with them today.

BLINDING LIGHT

Heavy storms had created a melting mess on the salty, sandy, slushy road. A straight stretch of road was banked on both sides by huge walls of snow. In front was a truck, and behind was another truck. Brownish slop was spraying up onto the windshield, which made driving difficult. The wipers and washer fluid rid the glass of only half its mess.

As the road bent, the sun shattered through the low-lying clouds and smashed down on the stained windshield. As the sun hit the caked slop, the driver became completely blind. He couldn't see anything in front of him except hardened slush and an intense spot trying to penetrate through the grime. Attacked by the sun, blinded panic rushed through the driver's brain and fingers as he clutched the steering wheel that controlled his life. "Go away!" he yelled at the sun. "I want the shadows!"

As the road bent again, away from the direct glare of the light, the driver developed a deep gnawing fear that the sun had found him.

And the judgment is based on this fact: God's light came
into the world, but people loved the darkness more than
the light, for their actions were evil.

JOHN 3:19

*Jesus, don't let me be comfortable with driving blindly through life. As difficult
as it is, help me give in to your brilliance. Amen.*

DIFFERENCE MAKER

The next time you're driving through winter weather, pray to Jesus.

TRADITIONS

Some people have developed strong Christmas traditions over the years. Some people read the Christmas story in Luke 2, while others put a present for Jesus under the tree. Some ask the younger kids in their families to tell the story of Jesus' birth, and still others go to special church services. Some simply rip open presents and gorge on good food.

Christmas traditions are supposed to do two things, really. They are to draw us to Jesus and draw us toward each other. We celebrate Christmas because Jesus has been born, because he has entered into history. We receive and give gifts because God gave his only Son so that we might have abundant life. By accepting presents together, we are reminded to be humbly thankful for the abundant life and the abundant fellowship we share in Christ Jesus.

Because of your stage in life, this might be an interesting year of change for you. Be sure to follow Mary's example. Even in the midst of visitors and transitions, she paused to treasure the birth of Jesus and made it a regular routine to remember.

They hurried to the village and found Mary and Joseph. And there was the baby, lying in the manger. After seeing him, the shepherds told everyone what had happened and what the angel had said to them about this child. All who heard the shepherds' story were astonished, but Mary kept all these things in her heart and thought about them often.

LUKE 2:16–19

Jesus, let me remember the meaning of this season—which is you. Amen.

DIFFERENCE MAKER

This Christmas season practice a tradition from your childhood and start a new one that will help draw you and your family to Jesus.

CHRISTMAS INFORMATION

Mary and Joseph weren't really into the Christmas spirit. They didn't decorate a Christmas tree. They didn't bake cookies or drink peppermint mochas or put up the mistletoe. Can you believe that they didn't go caroling either? Look, they weren't scrooges; they just had other things on their mind. There was no place for roasting chestnuts over a fire. They couldn't even find a place. Some (generous?) person allowed them to stay with their animals, but that was no place for a teenage girl who was going into labor.

Christmas is just a week away. Have you read—actually read—the account of Jesus' birth this year yet? Rather than just getting your Christmas details from carols or from reruns of old holiday TV programs, what if you were to read a couple pages of the Bible too? You might be surprised to find out that Father Christmas isn't real, Santa isn't in the Bible, and eggnog is not biblical.

Jacob was the father of Joseph, the husband of Mary.
Mary gave birth to Jesus, who is called the Messiah.
MATTHEW 1:16

Jesus, don't let me take you for granted this next week. Amen.

DIFFERENCE MAKER

Get some people together and read the first two chapters of Matthew and the first two chapters of Luke. Even try to pronounce any awkward names out loud. Talk about details you thought you knew that weren't there and other details you discovered but had never realized were there before.

VENITE ADOREMUS

For 2,000 years people have been celebrating the birth of Jesus. Actually, it has been longer than that, because even before Jesus was born people were anticipating his arrival. The prophet Micah had predicted his arrival in Bethlehem, Isaiah had foreseen his powerful ministry, and Simeon had waited his whole life to hold him. Celebrating the birth of the Messiah is one of the greatest traditions of history.

In the 1700s, John Frances Wade published a song known as *Adeste Fideles* in a collection of hymns known as the *Cantus Diversi*. He wanted the world to come and adore the birth of Jesus.

Adeste fideles,
Laeti trimphantes,
Venite, venite in Bethlehem.
Natum videte, Regem angelorum.
Venite adoremus;
Venite adoremus;
Venite adoremus, Dominum.

But you, O Bethlehem Ephrathah,
are only a small village among all the people of Judah.
Yet a ruler of Israel,
whose origins are in the distant past,
will come from you on my behalf.

MICAH 5:2

Jesus, let me, and countless others,
adore you this Christmas. Amen.

DIFFERENCE MAKER

Search the internet to figure out what these lyrics mean. Then watch a video of Andrea Bocelli singing this song. How could such grandeur be given to the birth of a baby in a small, backward town twenty centuries ago?

JESUS COMING TO US

Christmas is about Jesus coming to meet each one of us. The Christmas passages, and the rest of the whole Bible, tell us that Jesus came to the earth so that he could meet us and have an eternal relationship with us. For example, the book of Matthew is jam-packed with this concept of Jesus coming to meet us. In Matthew 3, John the Baptist references Jesus when he says, "Someone is coming soon who is greater than I am." In Matthew 5, Jesus urges people, "Don't misunderstand why I have come." In chapter 9, Jesus says, "I have come to call those who know they are sinners." And in Matthew 20 Jesus sums it all up for us when he says, "The Son of Man came not to be served but to serve others and to give his life as a ransom for many." Christmas is about Jesus coming to meet us so that we can have a relationship with him.

> "For the Son of Man came to seek
> and save those who are lost."
>
> LUKE 19:10

Lord Jesus, thank you for coming to give your life up for me. Amen.

DIFFERENCE MAKER

This Christmas season, where you will notice them frequently, set up both a manger and a cross.

US COMING TO JESUS

Christmas is about each of us coming to meet Jesus. The Christmas passages, and the rest of the whole Bible, share that each of us is to come and meet Jesus so that we can have an eternal relationship with him. For example, the book of Matthew is absolutely full with this concept of each of us coming to meet Jesus. In chapter 4, Jesus calls out to two brothers, "Come, follow me, and I will show you how to fish for people!" In Matthew 11, Jesus invites everyone, "Come to me, all of you who are weary and carry heavy burdens, and I will give you rest." In Matthew 14, when Peter asks if he can walk out to him on the water, Jesus simply responds, "Yes, come." And in chapter 28, after Jesus' resurrection, even the angels get into the action, saying, "Come, see where his body was lying." Jesus has come to meet you. Will you come to meet him today?

Jesus was born in Bethlehem in Judea, during the reign of King Herod. About that time some wise men from eastern lands arrived in Jerusalem, asking, "Where is the newborn king of the Jews? We saw his star as it rose, and we have come to worship him."

MATTHEW 2:1–2

Jesus, I come to you now and give you my whole life. Amen.

DIFFERENCE MAKER

Go meet with Jesus today. Seek him and find him, for he is inviting you to do just that. Set aside some time today just to worship him.

FAIRY-TALE VERSION

There's the fairy-tale version of Christmas: A quiet baby in a warm manger surrounded by a beautiful young mom and an incredibly gentle adoptive father, graced by gentle shepherds and cute little lambs, all the while a star hovers just overhead. Angels sing sweetly o'er the plain while the earth is placid.

Then there's the reality: A screaming baby, messy with an umbilical cord and misshapen skull, held by an unwed teenage mom who fled her family with her boyfriend, visited by terrified shepherds on a strange order from angels. The local king demands the baby's death, so soldiers descend upon the town and murder every young child present. The new family frantically escapes to Egypt, where his ancestors had been enslaved years before. Eventually the baby grows, gifted with authority to heal the sick and raise the dead. Crowds clamor for his kingship, but when he refuses to incite a revolt, the crowds betray him, beat him, and execute him—all while his mother wept at his bloody feet.

No wonder we like the fairy-tale version much better. The sweetness of a carnation is nicer than the shock of the incarnation.

> Then Simeon blessed them, and he said to Mary, the baby's mother, "This child is destined to cause many in Israel to fall, but he will be a joy to many others. He has been sent as a sign from God, but many will oppose him. As a result, the deepest thoughts of many hearts will be revealed. And a sword will pierce your very soul."
>
> LUKE 2:34–35

Jesus, you were willing to be real with me. I pray I will be real with you. Amen.

DIFFERENCE MAKER

In the next few days, consider the raw reality of Jesus' birth.

HELLO!

The award for the most awkward hello of all eternity should go to the simply spoken angel Gabriel. Luke tells us that God sent him to Nazareth to speak to Mary, a young virgin who was engaged to a carpenter named Joseph. Gabriel went to her and politely said, "Greetings." He then "delivered" the good news to Mary that the Lord had chosen her to conceive the very Son of God.

But Mary wasn't so sure his hello was a good thing. She was quite afraid of him and greatly troubled at the blunt verbiage of this supreme heavenly warrior. But with his amazing angel abilities, Gabriel must have sensed Mary's discomfort at his little announcement. So he decided he would try to reassure her with words that every unwed teenage girl wants to hear: "Don't be afraid, Mary. You're pregnant!"

I'm sure that calmed her nerves, Gabe.

Gabriel appeared to her and said, "Greetings, favored woman! The Lord is with you!" Confused and disturbed, Mary tried to think what the angel could mean. "Don't be afraid, Mary," the angel told her, "for you have found favor with God! You will conceive and give birth to a son, and you will name him Jesus."

LUKE 1:28–31

Jesus, don't let me be comfortable with the details of Christmas this year. Let its simplicity profoundly shake me awake. Amen.

DIFFERENCE MAKER

Write an encouraging note to someone who finds the Christmas season saddening or troubling to their heart.

CHRISTMAS EVE

Trying to help the poor…*er,* I mean "favored" girl understand her predicament—*er,* there I go again—I mean "blessing," the angel Gabriel went on to deliver to Mary information about her bundle of joy. He told her she would be with child, give birth to a son, and give him the name Jesus. Then Gabriel said, without shaking his wings, "Oh, and Mary, he will be very great." Uh, yeah.

No one could disagree one bit with Gabriel's assessment of Jesus. Jesus simply, no argument, would be great. Not kind of great. He would be the definition of and the very model of greatness. Masterfully great. Awe-inspiringly, knee-shatteringly, jaw-droppingly, arms-raisedly, angel-dumbfoundedly great. Gabriel couldn't have said it any simpler. Never before or since has one uttered such an eternal understatement.

To his credit, Gabriel did elaborate a bit. Besides the fact that Jesus would be great, Gabe casually reassured Mary, "Your son will be the Son of God and, by the way, his kingdom will never end. So, uh, don't be afraid, Mary."

> He will be very great and will be called the Son of the Most High. The Lord God will give him the throne of his ancestor David. And he will reign over Israel forever; his Kingdom will never end!
>
> LUKE 1:32–33

Jesus, you are greater than I realize. Let that sink into my heart tonight and tomorrow. Amen.

DIFFERENCE MAKER

In celebration of Jesus, for every Christmas gift you get, challenge yourself to give two gifts to others.

CHRISTMAS DAY

God used Caesar Augustus like a puppet, and he wasn't concerned about Quirinius complicating things or Herod stopping the show. He had set this plan in motion long before any of those men changed their diapers. A King, the only true King, was going to be born to a humble girl in a lowly corner of the world in the midst of fragility so that the broken people of the world could draw near and embrace their Almighty Savior.

At that time the Roman emperor, Augustus, decreed that a census should be taken throughout the Roman Empire. (This was the first census taken when Quirinius was governor of Syria.) All returned to their own ancestral towns to register for this census. And because Joseph was a descendant of King David, he had to go to Bethlehem in Judea, David's ancient home. He traveled there from the village of Nazareth in Galilee. He took with him Mary, his fiancée, who was now obviously pregnant. And while they were there, the time came for her baby to be born. She gave birth to her first child, a son. She wrapped him snugly in strips of cloth and laid him in a manger, because there was no lodging available for them.

LUKE 2:1–7

Lord Jesus, thank you for coming in a way that draws me to you. Amen.

DIFFERENCE MAKER

Gather together with people whom you love and read Luke 2:1–20 together.

GIFT

On December 25 of every year, people around the world celebrate God who took on human flesh. On December 26, people return their gifts. And by the New Year they've moved on. Should we leave Jesus, and our faith, in the manger? That isn't where Jesus stayed. He was wrapped in swaddling cloths and laid in a manger, but later he was wrapped in burial cloths and laid in a tomb. His incarnation is an intense story that encompasses his entire life: the Creator took upon himself blood and body and bones and entered humbly into the world of his created ones to sacrifice himself.

We are inclined to opt for a consumerist faith, selfish in its assumption of undeserved grace and shallow in its apprehension of the crude *carne* of Jesus Christ. That the holy God of the universe would take on the fragility of flesh in this violent, sinful world exposes God's determination to go to the most extreme lengths to love his people. How can we leave Jesus, and our faith, in the manger?

And so, dear brothers and sisters, I plead with you to give your bodies to God because of all he has done for you. Let them be a living and holy sacrifice—the kind he will find acceptable. This is truly the way to worship him.

ROMANS 12:1

Lord Jesus, let me be more and more like you every day of my life. Amen.

DIFFERENCE MAKER

Wrap up some simple but meaningful gifts and make arrangements to give them away in a soup kitchen, homeless shelter, prison ministry, nursing home, hospital, or group home.

POST-CHRISTMAS

When the child was born, angels declared peace on earth to humankind. So here's some good news: You are a kind of human, and you are on earth, so the angels declared peace for you. The post-Christmas peace comes from this: Jesus will destroy sin. He will obliterate distress. He will liquefy misery. And he will do all of this through the weapon he extends in his hands—forgiveness. Nothing can overcome forgiveness. It is the most powerful offense this world could ever embrace. It is futile to fight forgiveness. Everything surrenders or succumbs to Jesus' peaceful, abundant love.

Even though Christmas is past (and because it is it 363 days in the future), be careful not to resist Jesus. Embrace him. Pull him close to your heart. Let him overcome any shadow of death that you pass through. Let his victory break the chains in your life. Let his peace conquer the conflict in your soul. Let his wonder surpass your understanding. Let his counsel restore your heart. Let his might empower your passion. Let his everlasting life awaken you. Let his birth connect you to God.

> I am leaving you with a gift—peace of mind and heart. And the peace I give is a gift the world cannot give. So don't be troubled or afraid.
>
> JOHN 14:27

Jesus, Christmas is all about you, and yet you have gifted me. As much as this sinks in, there is still room for me to embrace you more. Thank you! Amen.

DIFFERENCE MAKER

Pray. Go to someone who is in conflict and creatively, effectively, and wisely share the peace of Jesus.

GOD REMEMBERS HIS PROMISES

God's house is full of joy. Do you know why? Because there is not one broken promise to be found anywhere within it. God not only makes promises to those he loves, but he also keeps those promises.

For instance, he told Abraham one of his future children would become a blessing as numerous as the stars. He promised David he would have a future son who would rule on his throne forever. He promised Mary she would have a child who would save the world from its sins. He promised Paul he would use him to bring the good news of Jesus to people who had never yet heard of it. He promised he would bring freedom and healing and joy and abundant life. He promised the Holy Spirit. He promised also to come again to judge evil and restore his creation. He promised to be with us always, even to the very end of the age.

God's house is full of joy because he keeps his promises.

He is the LORD our God.
His justice is seen throughout the land.
He always stands by his covenant—
the commitment he made to a thousand generations.

PSALM 105:7–8

Jesus, thank you for remembering me and for remembering your promises so many generations ago. I praise you today for keeping your Word. Amen.

DIFFERENCE MAKER

Tell people today how God remembers his promises for them.

WHAT A DAY

What an incredible day this is. Smack in-between Christmas and New Year's, this day cannot be overlooked. It's like the perfect blending of those two major holidays. Christmas marks the day we celebrate the birth of our Savior, while New Year's marks the celebration of our opportunity to start anew. It seems that December 29 is the bridge between them both.

At some point, we need to allow the birth of Jesus to change our lives so that we can start again, leave our sin behind, and resolve to pursue all that Jesus has planned for us. This is a day of renewal where we can prepare for works of service that will make a beautiful difference in the year to come.

> "For I am about to do something new.
> See, I have already begun! Do you not see it?
> I will make a pathway through the wilderness.
> I will create rivers in the dry wasteland."
>
> ISAIAH 43:19

Jesus, thank you for coming to give me new life. Guide me in the new directions you have for my life in the year ahead. Amen.

DIFFERENCE MAKER

You'll need a pen and a paper and a place to think. Old-fashioned style now. While praying with Jesus, brainstorm a list of what God intends for you in this upcoming year.

WRAP UP

At the end of the most famous sermon in history, Jesus looked back. He had offered world-changing thoughts through beatitudes, salt and light, teaching on anger and adultery, love for enemies, giving to the needy, the Lord's Prayer, ideas on money, instructions to not worry, to not judge; he encouraged people to seek and find, keep the Golden Rule, pass through the narrow gate, and discover who his true followers are. Some of the most famous sayings in history come from the Sermon on the Mount. History would say it was a pretty good message.

Jesus himself thought it was pretty good too. In fact, before he finished, he looked back on it all and encouraged everyone who heard his words to put them into action. If a person applied his teachings, he said, then they would have a stable foundation for life. So he wrapped up his words with one of the greatest analogies the world had ever heard.

Anyone who listens to my teaching and follows it is wise,
like a person who builds a house on solid rock.

MATTHEW 7:24

Jesus, thank you for making a difference in my life. Keep teaching me. Help me be changed even more so that I can change the world around me. Amen.

DIFFERENCE MAKER

Look back through the daily entries of this book that impacted you throughout the year. Highlight some of the Difference Makers that changed you or those around you, and then choose one of those to repeat today.

LAST DAY

The first book of the Bible, Genesis, launches our understanding of God's purpose in creating the world. The last book of the Bible, Revelation, has us calling for God to come back and re-create. We long to be fully restored to the relationship that God intended us to have in the world that God intended us to live in.

John, the writer of Revelation, can hardly wait for God's promised restoration. As he writes what will become the very last words of the Bible, he is filled with awe and anticipation. He chooses to respond to Jesus with a few wonderful words that capture his heart: "Come, Lord Jesus." John knows of no better way to conclude than this thought for his readers. The greatest blessing he could give to the world would be a prayer for Jesus to come back once again.

He who is the faithful witness to all these things says,
"Yes, I am coming soon!" Amen! Come, Lord Jesus!
May the grace of the Lord Jesus be with God's holy people.
REVELATION 22:20–21

Lord Jesus, in the year ahead, come to restore all things in my life and in this world. Amen.

DIFFERENCE MAKER

Gather some good friends or family and celebrate the last year, and look ahead to the upcoming year. But tonight add a twist. Stop to pray for Jesus' return so that the world will be remade as it was intended to be.

ACKNOWLEDGMENTS

To Kathy: You have made a difference in me and right beside me. You exemplify this book. You are the most consistent, most trustworthy, most sincere difference maker I know. Thank you. I love you.

To my amazing and unique kids, each one chosen by God to know him and do good for him: Each of you will be out from under my wings soon, a freedom you'll enjoy because nests can get exceedingly cramped and stinky if people don't get out of their parents' basement and start to fly. Zachary, may you always remember Jesus and lead people to him. Ben, may you serve God's right hand with grace and power. Elly, may you know God's promises and make them known. I love you all with more life than I knew I had.